D1488550

CRIME AND MYSTERY
The 100 Best Books

H.R.F. KEATING

CRIME & MYSTERY

THE

100

BEST BOOKS

Released from
Samford University Library

CARROLL & GRAF

Samford University Library

Copyright © 1987 by H.R.F. Keating
Foreword copyright © 1987 by Patricia Highsmith

All rights reserved

First published in 1987 in Great Britain by
Xanadu Publications Limited

First Carroll & Graf edition 1987

Carroll & Graf Publishers, Inc.
260 Fifth Avenue
New York, NY 10001

Library of Congress Cataloging-in-Publication Data

Keating, H. R. F. (Henry Reymond Fitzwalter), 1926–
   Crime and mystery.

   Includes index.
   1. Detective and mystery stories, English—Bibliography. 2. Detective and mystery stories, American—
Bibliography. 3. Bibliography—Best books—Detective
and mystery stories. 4. Bibliography—Best books—Crime
and criminals. I. Title.
Z2014.F4K43   1987   016.823'0872'08   87-17377
[PR830.D4]
ISBN 0-88184-345-8

Manufactured in Great Britain

2
2014
.F4
K43
1987

Foreword

BY PATRICIA HIGHSMITH

H.R.F. Keating, well-known as a crime writer himself and critic for *The Times*, has done crime and mystery fans a great service in creating this book, his choice of the hundred best of the genre. It is a pleasure to refresh one's memory of *The Moonstone*'s story, or a discreet part of it, and at the same time (in barely two pages, like all of these entries) have the novel appraised by so apt a man as Keating. What happened in Helen Eustis's *The Horizontal Man*, and why has it won a high place? Maybe more difficult, what happened in *The Long Goodbye* of Raymond Chandler, whose plots are said to be less memorable than some of his ripostes?

But Keating gives not so much concern to plot as to evaluation of the author and of one selected opus. The list begins with Edgar A. Poe and ends with the timely P.D. James' *A Taste for Death*; on the latter there is a remark from Keating that 'the central mystery of death is surely what comes after, the sustaining key to religious faith.' Is it? More food for thought and discussion. Among other entries are Dickens, Conan Doyle, E.W. Hornung, Rex Stout, Cornell Woolrich, Simenon, P.M. Hubbard. Some writers' names may ring the dimmest of bells or none at all, and perhaps lovers of such tales as these can make new friends, and significant ones, by learning here what these authors wrote. All the books that are mentioned are fairly readily available.

What makes this book more than merely a distinguished list or a who's who are the thoughtful words which H.R.F. Keating has for each writer's work. On Poe, for instance:

> He was a pioneer in the struggle that won for us today the notion that the individual has rights as an individual ... that established that great art can come from the self-expression of the artist and not only from following rules laid down in antiquity.

And on Dickens' *The Mystery of Edwin Drood*:

> ... this theme, the frightening duality of human nature, that

never-settled combat between our duties and our desires, is so woven into the story of the crime that the whole book is beyond doubt an example of what later became known as the crime novel.

The whole book? Of course not, writes Keating. He describes June 8, 1870, when, after working all day, Dickens at dinner abruptly got up from the table declaring that he had to go to London, and then collapsed. He lingered on for twenty-four agonised hours before dying. He never gave a hint of his intention for *Edwin Drood*'s ending. There is great affection in Keating's prose in regard to Dickens.

I now have a different view of Cornell Woolrich, thanks to the two pages on him here. Keating describes *The Bride Wore Black*, and Woolrich's curious and indirect methods of laying out his plot and his clues. A homosexual who apparently lived in the closet, Woolrich shared a life in residential hotels with a mother whom he both loved and hated. Could anything be worse? Yet 'books and short stories poured in a huge stream under his own name and those of William Irish and George Hopley.' And more, Otto Penzler and Chris Steinbrunner have hailed him in *The Encyclopedia of Mystery and Detection* as possibly 'the finest mystery writer of the twentieth century.'

To represent Maj Sjöwall and Per Wahlöö, whose ten novels were intended as a planned 'assault on Swedish society and by implication on all Western society,' Keating chooses *Roseanna*, 'because it most clearly stays within the bounds of crime fiction.' He has certainly read all the other nine.

One can open *The 100 Best* anywhere and be entertained by its contents, learn something new, or reinforce what is already in one's head. Keating modestly states in his Introduction that he may have left out some fine writers, for which he anticipates reproach. But who in our time could have done it better?

Contents

Introduction

Please, please don't prosecute me under the Trade Descriptions Act. But if I was to avoid that liability, the title of this book would have to be a little longer. Not *Crime and Mystery: the 100 Best Books*, but something like:

> *One Hundred Very Good Crime and Mystery Books, Taking into Account that No Author Should be Represented by More Than Three Titles (So As To Be Fair to Others) and Allowing for a Little Personal Idiosyncracy in Naming One or Two Whom the Majority of Other Commentators Might Not Have Chosen Very Readily*

—and even then there would be outcries. Where's Dick Francis? Charles McCarry? Stephen King? Daphne du Maurier? Mary Higgins Clark? The answer is that I have had to decide, quite arbitrarily, that by 'Crime and Mystery' I mean books with crime in them that are not pure thrillers, nor espionage novels, nor horror stories, nor stories of pure suspense. And certainly not novels proper that happen to have a crime in them. Sorry, Dostoiesvski.

And even here I have had to make some tricky decisions. The line that divides thrillers, books written to provide a succession of thrilling or exciting moments, from mysteries, books written to baffle readers, is at best an extremely wobbly one, as are the other dividing lines in our area. So some books I might have included I have kept out, and perhaps one or two that I have put in defy rigorous interpretation of my own definition.

Nor am I yet out of trouble. I hear outraged voices screaming 'Where's Fergus Hume?' (Fergus *Who*? You know, the author of *The Mystery of a Hansom Cab*, which some people claim as the father of all mystery stories and thus entitled to a place in the best hundred). And 'Where's Arthur B. Reeve?', yell others. Well, his Craig Kennedy may once have been the American equivalent of Sherlock Holmes as a scientific detective, but the sad fact is that Reeve is no longer an author easily found, and on those grounds I have excluded him, since I see little point in a book praising

8

authors if no one is going to be able to get hold of the books I have praised them for. On that count a number of other once-famous names, such as R. Austin Freeman, Alice Tilton, Freeman Wills Crofts and Stuart Palmer, are not to be found in the pages that follow, even if on an academic listing of the hundred best some of them might have made it.

But what anyhow constitutes the best? Is it those books with the most ingenious puzzles? Or the most exciting? Or is it the books that are best-written? And what's best-written? With the most convincing characters? With the most mellifluous prose? The funniest? The most grisly? No, there is no way of ranking the extraordinarily diverse products of the writing itch. Who's to say, turning out of embarrassment to another field, that Beethoven's Fifth is better than Mozart's 'Don Giovanni'?

And who said that there must be only a hundred best books? I confess that, owing to difficulties with simple arithmetic, I actually wrote one hundred and one pieces before I made my final count. (No, I do not intend to divulge the name of the unlucky author.)

Well, of course, my publisher issued that hundred-best decree in the interests of a snappy catch title, one preferable to my more comprehensive effort which would have caused some production difficulties in the way of necessitating a book with a spine three times its own width. You have, when it comes down to it, to make absolutely arbitrary decisions, just as I have had to make a hundred arbitrary decisions in my choices.

Ultimately, 'best' for me is simply the books I have most enjoyed. (What's enjoyment? Laughing aloud? Gasping in delight? Remembering long afterwards? Oh, stop, stop, stop.) A critic can do no more than depend upon his own feelings, when you come down to it. I was conscious as I pored over lists and indexes considering my possibilities that other critics and readers have views different from mine; that, say, Julian Symons would have produced in all likelihood a very different roll-call.

So I have to some extent taken into account the united voices of all the commentators I know of. And that has resulted, I think, in the book becoming, in outline at least, a sort of history of crime writing from Edgar Allan Poe to P.D. James, something I am glad to have arrived at. But, spoiling this a little, I have once or twice defied all those other commentators and included a personal favourite simply as such, though I firmly believe such choices are in fact very good books.

And then I am conscious, too, that I am a fallible human being. I have not read all the books in the world. Not even all the crime books. So I may quite easily be totally unaware of a book that ought to have ousted one of my choices. But which? Ah, which? Thank goodness, my ignorance has saved me from having to make that last, unkindest cut of all.

So what's left after all these quibbles? I'm afraid, really, no more than a hit-or-miss selection of crime and mystery books, all of which I fervently believe to have virtues that raise them out of the common run. And, looking over the complete list, I cannot help thinking that they are indeed a pretty splendid collection— best, next-best, fourth-from-best or what you will.

H.R.F. KEATING
London, 1987

Note

Details of first editions in Britain and the USA are given at the end of each essay. In every case the actual first edition is given first, and the succeeding transatlantic edition (if there is one) comes below. The 100 books have of course been chosen on account of their quality rather than their rarity (unlike some of the ones in *Queen's Quorum*, for instance), but a few of them are nonetheless extremely rare as first editions. Edgar Allan Poe's *Tales* of 1854, for example, published in New York by Wiley and Putnam, was the first to collect together all three Dupin stories and it is extremely valuable. But the first appearance of 'The Murders in the Rue Morgue' in a book was in *The Prose Romances of Edgar A. Poe* (Philadelphia: Graham, 1843) and *that* is one of the rarest of all books, with only a dozen or so copies known to exist. Anyone wishing to collect all of these 100 books in first-edition form may therefore be excused trying for the early Poes, and perhaps for *The Moonstone* and *The Adventures of Sherlock Holmes* too. Apart from those, happy hunting!

The bibliographical information has been compiled with the help of Camille Wolff of Grey House Books, 12A Lawrence St, London SW3, who has an excellent stock of rare and out-of-print crime books.

1

EDGAR ALLAN POE

Tales of Mystery and Imagination

Crime stories have always been with us, ever since huddled round the cave fire or squatting beneath the palm-tree men and women delighted to hear tales of how the bonds of society, even such simple bonds as theirs, could be broken by a hero of enough daring, and how when these bonds were broken and terror stalked there was another hero to put all things right. Or you can say that detective fiction began on the day in 1843 when one Edgar Allan Poe put pen to paper and produced a story called 'The Murders in the Rue Morgue'.

With this story, together with two others that appear in the book, and perhaps a couple more, this genius (or possibly part-genius) laid down almost all the basic tenets of mystery fiction. 'The Murders in the Rue Morgue' presented to us for the first time that figure who was to grow into a self-generating myth, the Great Detective. The story, too, adumbrated the locked-room, or impossible crime, situation.

In 'The Mystery of Marie Rogêt', where Poe attempted, with a certain amount of success, to solve the real-life mystery of the disappearance in New York of a certain Mary Rogers, transposing the whole to the Parisian world of his detective, Le Chevalier C. Auguste Dupin, he set out the principle of the 'armchair detective', the person who solves crimes by the pure use of intellect.

In 'The Purloined Letter' he put forward the device, afterwards much copied, of the object deceptively hidden in the most obvious place. Here, too, he put at its clearest the concept of the painstaking but limited police official opposed to the sideways-leaping, brilliant amateur detective. All three stories, too, sketched out what was to become known as the Holmes-Watson relationship, the all-seeing detective and the trailing-behind narrator.

Two other stories in the collection laid down minor aspects of mystery fiction: 'The Gold Bug'—the cryptogram defeating all but the genius—and, though it is essentially a melodrama, 'Thou Art the Man'—false clues left by the victim to implicate an innocent plus the least likely person murderer. In other stories in this collection there are further elements with crime fiction overtones, such as the theme of imprisonment and escape ('The Pit and the Pendulum'), and, working at a deeper psychological level, the theme of burial alive or the mind trapped in its own definition of its personality ('The Cask of Amontillado', 'The Fall of the House of Usher').

Poe's major achievement, however, was the creation of the Great Detective. He was able to seize on deep and complex patterns from a jumble of devices which hack writers had played with for years, unaware that they were using gold dust to fashion trumpery articles. He saw that the commonplace detective could be made into the romantic hero, the breaker of the false bonds of society. More than this, he created the man combining in himself the poet and the mathematician, the man of imagination and the man endowed with ratiocination.

You have only to look at the first pages of 'The Murders in the Rue Morgue' to see that it is something more than merely an ingenious story of detection. Before there is any mention of the mysterious deaths Poe gives us four mighty paragraphs of philosophy. There can be no opening words of a crime story more unexciting than 'The mental features discoursed of as the analytical ...' This opening is even followed by a long mental pen-portrait of Dupin. It is plain that here is a man aiming to do a great deal more than merely entertain.

Poe was, in fact, taking part in the great battle between the rising Romantics and the entrenched Classicists. He was a pioneer in the struggle that won for us today the notion that the individual has rights as an individual, the struggle that laid the foundations of democratic, equality-oriented societies. This was the struggle, too, that established that great art can come from the self-expression of the artist.

And the figure that embodied all this was the detective as super-hero, the investigator who in the hands of Poe's successors was to emerge definitively as the Great Detective.

First edition See note on page 10

First collected edition New York: Simms and McIntyre, 1852
as *Tales of Mystery, Imagination and Humour; and Poems*

2

WILKIE COLLINS
The Moonstone

The first, the longest and the best of modern English detective stories: thus did T.S. Eliot, guru-poet and, incidentally, detective-story fan who pinched words from a Sherlock Holmes tale for his verse-play *Murder in the Cathedral*, once describe *The Moonstone*. He was not altogether right, but he was right in that the book is the first work in English fiction to show a detective actually detecting.

Collins put into *The Moonstone* much that has been a staple of crime fiction ever since. His story provides the classic example of the innocent who must, despite all odds, prove he did not commit the crime. It actually put into the mouth of its detective, Sergeant Cuff, that since-done-to-death phrase 'the pieces of the puzzle are not all put together yet.' From Cuff, too, we get another phrase with a powerful echo, 'In all my experience along the dirtiest ways of this dirty little world, I have never met with any such thing as a trifle yet.' At once we hear Sherlock Holmes, 'You know my method. It is founded upon the observance of trifles.' And there is surely even a foretaste here too of the disenchanted private eyes many years in the future. Cuff was also a master of the throwaway remark. 'Nobody has stolen the diamond,' he declares, and immediately clams up.

So much for 'the first.' As to 'the longest', there are others longer, though I doubt if many readers have wished *The Moonstone* a page shorter. And 'the best'? Perhaps the term is more advocacy than elucidation and even more advertising than advocacy. But *The Moonstone* is certainly a very good book.

It is good as a detective story. The solution to the theft of the fabulous Moonstone is splendidly unexpected. And Collins was marvellously clever at slipping in clues in a fine fair-play way. Almost all you need to know is given in the first ten chapters. And what came to be known as 'red herrings' are, too, set up with delightful skill. Watch out for Franklin Blake's giving up smoking to please the beautiful Rachel Verinder. Listen carefully to the solid lawyer, Mr Bruff, talking about Franklin's notorious debts, and someone else's.

But the book is also a fine novel. It is full of splendid character studies, each of its various narrators realised in depth: Rachel shown as a 'good' girl but by no means a namby-pamby, and made to be genuinely in love, the crippled maidservant Rosanna Spearman never sentimentalised.

As a novel, the book has a theme of full significance, the irrational lying just underneath the apparently rational surface of life. The irrational is embodied, indeed, in the Moonstone itself, the stolen jewel that is the mainspring of the plot. It is described as a gem from mysterious India, worshipped under the moon's light, and when it is looked at it 'seemed unfathomable.' Then, a major symbol, there are the Shivering Sands, the quagmire that plays such a large part in the story, its surface 'glittering with a golden brightness,' hiding 'the horror of its false brown face.' Countless smaller details reinforce the feeling.

But, set against this, we have dozens of reminders of what Collins called the Actual. There is, to begin with, the comment that the Moonstone itself is after all 'mere carbon.' Or there is the delightful comic touch (Collins' recipe was 'Make 'em laugh, make 'em weep, make 'em wait') of staid old Betterage, the house steward, saying of the painter whose designs Franklin and Rachel copy, a business ingeniously used in the plot, 'the one, I mean, who stocked the world with Virgin Marys, and had a sweetheart at the baker's.' High art and low life in one.

It is curious that a book so packed with good things did not spawn a host of direct followers. Crime fiction had to wait a good many more years before it came into its own. Perhaps one reason for this is that *The Moonstone*, though it sold extraordinarily well, did not receive particularly enthusiastic reviews. The *Pall Mall Gazette*, indeed, could only say with high-toned disparagement 'In sliding-panels, trap-doors and artificial beards'—only one of these actually features in *The Moonstone*— Mr Collins is nearly as clever as anyone who has ever fried a pancake in a hat.'

But time has made amends. *The Moonstone* is a classic.

First edition London: Tinsley, 1868 (in three volumes)
First US edition New York: Harper, 1868

3

CHARLES DICKENS
The Mystery of Edwin Drood

Dostoievski's *Crime and Punishment* will not be found in this gathering of the hundred best crime books, though if ever a novel had murder as its mainspring that masterwork does. But it is a novel proper, an exploration first and foremost of an aspect of the human character. And the same bar withholds from us Charles Dickens's *Bleak House*, though it has a murder mystery and a first-class detective in its pages. Again, however, it is a novel before it is a crime story. But with Dickens's last book of all, *The Mystery of Edwin Drood*, the case is altered.

True, the book has, besides the mystery of what happened to the young man Edwin Drood one storm-shattered night in the ancient cathedral city of Cloisterham, a theme such as might power any novel. But this theme, the frightening duality of human nature, that never-settled combat between our duties and our desires, is so woven into the story of the crime that the whole book is beyond doubt an example of what later became known as the crime novel. Consider in this light Julian Symons's declaration, a hundred years after Dickens, that the aim of the crime novel is 'to show the violence that lives behind the bland faces.'

The whole book? But, of course, *Edwin Drood* is not a whole. All day on June 8, 1870, Dickens was hard at work on it, sitting in the little Swiss chalet that was his isolated writing hut at his home at Gad's Hill Place, near Rochester, otherwise Cloisterham. At dinner that evening he abruptly got up from the table declaring he had to go to London. And then he collapsed. He lay there, on the sofa in the dining-room, terribly ill for almost another twenty-four hours, and at last he died. He had completed only six of the twelve projected parts of his book.

I can remember with lasting vividness the London Exhibition in 1970 commemorating Dickens's centenary, where I saw the very last page he had written on that fatal day, and the very last words from his pen, '. . . and then falls to with an appetite.'

So, although as a crime novel *Edwin Drood* has a right to its place in these pages, should it—as only a 'haunting and broken vision', as James Wright of the University of Minnesota strikingly calls it—be here at all? I am altogether convinced that it should. And for exactly the reason indicated in James Wright's description. Because, though broken, its vision is haunting.

Dickens died before he was sixty, at the height of his powers. The pages of *Edwin Drood* are crammed with splendid things. There are pulsatingly vivid descriptions of the old cathedral city and, in glimpses, of the hidden side of the teeming metropolis of London. There is the extraordinarily skilful way in which we, the readers, are moved between scenes of humour, of farce, of sentiment, of brooding mystery. There is a host of different characters, each one standing out in sharp memorability.

But, more than this, the truncated whole gives us in full that theme, the inescapable duality of our nature, which Dickens wished to put into our heads as we attempt to solve the book's puzzle. And that is a puzzle, incidentally, that remains unsolved. Any new reader can join the dozens of commentators who have attempted to guess what solution Dickens had in mind.

Finding a satisfying answer, however, is a daunting task. Dickens had set for himself a situation of fearful complexity, and, though it is almost certain he knew before he had done much thinking about the book what solution he wanted, he had, as is the way of fiction writers, told no one what he had in mind. We have only a few tantalising hints, such as his correction of the drawing for the first draft of the title page.

But we should pay more attention to something Dickens' intelligent daughter, Mrs Perugini, once wrote: that no one would be 'able to detect any word or hint from my father that it was upon the Mystery alone that he relied for the interest and originality of his idea.' Dickens wanted to write the story, she goes on, because it was with 'his strange insight into the tragic secrets of the human heart, that he desired his greatest triumph to be achieved.'

Broken though the book is, it is yet a triumph, a triumph in the art of the crime novel. We can in our turn 'fall to with an appetite.'

First edition London: Chapman and Hall, 1870 (in parts)
First US edition Boston: Fields, Osgood, 1870

[1892]

4

ARTHUR CONAN DOYLE

The Adventures of Sherlock Holmes

On November 11, 1891, a not-very-well-known author, Arthur Conan Doyle, wrote to his mother to say he had just completed five more stories about his detective, Sherlock Holmes, to add to the seven he had produced for the *Strand Magazine* earlier. 'The twelve,' he said, 'ought to make a rather good book of sorts.' Considering that among them were 'A Scandal in Bohemia', 'The Red-headed League' and 'The Speckled Band', I think we can feel Doyle's modest claim was justified.

The stories as they appeared month by month in the then-new magazine became so much the rage that when, not much later, Doyle brought the series to an apparent end by killing off Holmes, groups of young men wearing black armbands marched on the magazine's office, and in various American cities 'Let's Keep Holmes Alive' clubs sprang up like mushrooms on a dewy summer morning. There was more than one reason for this extraordinary explosion of popularity.

First, perhaps, a detective who insisted on scientific method appealed to a new generation. It is not too much to say that until about this time the large majority sought explanations for almost any phenomenon in superstition. They believed in fairies. They had not been taught to trace back an event by logical stages to its mechanical cause. But in 1870 in Britain an Education Act had instituted reading, writing and arithmetic for all. Similar moves had happened in America. In consequence, by 1892 there was a large layer of society which could not only read but could tackle reasonably difficult material and had some grasp of scientific method.

On to this seedbed the Holmes stories fell, grew and prospered. But they would not have done so well, or lasted so long, were it not that Doyle had created in Holmes a figure to admire, even almost to worship. He was the hero. He was the lone bachelor untrammeled by everyday difficulties. But he was more than this. He was a recognisable human being, if one of a very superior sort. He was capable of human weaknesses, not only in his recourse to a stimulating seven per cent solution of cocaine, but also in his susceptibility to the prick of vanity. And he was a bundle of human contradictions.

He was an English gentleman, and yet a drug-taking, music-loving aesthete. He hated publicity, and yet subtly egged on Dr Watson to recount his exploits. He was a woman hater, yet he could show women 'a remarkable gentleness.' And to all this Doyle added something more. He made us see Holmes through the eyes of Dr Watson, an invention in some ways more remarkable than that of Holmes himself.

Watson, unblushing, can tell us Holmes was a genius. Watson can fail to see what Holmes has observed, and thus keep the nub of a story secret till its end. Watson is just a little more stupid than ourselves and thus gives us a feeling of quiet superiority. But Watson, though often something of a fool, was not a figure to despise. He was unquestioningly brave, unquestionably decent. He was, morally, ourselves as we hope we are.

Add to these assets a third, a technical advance, Doyle's invention of the series story, and you can see why the tales in this first collection merit the highest stature. But there is yet more to them. Tales I have called them, and this is what most of them are. Not concocted stories with a pay-off, but living entities which appeal to the depths in us.

Take the one called 'The Engineer's Thumb'. At first glance this is just a good story, curiously paralleling Edgar Allan Poe's 'The Pit and the Pendulum', with its hydraulic press, large as a room, and its last-minute escape. But look more closely and you see that both press and pit are prisons and represent prisons for minds. They tell of people locked into their own preconceptions.

And by whom in Doyle's story is the prisoner finally released when the press is located? By the Great Detective. In whom, thus, we find a figure of much more weight than any mere solver of simple criminal puzzles. In Holmes we find a figure of more than passing meaning. He is a true myth.

First edition London: Newnes, 1892
First US edition New York: Harper, 1892

5

E.W. HORNUNG
The Amateur Cracksman

At their best I rate E.W. Hornung's linked stories about A.J. Raffles, gentleman and burglar, squarely beside Conan Doyle's tales of Sherlock Holmes. Both, it seems to me, have an air of absolute rightness, the air that marks out the classic in any branch of literature. In many of the Raffles stories there are blemishes, but then so there are in not a few of the stories that Doyle, curiously Hornung's brother-in-law, wrote about Holmes. Yet in neither are they more than flakes of rust on engines that work with oiled perfection.

There is certainly no need to make more allowances than this for the Raffles stories in this collection. Although they date from so long ago, they can still be read today with pure pleasure. It comes not just from their period atmosphere, heady though that is. Unless you remember them exceptionally clearly, they can be re-read and still provide delightful and genuine surprises. Hornung knew the secret of telling the adventure tale. He had the trick not just of making us readers ask 'What next?, What next?' but of making us almost cry aloud: 'How on earth will he wriggle out of it this time?'

Hornung was a fine craftsman, and within the rigid limits of a short story craftsmanship is needed more than in the novel, where there is room for diversions that can cover up the sound of basic machinery inclined to clank. But look at the way Hornung varies a basic formula, the simple idea of a gentleman being a thief and getting away with his thefts despite all odds. On the face of it one might think that this would be good for two or three outings before it became obvious and boring.

But sometimes Hornung takes his Raffles out of his snug and snobby set of expensive flats, the Albany, to some different location, for example to Italy in 'The Fate of Faustina'. Sometimes he gives the usually cynical Raffles a tinge of being a righter of wrongs. Sometimes he makes the thrust of a story not 'How will Raffles wriggle out now?' but a duel with the truly formidable Inspector Mackenzie. Sometimes a story depends largely on Raffles as a master of disguise.

Yet Hornung was more than a clever craftsman. He possessed all the sensitivity of the good writer. George Orwell points out in one of the essays in *The Decline of the English Murder* that a lesser writer would have crudely made his anti-hero a lord or a baronet so as to get the maximum of showy contrast. But Hornung made Raffles a simple gentleman. And in the same way one comes across countless instances of Hornung preferring to the brutally obvious, and thus dull, something less than obvious but marked with the stamp of truth.

This avoidance of the crudely obvious is the reason why Raffles has lived when other heroes of crime stories of that era are long forgotten. Raffles is far more than a walking formula. He is a person one can believe in. Indeed, Hornung made him something yet more subtle than the simple gentleman. He is a gentleman who has not inherited the wealth needed to keep up, in those days, the gentlemanly show. He is a cricketer of renown, which on the face of it is an easy way of making him a hero, but he is no sporting hearty. Hanging in his Albany apartment are pre-Raphaelite etchings.

It is interesting, indeed, to compare him to that other figure who might have been a plaster hero and is a human being, Sherlock Holmes. Both were apt to act not for reward but for the satisfaction of exercising their art, whether detection or burglary. Holmes, like Raffles, was a sensitive man beneath a hard outer casing. And both had a companion through whose eyes we see them. For Doyle's Watson, Hornung gave us Bunny, not the brightest of brains but brave and all too loyal, a puppy to the bulldog Watson. And, to redeem anti-social traits, both Holmes and Raffles were ardent patriots in the days when such sentiments were natural among the great body of the public. Where Holmes had pistol-pocked his wall with 'VR' for Victoria Regina, Raffles in the story 'A Jubilee Present' sends his Queen a gold cup, stolen especially for the occasion.

Holmes and Raffles: they are the obverse and reverse of the same coin. Abiding heroes.

First edition London: Methuen, 1899
First US edition New York: Scribner, 1899

6
ARTHUR CONAN DOYLE
The Hound of the Baskervilles

In 1894 Conan Doyle, little realising what his inner mind had given to the world in the shape of that myth, the Great Detective, killed off Sherlock Holmes so as to have time to write more 'important' historical and moral novels. But from then on he was under pressure to revive his hero—from countless readers, from publishers and, almost certainly, from the internal power of his own genius. And at last the dam broke. On a postcard, with true Holmesean immodest modesty, Doyle wrote 'Very well. A.C.D.' Holmes was back.

The Hound of the Baskervilles, the book-length adventure that restored Holmes to us, claims to date from before his death struggle with Professor Moriarty. But from page one it gives us, with satisfying richness, the true Holmes as, first, he allows Watson to derive clues from a walking-stick left in their rooms, and then firmly squashes his deductions and goes on to create their as-yet-unseen visitor from the tell-tale marks on the stick. The dialogue simply crackles. You can almost see Doyle hopping in his head first to Watson (one side of his own character), then to Holmes (another, more mysterious, better-hidden side).

A hidden side. This, in fact, is the deeper theme that lies underneath what might have been a pretty kitsch sort of ghost story. The Victorians, and still more the Edwardians, priding themselves on a Britain that seemed to be progressing to ever-new heights, secretly feared something below the surface. They feared a violence below that might erupt, reducing the civilised beings they believed they had become to savages. The name they gave their fear was 'atavism', the recurrence of primitive characteristics from the remote past.

The idea of atavism permeates the book. When Watson looks up in the medical directory Dr Mortimer, their stick-leaving visitor—the Great Detective's suppositions about him having proved totally correct—they find he is the author of ' "Some Freaks of Atavism" (*The Lancet*, 1882).' Seemingly this is a touch designed merely to add plausibility to the directory entry, but already we have a pointer to the book's deeper purpose. Then, when the story takes Holmes to Dartmoor, we get the complicating presence of an escaped convict, his face 'all seamed and scored with vile passions', such that he might be 'one of those old savages' from the moor's primitive caves. Finally, the villain proves to be a throwback to a wild earlier generation.

So Doyle was putting a wince-inducing finger on a fear shared by many of his contemporaries, the dread of the violence within. It was something he recognised from his own depths. There is a curious poem he wrote that gives a lot away—just. It tells of the different beings who inhabit 'The Inner Room' of his mind, among them 'a stark-faced fellow/ Beetle-browed/ Whose black soul shrinks away/ From a lawyer-ridden day.' It is this self-knowledge that accounts for the power of the book.

But there are other things that account for the hold it has had on hundreds of thousands of readers. There is the legend of the black dog, a shiver-making ghost that has haunted people from the days of Ancient Egypt, where Anubis the jackal-headed undertaker-god roamed, to the many tales that have only in recent years faded from the British countryside. And there is Doyle's sheer good writing, from that often quoted 'Mr Holmes, they were the footprints of a gigantic hound' to the quieter, but almost as telling, 'there came no other sound but the chiming clock and the rustle of the ivy on the wall.'

On the other hand, the book has its share of errors. Doyle knew Dartmoor only from one brief visit. He has wild orchids flowering there in October (they don't); he has bitterns, those mournful-sounding birds, 'booming' at that time (they do so only in the spring); his Grimpen Mire is a bog a lot more dangerous than anything in actuality: and, worst of all, he put Baskerville Hall fourteen miles from Princeton prison, which would place it in the smiling Devon countryside.)

Yet none of these errors matter. The sweep of Doyle's narrative swishes us past them. He has used fiction-facts, things invented for the purpose of the story alone, a right established by the sheer story-telling power of this, one of the most gripping books in the language.

First edition London: Newnes, 1902
First US edition New York: McClure, 1902

7

JACQUES FUTRELLE
The Thinking Machine

The respected American critic, E.F. Bleiler, has said of Jacques Futrelle's story 'The Problem of Cell 13', the centrepiece of this book, that it 'is surely one of the dozen most famous detective stories ever written.' He adds that it has made its author familiar to almost everyone who reads crime fiction. Not so, I fear, to readers in Britain. The book was published in London in 1907, but when it was put out again in New York in 1918 under the title *The Problem of Cell 13* the edition was not picked up on the other side of the Atlantic. Since then, to the best of my knowledge, there has been only one British reprint, of an American edition called *Best Thinking Machine Stories* in 1973, though 'The Problem of Cell 13' has featured in anthologies.

This is sad. The story deserves all the praise it has received from Mr Bleiler and in Britain from Julian Symons, who in his magisterial survey *Bloody Murder*, parallels Futrelle's Professor S.F.X. Van Dusen with G.K. Chesterton's Father Brown, seeing the pair as the two most successful creations of the Golden Age of the detective short story and acknowledging 'Cell 13' as Futrelle's finest work.

Professor Van Dusen perhaps has failed to attain the world-wide fame of Sherlock Holmes, whom he much resembles for omniscience—and indeed excels—precisely because Futrelle sacrificed in him the human element in favour of the power of pure thought. Not for nothing is he called the Thinking Machine. Futrelle describes him as dwarf-like in stature, with a head big enough to need Size 8 in hats, though with a face that is small and white and overshadowed by a shock of yellow hair. He shares Holmes's heroic disdain of womankind ('I know nothing about women myself') but he has nothing of the sudden softening ability to make mistakes and acknowledge them that makes Holmes such a human figure.

So, though it is easy to step into the professor's shoes as we read and see ourselves for a short time as all-conquering geniuses, it is not easy at all to step into his mind.

Yet all-conquering genius he was, and Futrelle's great achievement is convincingly to show him solving problems that really do seem impossible. I refrain from analysing 'The Problem of Cell 13' since there will be, especially in Britain, many readers yet to meet its challenge. But let me spoil one other of the Thinking Machine stories.

In 'The Crystal Gazer', Futrelle first shows a somewhat sceptical American traveller named Varick, much interested in the occult, being allowed by an Indian seer in New York to peer into his crystal. In it he sees a room which he recognises as his own study, miles away in his apartment. He himself appears to be seated there. Then, more astonishingly, he sees a man enter and plunge a dagger into his back.

Varick does at least have the gumption to tell his fearful experience to the Thinking Machine, who questions him closely and then sends him into hiding. Later the professor's legman, a reporter called Hutchinson Hatch, seizes the seer in the act of attempting to knife a substitute victim whom the professor has provided. The professor explains: the fraudulent seer wanted to kill Varick for his money. To clear himself in advance he contrived a system of mirrors reflecting into his crystal from a room below an exact replica of Varick's study.

This is a foolproof explanation, and it would be a bright reader indeed able to hit on it. But the brilliance of the story lies not in the trick itself so much as in Futrelle's ability to envisage the whole idea. He must have had an extraordinary imagination. And he had other useful gifts to supplement it. He wrote fast-moving, direct prose. His characters were, at least on the surface, very well observed. He was able to embellish the stories with nice touches of humour.

Sadly, we were given less chance than we might have had to delight in these talents. Shortly after his thirty-seventh birthday Futrelle was on board the *Titanic* on the night she sank. He pushed his wife into a lifeboat, but refused to get in himself. He went down with the ship.

First edition New York: Dodd, Mead, 1907
First UK edition London: Chapman and Hall, 1907

8

MARY ROBERTS RINEHART
The Circular Staircase

'This is the story of how a middle-aged spinster lost her mind.'
Thus begins Mary Roberts Rinehart's *The Circular Staircase*, a
book which has been hailed as the best novel by the most
important American woman mystery-writer. Those opening
words point both to the common notion of what the book is
about, and to its real and long-lasting achievement.

First, how the book is commonly seen. To many casual
readers, and to more who have never actually read it, the book
appears to be the arch-example of a school of writing, mostly by
female authors and designed apparently for female readers
(though somehow males seem to have acquired considerable
knowledge of a good many of its products) that has been labelled
the 'Had I But Known' genre. It was epitomised in a poem by
Ogden Nash:

> Sometimes it is the Had I But Known what grim secret lurked
> beneath the smiling exterior, I would never have set foot within the
> door;
> Sometimes the Had I But Known then What I Know now, I could
> have saved at least three lives by revealing to the Inspector the
> conversation I heard through that fortuitous hole in the floor . . .

Indeed, at a superficial level this is what happens in *The Circular
Staircase*. Rachel Innes, the spinster, impulsively rents a lonely
country house and, when it seems to be haunted, she investigates
with increasing temerity until she has wrested its secret from the
hidden room no one else can find, and has witnessed five lives
'sacrificed in the course of this grim conspiracy.' And all to
create, in Julian Symons' words, 'an entirely comfortable shiver.'

For many readers that is all the book holds, or seems to hold.
But, whether they recognise it or not, it is a novel that operates at
a much deeper level than this, a more affecting level.

Despite the way—irritating to some readers—in which major
clues are withheld from the official detective, and despite what
others will see as the excessive use of coincidence, the book is, in

25

fact, a major example of the use and functioning of that figure of potent myth, the Great Detective.

Rachel Innes, middle-aged and at a point of mid-life crisis, a spinster (and in that at one with the lonely bachelors, Sherlock Holmes and Poe's Dupin), does just what the more obvious examples of the myth figure do. She combines the approach of logic with the approach of intuition. She climbs to the truth both directly up the straight line formed by a spiral staircase (and, note, there is no outward reason why the stairs in the house should take this form), and simultaneously by taking the winding, spiralling path of intuition, the path of the right-hand side of the brain as opposed to the logical left side.

And, more in the way of underlying symbolism, the story switches constantly between light and dark, between the light of logic and the night-side, the often feminine way of intuition, which comes marvellously into its own when at midnight the local electricity company shuts off the power and the old-fashioned lights fade slowly 'until there is only a red-hot loop to be seen in the bulb, and then even that dies away.'

Then we are in the realm that women writers from Mary Shelley fantasising Frankenstein and his half-mad monster to Daphne du Maurier and her haunting *Rebecca* have made their own. It is a world where women are frequently symbolically trapped in the twisting-corridored houses of their constrained lives. It is the world which Rachel Innes 'lost her mind' to enter and in the end to break out of.

It is a world, a book, that demands and gets complete emotional identification with its heroine, from male readers eased along by the author's splendidly readable prose as well as from women. And, note, it is a world where besides the murders and the horrors there is a constant reference to normality, partly from the warm and unforced humour that threads through it, partly from the presence of lovers gradually coming together and partly, again, from a strong sense of place and an even stronger ability to create believable characters at all levels.

No wonder that at one time Mary Roberts Rinehart was the highest paid writer in America. No wonder her book still lives.

First edition Indianapolis: Bobbs-Merrill, 1908
First UK edition London: Cassell, 1909

9

G.K. CHESTERTON

The Innocence of Father Brown

G.K. Chesterton was a spouting, ever-active volcano of spark-bright words, from his first collection of essays in 1902 to his autobiography published in the year of his death, 1936. And almost all those fiery particles have left, it seems, only dead ashes. With two exceptions. A handful of all the thumping verses he wrote lives on, and, above all, so do the stories he invented about Father Brown, the little Catholic priest who was somehow also one of the band of Great Detectives.

Towards the end of Chesterton's words-whirling life a good many of the Father Brown stories tended to be sparks that would soon end as cold ash. Told by his wife that the bank balance had shrunk low, he would sigh and say 'That means Father Brown again.' But the earliest tales of the priest-detective, the ones in this volume, have kept their fiery glow to this day and are hardly ever likely to lose it.

These are the ones he wrote *con amore*, with immense verve and splendid vividness; not for nothing was he also a highly talented artist, who originally trained at the prestigious Slade School. They sprang in part from his own simple delight in the detective story. The pockets of the huge cape he delighted to wear were frequently stuffed with what he called 'penny dreadfuls' and, ten years before he brought Father Brown to popping life, he composed a fine, fulminating 'Defence of Detective Stories.'

He hailed these then somewhat despised tales as 'the earliest and only form of popular literature in which is expressed some sense of the poetry of modern life.' Men, he said, 'lived among mighty mountains and eternal forests for ages before they realised they were poetical; it may reasonably be inferred that some of our descendants may see the chimney-pots as rich a purple as the mountain peaks, and find the lamp-posts as old and natural as the trees.' A prophecy which the novels of Margery Allingham in England and Raymond Chandler in California may seem to have fulfilled.

The detective, Chesterton went on, is 'the original and poetic figure, while the burglars and footpads are merely placid old cosmic conservatives, happy in the immemorial respectability of apes and wolves.' The image gives a good flavour of Chesterton's chief gift, his fecund paradox-making. And, note, a paradox is not simply something turned upside-down: it is something turned upside-down to bring to light a forgotten truth.

Chesterton's gift of paradox came most into its own, perhaps, in his detective stories. The ability to see paradoxes is something any detective-story writer might well ask as a gift from his fairy godmother. Essentially, detective stories depend on a sudden seeing of something the right way up, which often means turning it upside-down. Poe showed us that the best place to hide a letter is in a letter-rack. Conan Doyle told us that the really significant thing was that the dog did *not* bark in the night-time.

The gift was all the better in Chesterton's case for being powered not just by a puzzler's delight in producing conundrums but by the whole man and his beliefs. He saw everything, as often as not, upside-down. And nowhere is this more so than in his running portrait of Father Brown.

Though based on a real priest whom Chesterton knew, Father Brown is, in fact, not a portrait-in-depth. He is rather a walking idea, an immensely lively and paradoxical doll, the tame little priest who both knows more about human wickedness than any policeman and can defeat the most murderous of evil men. He is, indeed, a Great Detective.

The paradoxical method of this innocent priest is to put himself heart and soul (and 'soul' is the word) into the minds of his suspects. Then, when he has bent himself into the murderer's posture of 'hunched and peering hatred', he knows who done it. At that moment of truth we see him, in 'The Secret Garden', looking up 'with a face quite fresh and serious, like a child's.' He has the wisdom of the child, the directness to go to the heart of things and see them as they are; to see them, often, the other way up from the angle that adults have taught themselves to look at things.

First edition London: Cassell, 1911
First US edition New York: John Lane, 1911

10
MELVILLE DAVISSON POST
Uncle Abner

'It is a law of the story-teller's art that he does not tell a story. It is the listener who tells it. The story-teller does but provide him with the stimuli.' So comments Melville Davisson Post some-where in the middle of the first of the linked stories that make up his magnificent novel *Uncle Abner*. For me, certainly, the stimuli he provides in each of the book's eighteen detachable chapters make me tell myself stories of wonderful puzzlement and, more, of thunderous power.

It is sad, even astonishing, that these stories are not household tales in every English-speaking land, like those of Sherlock Holmes. But although Post wrote them for magazines in Amer-ica in the years before 1918, when they were collected together in the USA, they were not published in Britain until 1972 and now fifteen years later they have dropped out of sight once more. This cannot be because Post was not an extremely skilled story-teller, as witness his observation above, let alone his commercial success which was without parallel in his day, whether he was writing about the unscrupulous lawyer Randolph Mason, who later became like Simenon's detective a 'corrector of destinies', or about that monumental figure Uncle Abner.

Uncle Abner performed his feats of detection in the back-woods of Virginia in the early days of the nineteenth century when, in the area protected by the towering Allegheny Moun-tains, the law hardly ruled. He brought to his occasional and self-imposed task two sterling attributes: keen observation (as evinced in the tale 'An Act of God', when he explains that a deaf man could not have written a certain letter because a word in it was mis-spelled phonetically) and, more powerful, a deep know-ledge of and love for the Bible.

But Abner is no milksop religionist. Physically he is tremendously strong, huge in stature, sinewy, bearded. When he is mocked for sitting in a tavern reading his Bible, after the ensuing fisticuffs it is Abner alone who is able to get astride his horse and depart. And he is, above and before all, a man of good. Challenging all-comers with what he knows to be the truth, he stands there 'like the shadow of a great rock.'

His goodness, however, is shown always in the strict terms of his Bible-based religion. Asked what the motive for the crime was in the story 'Naboth's Vineyard' (a courtroom drama as packed with surprises as any of Perry Mason's, but with much greater power), he replies simply that it is to be found 'In the twenty-first chapter of the Book of Kings.' And that is, of course, the story of Naboth's vineyard, which was coveted by one prepared to use any means to acquire it.

And in the truly magisterial first story in the book, 'The Doomdorf Mystery' (incidentally one of the best of all locked-room tales), when his Watson, the pompous yet courageous Squire Randolph, asks under what statute of Virginia the crime should be prosecuted, Abner replies 'under an authority somewhat higher.' He refers, he says, to the Bible's injunction 'He that killeth with the sword must be killed by the sword,' and goes on to add something yet more significant. 'Must! Randolph, did you mark particularly the word "must"? It is a mandatory law. There is no room in it for the vicissitudes of chance or fortune. There is no way round that word. Thus, we reap what we sow and nothing else.' Tough talk, from a tough man.

In that splendid story we see, too, plodding Squire Randolph, the semi-official examining magistrate, attempting to solve the mystery of the death of the rot-gut seller Doomdorf solely by linear thinking, and ending baffled. In contrast we see Abner, hearing one of the suspects, a fiery hill preacher, rant that he had prayed to have the evil man destroyed 'with fire from heaven', take on 'a deep, strange look.' The typical Great Detectival trance has come upon him, in which he combines rational observations at the scene of the death (where all is laid out with scrupulous fairness) with an intuitive understanding, to arrive at the solution of an 'impossible' mystery.

First edition New York: Appleton, 1918
First UK edition London: Tom Stacey, 1972

11

EDGAR WALLACE

The Mind of Mr J.G. Reeder

The author of crime novels at one time so popular that every fourth book sold in Britain came from his pen surely deserves a place in a list of the hundred best. Some of his output, certainly, should never get near it. Edgar Wallace wrote at enormous speed. *The Coat of Arms* (*The Arranways Mystery* in the U.S.), was written from start to finish over one weekend. And he wrote enormously copiously, a total of 88 crime novels, some 62 volumes of short stories, six straight novels, 28 plays and four volumes of verse, plus quantities of journalism. So it will come as no surprise to learn that he was capable of changing the name of a character half way through a book, or that he could perpetrate howling errors of fact.

But amid all the plethora of the meretricious there are books of real merit. His stories of Sanders of the River in West Africa had so much power they induced a cousin of mine to make a career in overseas administration. And some of the crime novels can be ranked equally high. The one I have chosen is actually a series of linked short stories detailing the methods of Mr J.G. Reeder, 'something over fifty, a long-faced gentleman with sandy-grey hair and a slither of side whiskers that mercifully distracted attention from his large outstanding ears.'

In this description one can see several of Wallace's qualities. There is the economy of the writing. We get a good picture, both physically and mentally, of our hero in some three lines. There is an easy vividness in that 'slither of side-whiskers'. Not for nothing did Edgar, aged about twelve and playing truant from school to sell newspapers at a windy corner of London's Fleet Street, keep himself warm by jumping up and down reciting Shakespeare. And there is a nice touch of humour in that reference to our hero's ears. Wallace has been compared, perhaps a trifle ambitiously, to his friend P.G. Wodehouse.

Mr Reeder, once some sort of private inquiry agent specialising in fraud, is transferred at the start of the book to the office of the Public Prosecutor, an individual and a post invented by Wallace, with a certain quick plausibility, for the occasion. As such Reeder is set to investigate crimes which for various rather vague reasons do not come within the purview of Scotland Yard, an organisation which, incidentally, Wallace in defiance of fact saw as the headquarters of a national police force. Before much of the book has passed Reeder has become the secret terror of a large part of the criminal community.

It is, in fact, in describing this community and the dodges its members can get up to that Wallace comes into his own. He knew that world well. Not only had he reported court cases, but he had been brought up—he was the illegitimate child of an actress—in a Billingsgate fish porter's family in the 'lower depths' of London, (where, however, he was taught to be ferociously honest.)

'The criminal mind is a peculiar thing,' Mr Reeder is once made to remark. 'It harbours illusions and fairy stories. Fortunately, I understand that mind.' Wallace, too, understood that mind, and its curious link to illusions and fairy stories. He understood, as well, the curious link between crime stories and fairy stories. They both need to be set in worlds which do not really exist. Their readers want the happy endings that only very occasionally come to pass in the dirty, grim real world, and are prepared to suspend a good deal of disbelief in the cause.

Thus in reading the stories of Mr J.G. Reeder one must, first of all, accept that such an unlikely person does exist. (He is a deadly shot with a pistol despite being 'a gentleman who liked to work in an office where the ticking of the clock was audible and the turning of a paper produced a gentle disturbance.') Then one must occasionally suspend yet more disbelief at some pretty unlikely turns of events.

But give in to Wallace's happy blend of excitement, mystification and humour and these stories, written no doubt in some haste all of sixty years ago, still amuse, intrigue and notably entertain.

First edition London: Hodder and Stoughton, 1925
First US edition New York: Doubleday, Doran, 1929
as *The Murder Book of J.G. Reeder*

12

AGATHA CHRISTIE

The Murder of Roger Ackroyd

The Murder of Roger Ackroyd is one of the landmarks of detective literature. I am not going to be able to write about it without giving away its fundamental idea, a notion in part suggested to its young author by the man who was to become Earl Mountbatten, Viceroy of India, and who was at last to be assassinated in Ireland. So, reader, beware. In the unlikely event that you do not know the trick, don't read on.

The idea is simply that the narrator-Watson turns out to be the murderer. It is a notion that might seem to flout the agreed conventions of the detective story. But, in fact, it merely takes advantage of these conventions in order to create a puzzle that is a peak of the genre's art. To bring off the feat Mrs Christie had, of course, to abandon the faithful Watson she had put alongside her regular sleuth, Hercule Poirot. For Captain Hastings, no great loss, she substituted a neighbour of Poirot's in his ill-advised attempted retirement to the country, one Dr Sheppard.

The book's story is told totally in his words and, with extraordinary cunning, Mrs Christie contrived that not a single thing he says is other than true. Only occasionally did she arrange his prose in such a way as to conceal from the reader that a period of time has elapsed.

Consider the classic instance of this clever word use. Sheppard, accompanied by Parker, the butler, has broken into the study where they have found the body of Roger Ackroyd. Sheppard recounts how he sent Parker for the police. 'Parker hurried away, still wiping his perspiring brow. (Paragraph) I did what little had to be done. I was careful not to disturb the position of the body, and not to handle the dagger at all.' That 'what little had to be done' is taken by almost every reader to mean some small task of medical tidying up. In fact, Sheppard has stowed the dictaphone that simulated Ackroyd's voice into his doctor's bag and has restored the chair which concealed it to its proper place.

But the splendid cunning of the plot is not the only merit of

Roger Ackroyd. The book embodies at least one fine character study; (commentators on Christie's art have too often, in lavishing praise on her cunning, neglected her considerable skill as a straightforward novelist). The successful portrait is of Dr Sheppard's spinster sister, Caroline. Caroline is, simply, a gossip. As such she is a standard character, one that might have been included in Ben Jonson's theatre gallery of 'humours'. But Mrs Christie succeeded in drawing her so well that she takes on a life of her own, a life as vivid as those characters who are created by the author putting in the contrasts to the 'humour' that is their basic reason for existence. It is a considerable feat.

But the book on its first appearance created a sensation solely because of its plot. Those were the days when detective fiction was the staple entertainment of the reading public, occupying a place comparable to that of the most popular television programmes of today. So sides were taken up in no uncertain manner over Mrs Christie's daring device.

Opinions ranged from 'a rotten, unfair trick' to 'a brilliant, psychological tour-de-force.' In America condemnation came from Willard Huntingdon Wright (S.S. Van Dine, creator of Philo Vance); in Britain Dorothy L. Sayers, Mrs Christie's rival, leapt to her defence. The London *News Chronicle* called the book 'a tasteless and unforgiveable let-down by a writer we had grown to admire.' Its Fleet Street fellow, the *Daily Sketch*, countered with 'The best thriller ever!'

The row brought about a quite unexpected consequence. Coupled with the fact that Agatha Christie's beloved mother had recently died, and that her husband had just announced that he was cancelling their much-needed holiday because he had fallen in love and wanted a divorce, the brouhaha caused the young author to suffer a severe nervous breakdown. It was on one evening during this period, and after a row with Colonel Christie, that she got into her car and drove off. For nine days she was seen no more. A huge manhunt was mounted. Headlines proliferated. Edgar Wallace was asked for his opinion. Then Mrs Christie was found, living under another name, in a hotel in distant Harrogate. She never got over the experience, and in her autobiography she passes over it without a word.

First edition London: Collins, 1926
First US edition New York: Dodd, Mead, 1926

13

DASHIELL HAMMETT
Red Harvest

To appreciate Dashiell Hammett's first novel to the full it is necessary to know something of his life. Though a man of considerable intelligence, he had left school at fourteen and made a higgledy-piggledy living in a variety of jobs, ending up as an operative for the famous Pinkerton detective agency. Then in the course of war service he contracted tuberculosis and did not expect to live long. About 1922 he decided to try to make a living writing.

He contributed to pulp magazines stories about an unnamed operative working for an agency much like Pinkerton's called the Continental. So his hero was, baldly, the Continental Op, and was based on a fellow Pinkerton man. In the stories Hammett endeavoured to tell it how it was. He kept out of them any trace of the authorial voice and any of the thoughts in the Op's head.

His objective was to give his readers the genuine thing. Commenting on his method later, he said: 'The contemporary novelist's job is to take pieces of life and arrange them on paper. And the more direct their passage from street to paper the more lifelike they should turn out.' But some time in 1927 he began to feel that the pieces of life he was arranging as short stories were not enough. He began work on *Red Harvest*.

In it he did more than present directly chunks of life. Indeed, the book can be seen as an allegory, or a morality story from the earliest days of print. It tells of the Continental Op being summoned to a grim mining town called Personville (allegorical point one), a place customarily referred to as Poisonville (allegorical point two) and corrupt from top to bottom, with every member of its police department on the take. The Op has been called there by the town boss, Elihu Willson (another possible allegorical point in the first syllable of that surname) to pin the murder of his son on a rival set of gangsters. But when the Op finds the killing was one of passion, he takes Willson's ten thousand dollar fee and says he is going to use it 'opening up

Poisonville from Adam's apple to ankle.'

This he proceeds to do by the simple expedient of setting one group of crooks against another. The deaths pile up. There are twenty-five of them directly described, and more obliquely implied. But, though the bullets fly, the Op appears to be invulnerable. Indeed this quality, which makes him somehow an avenging angel, or avenging demon, is emphasised by the two tiny injuries he does receive. One bullet just creases his hand. A chair-leg in a fight bruises his arm.

Yet, despite this almost fairytale unlikeliness, the book is splendidly real. I suppose it could be described as an example before its time of late twentieth-century 'magic realism.' Hammett discovered for it a power of visual description not only riveting in itself but laying out characters in front of one with wonderful clarity.

Add to this a stinging humour, and as a reader one is in no danger of feeling caught up in a dreary morality. It is an achievement to parallel John Bunyan's *Pilgrim's Progress*, though the humour is far from Bunyan's delightful innocence. 'I haven't laughed so much,' the Op says once, 'since the hogs ate my kid brother', while the town's bootleg bourbon is described as tasting 'a little bit like it had been drained off a corpse.'

But there is yet one more level of reality to take into account. The Op is seen eventually as more than an avenging angel/demon. He is shown as being, despite his immunity from bullets, liable to fail. It will be a failure from within. He recognises in himself a growing tendency to go 'blood-simple'. He begins to see in every common object a deadly weapon, an ice-pick, a length of wire, a lighter that could be filled with gelignite.

In this he can be likened to Sherlock Holmes, whom Conan Doyle made occasionally fallible. This recognition makes of two towering figures of crime fiction something more than unreal gods. It makes them figures whom ordinary readers can yet see as part of themselves.

First edition New York: Knopf, 1929
First UK edition London: Cassell, 1929

14

C.H.B. KITCHIN

Death of My Aunt

C.H.B. Kitchin was a man loaded with talents, especially perhaps a talent for using words. His obituary in *The Times* called him a man of uncompromising intellectual honesty, of wide erudition and of iridescent wit. So it might have been expected that when he turned his hand to plaything literature, as crime fiction was in the Golden Age of the detective story, he would produce a book well above the common ruck. And so *Death of My Aunt* was.

In fact, Kitchin somewhat overshot the mark, at least as far as his own ultimate satisfaction was concerned. The book was acclaimed, and the public expected him to do it again, and again. But he by no means wanted to be put on this treadmill. He wanted to go on writing his mainstream novels, fastidious blendings of shimmering humour and quiet lyricism, far from even the civilised murder of *Death of My Aunt*.

This he did, earning himself a small band of devoted admirers only—many of them, like L.P. Hartley, fellow writers. He came to refer to his single detective story as 'that wretched book.' But after five empty years he did produce another, *Crime at Christmas*, and after another five years he yielded again with *Death of My Uncle*. Finally, ten years later, there came his last venture, *The Cornish Fox*. Luckily, he did not need the financial rewards of bestsellerdom. He had private means, and, like the hero of his detective stories, Malcolm Warren, he was a member of the Stock Exchange as well as being an adroit and successful collector of Georgian silver, Meissen teapots, French paperweights.

From this it can be seen that he was very much an amateur writer in detection, as his Malcolm Warren is an amateur detective of the most unprofessional sort. In so far as he is the hero of *Death of My Aunt*—and he would be the first fastidiously to jib at such a description, which is one of his great attractions—he is very much a part-time hero. He has a way of standing back from the hurly-burly which, while it endears him to some, must have helped to ensure that Kitchin's detective stories, like his novels, were never to have wide popular sales.

Added to his delicate sensitivity there is, too, in him a streak of the sharply sardonic, something that must have alienated a few more readers. Right at the beginning of *Death of my Aunt* you come across him saying of that lady, 'Nothing was more galling to her than that one should mention . . . a play which she had not seen.' A bitter little pill for anyone with any intellectual pretensions.

But that tiny, acute observation demonstrates Kitchin's virtue as a crime writer. He had a fearsome knowledge of the crevices of human nature. 'I see,' Inspector Glaize says to Malcolm Warren, with intent to crush, 'that you are a student of human nature.' It is what Warren is, and behind him it is what Kitchin is. And it is his being such a sensitive and sharp student of humankind and its follies that lifts the book out of the realm of the detective story and into that of the detective novel. Kitchin was a writer ahead of his day.

It is this which, to my mind, puts *Death of My Aunt* into the topmost category. As a detective story pure and simple it is no match for the best of that sort. Malcolm Warren is altogether too unpressing an investigator. But among the crime fiction that depends less on any cunning laying-down of clues and ingenious recognising of their significance than on crime revealing characters as recognisably real people, Kitchin can hold his own.

After his day it came to be seen that there was a type of crime fiction which had, as it were, two separate solutions: the one an answer to a basic factual mystery, the other an answer to some aspect of the greater mystery of what people are truly like. *Death of My Aunt*, for all its waywardness, is firmly of this second sort and as such deserves enduring life.

First edition London: L. and V. Woolf, 1929
First US edition New York: Harcourt, Brace, 1930

15

DOROTHY L. SAYERS

The Documents in the Case

The Documents in the Case, which Dorothy Sayers wrote in collaboration with Robert Eustace, adviser on the science aspect of the story, is first of all a classical detective story, or a variant at one remove. It tells the story of the murder of George Harrison, a comfortably-off electrical engineer, first detailing the circumstances prior to his death and then exposing the murderer. There is never more than one suspect, but the element of mystery is fully present in what seems to be an unbreakable alibi. But the book is also a novel, a rumination on a philosophical theme, no less.

This theme is, in fact, an age-old and basic crux of philosophy, the problem of perception. What is the real? Since the evidence of our senses is notoriously fallible, what can we believe of what they tell us?

The book is largely presented in the form of letters, the documents in the case. It opens with one from Miss Agatha Milsom, Mr Harrison's genteel housekeeper, a fussy, doctor-bound, Freud-flirting spinster, who garrulously compares her new doctor and her old one. Innocuous scene setting stuff? Not at all. Miss Sayers used it to play a little trick. By stating clearly that the new doctor is a man and by using only the surname of the former one she plants in our minds the notion that that person also was a man, only, after some eight lines, to explode the idea with a sharp little 'she'. Things are not always what they seem, it warns us.

The second correspondent whose letters we read is one of two bachelors sharing a top-floor flat in the Harrison house, John Munting, an author who is writing a biography. This gives Miss Sayers another lever on her theme. What is a biography but the asking 'What exactly was such-and-such a person?'? And she adds to this by making the subject of the biography a Victorian worthy, so we get references arising from the typically Victorian belief in man's over-riding importance. 'We say,' the intelligent Munting writes to his fiancée, 'it is important when we have a magnum opus to present to an admiring creation, and unimportant when it suits our convenience to have our peccadilloes passed over.' This lack of objectivity proves to cast a shaft of light on to the motive of the murderer, the artist who is Munting's flat-mate.

At the book's climax Munting goes to dinner with the local vicar, who happens to have as his guests old university friends, a physicist, a biologist and a chemist. They discuss—what else?—the origin of life, what makes the organic different from the inorganic. The talk is, frankly, rather too long-winded, but in the middle of it Munting sees that something said could solve the Harrison murder, the possibility of distinguishing an artificial substance from a natural one with exactly the same chemical formula. Real-life is lop-sided, and this will show up in the beam of light from a polariscope.

Munting hurries off with the chemist and tests the meal the victim has eaten to see whether the poison is artificial and could thus have been added to some beef stock in advance, depriving the murderer of his alibi, or whether it is the natural poison from a fungus picked by Mr Harrison himself. In a passage of considerable excitement a shaft of light shines out and the proof is obtained.

So the plot of the book as a whole is made to serve both the puzzle element and a symbolic structure, the symbolism being complemented by the choice of major characters to reflect aspects of the theme as well as by countless incidental details, such as Miss Milsom's doctor. It is a remarkable feat, and all the more so for coming in what is generally seen as the heyday of the pure and simple detective story.

The book is a telling demonstration that this formal detective story, perhaps because of its formal qualities themselves, can make an excellent vehicle for expressing an author's beliefs, even about a major theme. It might be asked whether the addition to a piece of 'mere entertainment' of such profundities is worth the effort. But symbolism works in secret, and is at its most effective when it is least noticeable. So perhaps crime fiction is the best way of putting into readers' minds an author's deepest thoughts.

First edition London: Benn, 1930
First US edition New York: Brewer, Warren, 1930

16

DASHIELL HAMMETT
The Maltese Falcon

Dashiell Hammett's *The Maltese Falcon* is in many ways the archetypal private-eye novel, America's distinctive contribution to mystery fiction. Its hero, Sam Spade, was enshrined in cinema history in the person of Humphrey Bogart as the very type of the 'tough guy' in what the critic James Agee called 'the best private-eye melodrama ever made.' But Sam Spade is more, much more, than a figure of celluloid melodrama. There had been hard-boiled heroes, as they were called, before him. But into these stereotypes Hammett put a charge that made of Spade a folk hero for his times, and perhaps still for ours.

He saw that the private eye could be portrayed, in his own description of Spade, as a 'blond satan.' A satan he is, a man free of almost all the clinging softnesses that impede ordinary people. He is free, most notably, from sentiment. He is free from the fear of death, that unfaceable thing that keeps the majority of us in our place. He is free of the temptation of money, something many of us like to feel we are safe from but which, if offered enough of the stuff, we might well succumb to. Finally, he is free from the lure of sex, a yet more powerful bribe, though of course he is no asexual nonentity, ending as the book begins an affair with his partner's wife.

In *The Maltese Falcon* we watch him flinging aside one by one each of these sticky trammels. We see him reject the advances of the sexy Brigid O'Shaughnessy, taking her to the bathroom and making her strip to be searched in a spirit of calculated coolness. We see his wretched office—he can afford no better—where 'a buff-curtained window, eight or twelve inches open, let in from the court a current of air faintly scented with ammonia.'

We see him, in the curious long tale he insists on telling Brigid, the story of a man named Flitcraft, as prepared for death at any moment. Flitcraft, he tells the uncomprehending Brigid, was a man 'in step with his surroundings' till one day a beam fell from a building and came within an inch of killing him. Converted as dramatically as Saint Paul on the road to Damascus, Flitcraft disappeared. 'He knew that men died at haphazard like that, and lived only while blind chance spared them.'

Spade, the working detective, was sent to locate Flitcraft and found that after some years of free wandering he had simply got himself another wife as like his first in her bourgeois outlook as possible and had settled down to raise a new family. Here Spade is telling Brigid, whom he has already fingered as the killer of his partner, Archer, that he himself is the Flitcraft of the free years, the man who never forgets the beam that fell out of a blue sky. So that no threat of death—and these come—can really touch him.

But, above all, it is sentiment the blond satan is free from. The whole book can be seen as his battle with Brigid, the 'vamp' who ought to be beyond sentiment but who sees life as being dictated by the softer emotions. All through we get Spade's wisecracks—more than just decoration—mocking Brigid's sentimental platitudes. Hammett is portraying a new man for new times—at the beginning, incidentally, of a new decade, the 1930s.

But on top of this theme there is a subject, Spade's obligation to find out who shot his partner, the not very admirable Archer. 'When a man's partner is killed,' he says, 'he's supposed to do something about it.' And on top of that subject there is a story, the story of Spade's search for the Maltese Falcon, the bird statue which, rumour has it, is of incalculable value. The ins-and-outs of this produce for us a memorable gallery of figures from the California underworld, from the fat Gutman to the homosexual gunman Wilmer (a character it was more than a little mould-breaking to portray in 1930). And there is, too, near the start of the book, as fine a detective-story clue—shan't tell you—as any in Agatha Christie.

First edition New York and London: Knopf, 1930

17
ARTHUR W. UPFIELD
The Sands of Windee

Here among my hundred best mystery books is one which is, frankly, written in leadenly ponderous prose. Why have I chosen it? Because it features a very remarkable detective, Inspector Napoleon Bonaparte of the Queensland Police in Australia.

If Bony, as his creator Arthur Upfield says he insists on being called, were no more than an example from Australia of the Great Detective or even of a fine police detective, I would not have given him his place in this century of crime writing. But Bony is more than a mere Australian detective, although what makes him more is, paradoxically, his Australian quality.

Bony is a combination of the two main strains of Australian life in his day, the British settlers (by no means all transported convicts) and the original inhabitants of that sparse-centred continent, the aboriginals—or, as they were called in Bony's time, the blacks. It is the combination of European logicality with aboriginal intuition and observation that puts Bony on a par with Sherlock Holmes or Poe's Dupin, despite the thumping prose with which his creator depicted him.

It was a stroke of luck, or of sudden inspiration, that brought Bony into existence. Arthur Upfield was one of those people who have a tremendous desire to see themselves in print but lack the twist of originality which is, almost always, the passport into fiction authorship. As a young man, sent by his English family to make good in Australia, he had produced a book, *The Barrakee Mystery*, which had failed to find a publisher. Then, spurred on by actually getting into print a mystery called *The House of Cain*, he decided to replace the detective of *The Barrakee Mystery* with a figure he had met in his days of working as a trapper, miner, cook and boundary rider in the outback, one Tracker Leon, a half-caste attached to the Queensland Police.

On to this acquaintance he grafted a rather more romantic background. He gave him his mildly absurd name by stating that he had been found as an abandoned baby and had attempted to eat a Life of Napoleon. He gave him, too, a university education, a wife and family (scarcely seen) and a naïve boastfulness which, if it were not laid on with so heavy a hand, would be more endearing than it is.

In *The Sands of Windee*, in which Bony investigates a 'perfect murder' in the sheep station country of New South Wales, one gets example after example of a tracker's magnificently close observation, combined with European ratiocination and flashes of intuition. At one point Bony's eye falls on an ants' nest and he works out why the creatures are methodically carrying tiny pebbles up from below and replacing them with others from the surface—it is what they do to keep their nest at the right temperature, constantly swapping cold pebbles for sun-warmed ones. And one of these minute stones proves to be a sapphire, and a clue.

There is an interesting story about this book. Upfield had spent a long time devising a really tough case for boastful Bony to crack, and had come up at last with the notion of burning a body, pounding the ashes to powder in a 'dolly pot', sieving them to remove any tell-tale dental work or metal pieces from the clothes and then mixing the remains with those of the kangaroo victim of a bush fire. So 'perfect' was this murder that Upfield was unable to work out how Bony could solve it.

A young man called Louis Carron suggested a hole in the sieve which, unnoticed, lets one tiny clue slip through, and Upfield gave him a copy of *The Sands of Windee* when it came out. Some time later Carron disappeared in mysterious circumstances. Upfield, convinced he had been murdered, eventually found at a likely spot in the bush the copy of the book, badly burnt, but not so badly that he was unable to see that the four pages describing the 'perfect murder' method had been torn out.

Eventually, by the rather more mundane process of seeing who was spending more than their earnings, the murderer who had employed the Windee method was brought to justice. A justice that vindicates the book as a masterpiece of authenticity.

First UK edition London: Hutchinson, 1931
First US edition New York: British Book Centre, 1959

18

FRANCIS ILES

Before the Fact

Before the Fact is one of the key texts in the history of crime fiction. It was called a 'masterpiece' in Howard Haycraft's listing of detective-story cornerstones in his pioneering *Murder for Pleasure*, and even at its first appearance Christopher Morley, the novelist, spoke of it as 'one of the finest studies of murder ever written' adding, pre-echoing Haycraft, 'it is a masterpiece of cruelty and wit.'

The book owes its fame, basically, to the fact that it reversed totally the accepted pattern of the detective story, telling you who done it from the very start. Yet it would not have found its high place had it not also been extremely well-written. It was not the first crime story to turn the genre topsy-turvy. It was preceded, indeed, by the author's own *Malice Aforethought* with its wonderful opening words, 'It was not until several weeks after he had decided to murder his wife that Dr Bickleigh took any active steps in the matter.' And even that was not incontrovertibly the first of the strain.

Iles, in the preface to his own *The Second Shot* (1932, written under his other pseudonym of Anthony Berkeley), draws attention to R. Austin Freeman's collection of short stories *The Singing Bone* of 1912, in which the criminal is seen first actually doing the deed and then the detective is seen at work. In that same year, too, Mrs Belloc Lowndes, author of the Jack the Ripper novel *The Lodger* and creator of a detective called Hercules Popeau, had produced a murder novel seen from the victim's viewpoint, *The Chink in the Armour*.

Yet *Before the Fact* deserves its place in the history of the genre, despite these predecessors, for two reasons. First, for taking the victim's view, an advance on taking the murderer's standpoint, and for being influential as such (Mrs Belloc Lowndes had no followers); and secondly, and more importantly, because it shifted the whole genre towards an increased interest in character. It put people before plot.

In the preface to *The Second Shot* Iles claimed that 'the days of the old crime-puzzle pure and simple, relying entirely upon plot and without any added attractions of character, style or even humour, are, if not numbered, at any rate in the hands of the auditors.' The detective story, he said, was already developing into the novel with a detective or crime interest. 'The puzzle element will no doubt remain but it will become a puzzle of character rather than a puzzle of time, place, motive and opportunity. The question will not be "Who killed the old man in the bathroom?" but "What on earth induced X of all people to kill the old man in the bathroom?"'

But, as Christopher Morley pointed out, the book has more to it than this, a good deal more. It is something of a masterpiece of wit, often very savage wit. Hear this: 'She had never realised that the percentage of happy marriages among the population of Great Britain is probably something under .0001.' Or, less savage but stinging enough, there is the jibe at Iles's fellow member of the Detection Club, Dorothy L. Sayers, lightly disguised as Isobel Sedbusk, whom the heroine wishes had been 'fitted with a volume control, like the wireless.'

Nowhere, perhaps, is Iles's unblinking perception of humankind's follies and weaknesses more evident than in his treatment of sexual relations. The vast majority of the detective stories of the 1930s in England scarcely referred to sex. Occasionally for plot purposes a young couple would be 'in love'. There might even be a guarded reference to adultery. But Iles snapped the taboo like a piece of dried stick. We have Johnny, the murderer, trying 'terrifyingly improper things' with Lina, the victim heroine. We have him calling her 'a stingy bitch in bed' and saying he would 'sooner have a wet fish in my bed'.

The note of reality sounds out. And it is Iles's triumph that he creates believable people in some depth, and people not only believable as first described but capable, too, of changing and developing in a believable way. Here is not only the detective story turned upside-down, but the detective story very much as 'a puzzle of character'.

First edition London: Gollancz, 1932
First US edition New York: Doubleday, Doran, 1932

19

ERLE STANLEY GARDNER
The Case of the Sulky Girl

Erle Stanley Gardner may be said to have made one important contribution to the shifting history of crime fiction. With his immensely successful creation of Perry Mason, lawyer first and detective afterwards, he put a final nail into the coffin of the brilliant amateur sleuth in American crime writing. S.S. Van Dine's Philo Vance (who, as Ogden Nash famously stated, needed 'a kick in the pants') is dead: long live Perry Mason.

And long Perry Mason did live. There are eighty-two investigations, from *The Case of the Velvet Claws* in 1933 to *The Case of the Postponed Murder*, published posthumously in 1973. By and large any one case is hard to distinguish from another, though over the years some change did take place. Gardner came to Perry Mason from writing stories for the famous *Black Mask* magazine, cradle of Dashiell Hammett among others, and the early Masons have a toughness which when Gardner started writing serialisations in the *Saturday Evening Post* vanished away, leaving Mason an out-and-out goodie instead of part-goodie, part-toughie.

Each plot is, of course, different, with some being more complicated and ingenious than others. But the progress of the story, whether written in the 1930s or the 1960s, is almost always exactly the same. A client enters Perry Mason's office, ushered in almost invariably by his secretary Della Street, who is usually described capsulewise—I quote here from *The Case of the Sulky Girl* itself—as 'about twenty-seven years old. Her manner radiated assurance and efficiency.' Mason questions the client, often with more than a little aggressiveness. A murder soon comes to light.

Mason, with the aid of various minions, investigates the circumstances. Generally the client is arrested. And always there is a court scene at the end of which Mason by some tremendous dramatic stroke reveals one of the witnesses as being the true murderer. End of book, bar a final piece of swift moralising, doubly assuring a happy conclusion.

This is formula fiction at its most—word beloved of academic critics—formulaic. But formula fiction should not be despised. Many readers—*millions* of readers, as Gardner has proved—want just this sort of book. A book you can rely on, a book that is going to give you what you expect and nothing more. In short, pure and simple entertainment. And many more readers who customarily ask more than this from their fiction can find times in their lives when what they want is something altogether undemanding.

Because Gardner makes, really, only one demand: that the reader should outguess Perry Mason. And even this is never pressed. You can read a Perry Mason and make no effort at all to arrive at the properly clued solution, and I hazard that the majority of Gardner's readers do that. But for those who want the small stimulation of a puzzle set and a puzzle solved Gardner plays strictly fair.

One character Gardner did create in some depth, and that was Perry Mason himself. Generally his characters are introduced with no more than a brief description. In *The Sulky Girl*, for example, the girl's lover, Robert Gleason, is described: 'A man came into the room who radiated restlessness. He was a thin man, with a very pointed nose and large ears. He walked with nervous, jerky steps. He was in his late twenties or early thirties.' From which you can see that Gardner was no stylist, though he is a splendid rush-on, non-stop storyteller.

But Mason receives slightly better treatment, and from all one reads about Gardner himself, who had to leave college by his own account for bopping a professor on the nose, he and his creation were not unlike. Mason, Gardner says here, 'gave the impression of bigness; not the bigness of fat, but the bigness of strength. He was broad-shouldered and rugged-faced, and his eyes were steady and patient. Frequently those eyes changed expression, but the face never changed its expression of rugged patience.' From such clumsy but well-meant words a myth was created; not a myth of any great subtlety or deep meaning, but a myth nevertheless, and one which is here to stay.

First edition New York: Morrow, 1933
First UK edition London: Harrap, 1934

20

AGATHA CHRISTIE

Murder on the Orient Express

Sir Max Mallowan, Agatha Christie's second husband, relates in his book *Mallowan's Memoirs* how his wife nearly lost her life under the train called the Orient Express shortly before she wrote this book (published in America as *Murder on the Calais Coach*). It was in Calais that the incident occurred. Sir Max wrote: 'It was lucky she lived to write the book, for not long before penning it, while standing on the railway station at Calais, she slipped on the icy platform and fell under the train. Luckily a porter was at hand to fish her up before the train started moving.'

Perhaps it was this escape which prompted Agatha Christie to make this book rather more than just her usual puzzle. She was too much of a craftswoman, however, to let the injection from life affect the story. One of her great virtues is that she always knew her limitations and kept firmly to what she knew she could do.

And cunning with plot was one of her greatest strengths, though curiously enough the plot for this book, which matches that of *The Murder of Roger Ackroyd* for the daring advantage it takes of the conventions of the detective story, was suggested to her by Sir Max. The handling of it, however, was entirely her own and is of its kind masterly.

In it we see her chief sleuth, Hercule Poirot, at his most characteristic. Poirot is the Great Detective as a purely literary conceit. He possesses everything that Edgar Allan Poe laid down as necessary for this figure, and, since his creator described in her autobiography how she came to him directly from considering what went to make Sherlock Holmes, this is not surprising. Poirot is, if you like, the pure essence. As such he has little of a real person about him. There is only an indiscriminate collection of engagingly eccentric traits, none of them too far from the imagination of the ordinary reader. Agatha Christie was wise in the latter days never to allow him to appear on any dust jacket: the various traits would not add up.

However he does possess the key characteristics. He is observant (at least of that which plot-clever Christie wishes him to observe). He is shrewd: a quality, I suspect, he derives from his creator herself. And then, at the height of a case, comes his intuition. There will be a short withdrawal, and, emerging as it were from a trance, the words 'I know.' And Poirot has, probably another inheritance from his creator, a strong, even bourgeois, feeling for right and wrong.

It is this that allowed Agatha Christie to touch in this book on real life, if discreetly. Its story of a murder in a cut-off coach of the Orient Express, delayed and isolated by snow on its journey from Istanbul to Calais, a murder which not one of the possible suspects could have committed, was clearly based on the inadmissible Lindbergh kidnapping case. Poirot's solution, after which revelation he allows the train to proceed with no arrest made allowed his creator to say something about life, to set forth her own beliefs.

In discussing in *An Autobiography* the various sorts of crime fiction she came to write—they are more varied than is often supposed—Christie draws attention to 'what I can only describe as the detective story that has a kind of passion behind it—that passion being to save innocence. Because it is *innocence* that matters, not *guilt*.'

Yet, for all the underlying thread of passion, the book is still primarily a most cunning puzzle. The plot, though perfectly logical, is in fact immensely unlikely. So much so that it aroused the particular ire of Raymond Chandler in his famous essay 'The Simple Art of Murder'. But Agatha Christie was ever one to put entertainment first. While you read you are willing to suspend disbelief and to be caught out magnificently by her simple cunning.

First edition London: Collins, 1934
First US edition New York: Dodd, Mead, 1934
as *Murder on the Calais Coach*

21

JAMES M. CAIN

The Postman Always Rings Twice

No mystery in *The Postman Always Rings Twice*, except the mystery of human behaviour. But crime there is, certainly. And crime written, I venture to think, for all the background seriousness of the book and for all the mainstream novels Cain was later to produce, primarily as entertainment; even if it is entertainment of a fairly grim kind.

The book is the simple tale, the sordid story even, of how Cora, a young woman of blatant sexuality who has left her home in a small town in Iowa for California and the hope of Hollywood stardom, marries the gross Greek owner of a rundown roadside cafe, a man much older than herself, and of how, not long after, when a wandering bum called Frank Chambers comes by, she is led by lust to betray the husband who has given her at least some security, to collaborate in his murder with Frank an' at last to make love beside his dead body.

And there is no postman in the book, either. It owes its strangely memorable title to Cain's sideways acknowledgement of the power of fate, of chickens coming home to roost.

Though the book eschews all comment and authorial moralising, it is by no means the simple storytelling of an untutored, unambitious writer. It is not one of the many products of the 'hard-boiled' school of American popular writing of the 1930s, into which Cain, against his expressed opinion ('I belong to no school, hard-boiled or otherwise') is often placed.

Cain's simplicity and bare straightforwardness arise from sources other than the demands of popular magazines. This style was the conscious choice of a man, then aged forty-two, who wrote this his first novel from an individual motive. He believed that this was the way books should be written in America at the time of the Depression. He was no untutored hack, but a college product (B.A. and M.A.), a skilled journalist (Editorial writer for the *New York World* from 1924 till 1931) and a professor of journalism. His books came to be an acknowledged influence on

51

the Nobel prizewinner Albert Camus' *L'Étranger*.

So Cain deliberately wrote this book in a spare, basic style which has often been compared to Hemingway's. He shied away from anything in the nature of an abstraction and he used very few adjectives to modify the planked-down nouns which tell the story he wanted to make people read. And in 1934 to write about the sexual coming-together of two human beings in these terms was the cause of much scandal, if nowadays what he wrote may seem merely run-of-the-mill.

But at the time even a fellow writer like Raymond Chandler, for all his talk of putting murder back where it belonged, was shocked. Writing to his publisher about *The Postman*, he yelped: 'Faugh! Everything he touches smells like a billygoat. He is every kind of writer I detest, a *faux naif*, a Proust in greasy overalls, a dirty little boy with a piece of chalk and a board fence and nobody looking.'

Even Chandler's literary judgment was sent astray by the violence of his objection. There is nothing falsely naïve about a narrative which Cain cast in the form of Frank Chambers's first-person confession. This is told to us, with all the hypnotic grip of Coleridge's Ancient Mariner, as if by Frank in the death cell, when at the end of the story he has received the rough justice of the book's dénouement.

This is, and it is Cain's point, justice imposed implacably by the ironies of chance. It is this which gives the story a universality which a mere recounting of the lusts and viciousnesses of two ordinary, unremarkable people—Frank and Cora actually yearn for respectability—would otherwise not possess.

Cain's handling of this first-person narrative put him at once into the front rank of American storytellers, but to it can be added an almost equal mastery of place. The run-down café that is the chief locale of the book seems engraved on the mind after even a single reading. And the set scenes, the big encounters, are almost as vividly memorable. The reader feels the sexual attraction between Frank and Cora almost as a tangible heat coming off the black and white of the page. From out of nowhere, in 1934, a journalist-turned-writer produced a kind of masterpiece.

First edition New York: Knopf, 1934

First UK edition London: Cape, 1934

22

DOROTHY L. SAYERS

The Nine Tailors

Dorothy L. Sayers made two great contributions to the art of crime writing. She moved the conventional detective story, the pure puzzle, forward towards being a book in which a whole social milieu could be examined and chronicled with characters much more real than cardboard cut-outs. And she created Lord Peter Wimsey.

Coolly invented to be a detective-story hero who would sell books by the thousand, Lord Peter eventually became a cross between his creator at her most perceptive and the man she would have liked to have loved. He had, in fact, a short, never-seen pre-existence in an unfinished story designed for a crude Sexton Blake series. But from his proper beginning, in *Whose Body?* in 1923, he was a character to be adored, or derided, and clearly one of the élite of Great Detectives.

Sayers made him the second son of a duke, since everybody loves a lord as the saying was. She gave him, too, all the money he could ever need, since, she said, 'at that time I was particularly hard up, and it gave me pleasure to spend his fortune.' He had a fine war record behind him, masked by a 'silly ass' manner. He had a Jeeves-like 'man', Bunter, at his beck and call. Every Chief Constable and lesser policeman was eager for his assistance, and when that failed he was able aristocratically to poke his nose in wherever he liked, thus overcoming a particular difficulty of amateur sleuths less nobly born. He was strikingly and convincingly intelligent, as well as thoughtful and considerate. He also had an unpleasant contempt for Jews and especially 'bolsheviks', traits which were perhaps excusable, just, in the days before Hitler's war.

Various men whom Dorothy Sayers knew and admired have been put forward as the model for this pretty well superhuman soul. There was John Cournos, a now forgotten novelist, with whom she had once been in love. There was a chaplain at Balliol College. There was Eric Whelpton, a handsome ex-Army undergraduate at Oxford for whom she later acted as secretary in France. But, more and more, Lord Peter became Dorothy Sayers, transvestited so to speak and magnifying her passing moods and thoughts into the stuff of fiction.

Something that she said of her creation in an essay she contributed to a book called *Titles to Fame* ought to be added. 'The essential Peter,' she wrote, 'is seen to be the familiar figure of the interpretative artist, the romantic soul at war with a realistic brain.' This is remarkably close to Edgar Allan Poe's great hammered-out definition of the detective as genius, the man combining in himself the poet and the mathematician.

So much for Dorothy Sayers' hero. In *The Nine Tailors* he does not appear as a sleuth until quite late in the affair, having established himself in the opening pages merely as a snowbound traveller. In the book Dorothy Sayers was aiming, and not without success, to do more than add to her continuing portrait of the much-loved Lord Peter. She was revisiting her own childhood, much of which was spent in the East Anglian fens, that curious, flat, windswept region through which Wimsey and the faithful Bunter tramp. 'To the left of them, the drain ran straight as a rule could make it, black and sullen, with a steep bank shelving down to its slow, unforgiving waters. To their right was the broken line of the sunk hedge, with, here and there, a group of poplars or willows.'

This bleak countryside, described with an undertow of love, allowed Dorothy Sayers to do more than produce a jolly setting for the book, with its background of the art of bell-ringing, causing the 'nine tailors' to peal out in a long and complex pattern. It allowed her—the book was to be 'a labour of love,' she wrote to her publisher—to say things about the old, traditional England in whose strengths she fervently believed and whose noble churches, nowhere more noble than standing up in this flat rich country, had given her the religious faith that was her mainstay in a life not without troubles.

First edition London: Gollancz, 1934
First US edition New York: Harcourt, Brace, 1934

23

JOHN DICKSON CARR
The Hollow Man

No collection of the hundred best crime and mystery books would be complete without the one example of that special corner of the field known as the 'Locked-Room Problem' which is recognised by almost every commentator as supreme: John Dickson Carr's *The Hollow Man*, or as it is called in the U.S. *The Three Coffins.*

The book contains not only two murders committed in, to use the words of Dickson Carr's detective Dr Gideon Fell, 'hermetically sealed chambers', but also, in its much-written-about seventeenth chapter, a monstrous and unashamed digression entitled 'The Locked Room Lecture.' In this the author, through the rumbustious sentences of Dr Fell, magisterially outlines the seven types of explanation for what seem to be impossible crimes.

He does more than this, even. He produces a fine and robust defence of the classical puzzle story in general and of its apotheosis, the locked-room problem, in particular. Carpers, he says, have for long denigrated the detective story on the grounds of its improbabilities. But, Dr Fell trumpets, speaking for his creator, improbability is in fact the chief glory of the detective story, and even more so of its culmination in the hermetically-sealed chamber mystery.

The good reader, he says, wants improbabilities; wants indeed to have proposed by the author a situation of marvellous improbability and then to be shown that it is not impossible, not quite impossible, if the author is allowed a series of unlikely but actually just-possible events and coincidences. Thus in *The Hollow Man* itself—I give away little or nothing—it has to be accepted that no fewer than three reliable educated witnesses do not, in the year 1935 in up-to-date London, carry watches, but rather rely on a street clock, a street clock that proves not to be telling the right time.

'When the cry of "this sort of thing wouldn't happen!" goes

up,' Dr Fell says, "You are merely saying "I don't like this sort of story." That's fair enough. If you do not like it, you are howlingly right to say so. But when you twist this matter of taste into a rule for judging the merit or even the probability of the story, you are merely saying "This series of events couldn't happen, because I shouldn't enjoy it if it did."' The case may not be perfectly logical, but it is well put.

One cavil to this theory of improbabilities. On the dust-jacket of the early American editions of *The Three Coffins* its author defended, very properly, fiction against fact. Mysteries such as he delights in, he said, do not happen in real life, nor should they. 'I have prowled around Limehouse,' he wrote, 'and the gummiest sections of Paris, but I have never yet seen a really choice murder in a locked room.' Yet life does occasionally imitate art.

Even before Dickson Carr's book came out, a Chinese laundryman in New York was murdered in precise locked-room conditions. Furthermore, many years later I myself heard a forensic scientist in California describe a real case which came neatly under Dr Fell's fourth heading in 'The Locked Room Lecture', a suicide in which the victim 'shoots himself with a gun fastened on the end of an elastic.' Eagerly in my next Inspector Ghote book, set in California, I adopted the hoary device. It seemed to work, given a few of Dickson Carr's readers longing for improbabilities.

It worked because it remains true that the speed of the hand deceives the eye, or, to put it in writing terms, the speed of the prose deceives the reader—as Dickson Carr himself showed time and again in his books, especially in the wonderfully daring *The Crooked Hinge*, and in *The Problem of the Wire Cage* (in which a man is found strangled in the middle of a wet tennis court with only his own footsteps leading to the body). In such books you give your reader the essential clue and at the same time neatly distract his attention from it—even, if necessary, by having the stately *alter ego* to Dr Fell, Sir Henry Merrivale in the books written as by Carter Dickson, slip on a banana skin. Delightful improbability.

First edition London: Hamish Hamilton, 1935
First US edition New York: Harper, 1835
as *The Three Coffins*

24

REX STOUT

The League of Frightened Men

When Rex Stout died in 1975 he left behind, among other writings, a *corpus* of some forty novels and as many short stories featuring Nero Wolfe, a figure it is not unjust to call the last of the Great Detectives. Stout's rolling river began to flow in 1934 with *Fer de Lance*. It ended with the posthumous *A Family Affair*, in which, through Wolfe, his creator had some trenchant things to say about an America that had spawned Watergate. I have chosen *The League of Frightened Men* as Stout's best book, though I might have picked on half a dozen others. But this early work has Wolfe fully established and also has the virtue of being, as it were, time-hallowed.

Wolfe has been neatly characterised as the most eccentric fictional sleuth to stay this side of being human; but he gets on to that right side, though only just. To begin with, he weighs an almost incredible one-seventh of a ton, has the greatest difficulty in crossing his legs owing to the enormity of his thighs and needs especially strong chairs when he sits. So, naturally enough, he seldom stirs from the brownstone house on New York's West 35th Street which he inhabited for the full length of his career.

In *The League of Frightened Men*, Archie Goodwin, his legman, suggests that Wolfe step out into the street in front of the house to bring his powers to bear on an important witness, a cab driver stationed just there. 'Out?' Wolfe looks at Archie in horror. Archie explains that his employer would not even have to step off the kerb. 'I don't know, Archie,' Wolfe is made to say, 'I don't know why you persist in trying to badger me into frantic sorties.'

Did I say eccentric? To add to this, Wolfe has a collection of ten thousand orchids and is a gourmet's gourmand who once ate a whole eight-pound goose in the course of a single day. He has, too, a routine which has to be adhered to with the utmost strictness, come hell or high water: a murderer with a confession or a man with a gun.

57

Much of *The League of Frightened Men* is concerned with describing this routine, with the arrival at intervals during any confrontation of glasses of beer for the great man (though it is never stated just how they materialise), with his method of entering a room, his method of sitting at his desk. The effect is curious. It is rather like looking at one of those late twentieth-century buildings where the architect has put all the plumbing on the outside. You see the workings, and not only the workings of the story (you don't see the workings of the *plot* till in the last pages Stout launches his surprises), but also of the building-up of the central figure, of the self-proclaimed genius.

Wolfe has often been compared to Sherlock Holmes, with Archie Goodwin cast in the role of Dr Watson, though a Watson whose task in life, or in books, is more than to ask the right questions. Archie has work to do. If Wolfe will not leave the brownstone, Archie is frequently and unceremoniously de-spatched to do the sort of things a Californian private eye does.

But Wolfe collects the fees, and Stout makes a point of naming them. Here lies a notable difference between Wolfe, the American Great Detective, and the various English examples of the breed who almost always work for the love of the chase or some other high-minded motive. The cash nexus, as they used to call it, gives just a thin lining of real steel to a figure that otherwise would be too much beer-inflated flesh to end on that right side of being human.

Yet Wolfe is not all that real. In this early book he is aided by a variety of hired-hand detectives, not much characterised but named as Saul Panzer, Fred Durkin and Orrie Cather. Thirty years later, in *The Doorbell Rang*, what do we find? A pushy female client pointing out to Wolfe, who for his own reasons has stated he has only Archie to assist him, 'You have Saul Panzer and Fred Durkin and Orrie Cather.' So we see that Wolfe himself, Archie, the brownstone and all the subsidiary characters are, in fact, timeless.

First edition New York: Farrar, 1935
First UK edition London: Cassell, 1935

25
ETHEL LINA WHITE
The Wheel Spins

Not many books can stand up to being read simply for themselves fifty years after they were written. But among those that
can, *The Wheel Spins* certainly earns its place. What keeps it
fresh, despite more than a few topical references such as that to
Diana Wynyard as a current cinema delight, and the frequent use
of 'topping' as an exclamation of pleasure, is writing of an
unobtrusively high order. This is the salt that preserves, when
books from that period as exciting or more puzzling are long
forgotten.

What enabled Ethel Lina White to put so much energy into her
writing was that she had something to say beyond the simple tale
of a girl in a train finding that an elderly woman fellow-passenger
seems to have disappeared, even though there have been no
stops. The title given to the Hitchcock film based on the book
was *The Lady Vanishes*, which is also used on many later
editions. This is in many ways a pity. *The Wheel Spins* points
plainly to the book's theme, to what Ethel Lina White wanted to
say.

Which is that chance plays an extraordinarily important part in
the lives of all of us, even those, like the Mr Flitcraft of Dashiell
Hammett's *The Maltese Falcon*, who lead the most humdrum of
existences. The theme is a difficult one for the novelist, since
novels are in essence rational orderings of the chaos of human
existence. Conrad tackled it in his novel named, simply, *Chance*.
Patricia Highsmith has also, many years after Ethel Lina White,
succeeded in using the theme effectively in a novel of suspense,
Ripley's Game. But few other novelists have been courageous
enough to tackle it.

Perhaps it is in the novel of suspense, which *The Wheel Spins*
partly is, that chance can most easily be handled as a theme.
When a high-tension situation has been successfully contrived, as
it most certainly is here, the effects of chance come into play with
perfect naturalness.

Take one example from *The Wheel Spins*, a tiny episode made to say much. Max Hare, a man who befriends the heroine, Iris, without consistently believing her story of the vanished Miss Froy, is bringing her a cup of soup into which he half-intends to put a sleeping draught given him by the enigmatic local doctor. He decides that if he can carry the brimming cup through the crowded, swaying train without spilling it he will use the draught, a notion typical of the irrational way we often go about our business.

Max almost succeeds in getting the soup to Iris unspilt. But at the last moment a child buffets into him. Chance. But—and this is where Ethel Lina White scores over less sophisticated rivals—Max, put out by the nearness of his success, returns to the train kitchen and collects a second cup which this time he does succeed in conveying intact. So Iris, by a double mischance, is given the draught which almost prevents her pursuing her search.

None of that got into Hitchcock's film, excellent though it is, of its kind. And indeed a lot more of the book is missing from the film. In Ethel Lina White's story Iris does not board the express, taking her from a holiday in a remote corner of Europe where royal extravagance goes hand in hand with primitive sanitation and deadly power politics, until we have read sixty pages.

These pages do much more than describe the sunstroke which is the necessary preliminary to Iris's disoriented state as her journey takes its nightmare course. We see her among a noisy, rather unpleasant, group of hedonistic young people, some as wealthy as she is, others spongers, all careless of others—as Iris herself is at this stage of the story.

So the subsequent adventure on the train is an account of how Iris reaches maturity, and the book benefits from a deeper layer below that of the theme of the spinning roulette wheel of chance. No wonder it is as readable today as it was when it was first published.

First edition London: Collins, 1936
First US edition New York: Harper 1936
Subsequently published as *The Lady Vanishes*

26
NICHOLAS BLAKE
The Beast Must Die

The title of this detective story is taken from the text of Brahms's *Four Serious Songs*, a paraphrase of the Book of Ecclesiastes, 'The beast must die, the man dieth also, yea both must die.' The author, whose pseudonym concealed the poet (eventually Poet Laureate) Cecil Day-Lewis, had learnt the music while an undergraduate at Oxford, his 'loud, confident but wonderfully inaccurate' pianist being the poet W.H. Auden, who later became the primary model for Nicholas Blake's detective Nigel Strangeways.

All of which is perhaps a clue to the fact that, under the outward show of being a straightforward detective story, *The Beast Must Die* is a good deal more. Seriousness was shouldering its way into the plaything genre. You can tell from the very opening page of the book that you are in the hands of a writer who has something of weight to put before you, however apparently light-hearted the means.

The book begins with a declaration: 'I am going to kill a man . . . I have no idea what he looks like. But I am going to find him and kill him.' Then, at once, with a nice play on the old phrase 'gentle reader', the narrator steps down from his melodramatic note, only within a couple of hundred words to step up again, not into melodrama but into a consideration of modern man's predicament, no less. 'Deep inside us all there exists,' he says, 'that compulsion to make atonement—a sense of guilt, the traitor within the gates.'

It is, incidentally, this sense of guilt which, according to Day-Lewis's friend Auden in his essay 'The Guilty Vicarage', accounts for the enduring popularity of the detective story, which Auden saw as absolving us temporarily and in miniature from that sense of guilt. It was a view shared by Day-Lewis, who spoke of the detective story as a substitute religious ritual at a time when the religion of the churches was at a discount. The detective and the murderer, he thought, represented the light and dark sides of our divided nature, and the detective's eventual and mandatory triumph was an assertion of our hope that in the end good must triumph.

There is also another and different element of seriousness in *The Beast Must Die*. The reason its narrator is going to 'kill a man' is that the unknown man, a hit-and-run driver, was responsible for the death of the narrator's seven-year-old son. And that loss, and its effect on the widower father, is wonderfully brought to life. Here, one feels, is no play-acting but what seem entirely to be real thoughts, real mourning.

So it nearly was. The idea of the book came from a terrible moment in the poet's own life when his small son was almost run over in similar circumstances.

On virtually every page that follows it is evident that one is in the hands of a fine novelist, from the moments of affecting seriousness to the moments of glancing wit, as when the narrator, himself a writer of detective stories who has kept his identity secret, pretends that he is busy with a biography of Wordsworth, although 'I'd as soon eat a hundredweight of solid glue as write his Life.'

Amusingly, this concealed identity which Nicholas Blake makes such good use of in his story was also based on real life. When Day-Lewis wrote his first detective story, in order to scrape together money to repair the roof of the tumbledown cottage he was then living in, his agent, the formidable A.D. Peters, advised him that it would be best for his career if the up-and-coming poet and the lightweight detective novelist were separated. Alas, though considerable precautions were taken, the disguise proved not to be as effective as that of 'Felix Lane' adopted by our narrator, Frank Cairns.

Nor was Cairns's disguise eventually proof against the pertinacity of Nigel Strangeways. The 'beast' of the book's opening words is indeed killed, but Strangeways is able to lay his finger on the executioner. He lets him choose his own way out, however, allowing Cairns to set sail in a tiny dinghy into the storm-tossed Channel, thus lending a fine touch of irony to the book's title quotation: 'The man dieth also.'

First edition London: Collins, 1938
First US edition New York: Harper, 1938

27
CORNELL WOOLRICH
The Bride Wore Black

Never take your child aged eight to Puccini's tragic opera *Madam Butterfly*. Or perhaps you should. Because, it has been argued, this experience gave Cornell Woolrich his deep and pervasive feeling for tragedy and was ultimately responsible for such a landmark book as *The Bride Wore Black* and the succession of titles that followed, each containing the significant word 'Black'.

On the other hand, Woolrich himself lived a life of reclusive misery which may also have been triggered by that too-early experience of the lush sadness of Puccini and his doomed Japanese heroine, though it was doubtless also much affected by the collapse of his parents' marriage, by his own extremely short-lived marriage and by his homosexuality in a period when such an inclination could not be flaunted.

Together these afflictions sent Woolrich to live the life of a recluse in a series of New York residential hotels, with a mother he both loved and hated. Nevertheless the experiences also gave us his books and short stories. Both poured out in a huge stream under his own name and those of William Irish (*Phantom Lady*, 1942) and George Hopley (*Night Has A Thousand Eyes*, 1950).

The Bride Wore Black, his first mystery novel following five straight novels in the manner of F. Scott Fitzgerald, an early hero, is the story—though this is hardly the word for Woolrich's particular method of holding the reader—of a series of murders of young men-about-New York, at first apparently unconnected, and of the tenacious pursuit of the criminal by a detective named Lew Wanger.

Wanger is described almost solely in the following terse terms: 'Lew Wanger left the cab with its door teetering open and elbowed his way through the small knot of muted onlookers.' The brevity is typical of the driving speed which Woolrich got into his stories, as well as being typical, with that word 'teetering', of the vividness of his writing.

Woolrich was later to coin the term 'the line of suspense' to describe his method. Unusually and daringly he abandoned the 'line of story', the 'what next, and what next?' that most crime writers and many straight novelists rely on. Instead he asked himself: 'What will snatch up my readers next into a state of nail-biting suspense?', and by laying out situation after situation of that sort he constructed in the end books that hang together, though along the way you have to give him a good deal of trust.

So, here we get first a short unexplained scene of a woman leaving a house, being called after, pathetically, by an unnamed friend, and then carefully buying a rail ticket for a distant destination—and getting out of the train at the first stop within the confines of New York City. Then we are lifted up and dumped down in what might almost be a self-contained short story about a socialite at whose apartment block a mysterious and beautiful girl calls. We next see this girl gatecrashing the socialite's engagement party at his fiancée's penthouse and manoeuvring herself out on to the high balcony alone with the socialite, who appears not to know her. This section ends swiftly with a phone call telling us that the socialite's body is lying on the pavement below. Enter Lew Wanger.

Similar short episodes follow, each unexplained. Only in the book's final pages do they all come together. The result is extraordinarily satisfying.

It well accounts for the high praise, often laced with sharp criticism of much of the output, that has been heaped on this writer, a writer much better known and appreciated in his native country than in stodgier Britain. He has been called by his biographer Francis M. Nevins, with only a little exaggeration, 'the Poe of the twentieth century and the poet of its shadows.' The *Encyclopedia of Mystery and Detection*, edited by Chris Steinbrunner and Otto Penzler, hails him as 'possibly the finest mystery writer of the twentieth century', and Ellery Queen, fine writer himself, has said that few other books make the reader share so deeply 'the agony of the hunted and the terror of the doomed.'

First edition New York: Simon and Schuster, 1940
First UK edition London: Hale, 1942

28

NGAIO MARSH

Surfeit of Lampreys

The murder in this book (tamely known in America as *Death of A Peer*) occurs on Page 71, out of a longish total of 284. Its coming as late as this is not without significance. Ngaio Marsh had undertaken to provide a conventional detective story, with a puzzle to solve before she produced the answer, but what she wanted to do was to paint a pen portrait of a group of characters.

That group is the Lamprey family, English aristocrats of a delightfully feckless sort, seen through the eyes of a quiet, intelligent New Zealand girl. Ngaio Marsh was always more interested in character than in crime, though as a conscientious upholder of the still-viable detective story she provided her readers with, generally, a puzzle to be solved, often an extremely complex one (as in the business here of the lift at Pleasaunce Court Mansions, Cadogan Square, London S.W.) which typically was clued with scrupulous care. But here, as elsewhere, it is the people who most interest her.

It is in this book that her group portraiture is seen at its best no doubt because the Lamprey family was closely based on an actual English family the young Ngaio had become friendly with in New Zealand and had subsequently stayed with in London. She succeeds in painting a whole family united in the possession of one quality, charm.

It is difficult to indicate in a few words the nature of this charm, for only Ngaio Marsh could succeed in communicating it complete. It consists partly in the hilarious contrast between the family's exalted station and their constantly recurring bouts of poverty, during which they are apt to buy a second car so as to be able to economise by using the Rolls a little less. It hardly consists of wit, though there is an abundance of family jokes. A little of it is to be found in the Lampreys' universal habit of gaily and inconsequentially speaking the truth ('Gabriel's our uncle. He's a revolting man'; in due course Gabriel, otherwise the Marquis of Wutherwood and Rune, is murdered). But principally it consists in the undoubted niceness of each and every one of the Lampreys, including even Old Nanny and the butler.

Niceness, indeed, is the quality that this book brims over with, even to the point of somehow softening the gruesomeness of the murder when Lord Wutherwood's eye is put out, leaving him not dead but noisily dying. Ngaio Marsh's murders are apt to be of this sort. They reflect her abiding interest in the theatre in general and in particular in Shakespeare, (who has Gloucester's eyes put out on stage in *King Lear*). But niceness is what, fundamentally, makes all Ngaio Marsh's output so enjoyable.

Above all her detective, Roderick Alleyn, is 'a nice chap.' He is of the breed of 'noble' detectives which the English school of detective-story writers made its own. Though a policeman, he is a gentleman to his fingertips, with an incidental elegance learnt no doubt during his Eton schooldays. And he is invariably courteous, to witnesses and suspects alike. Yet it is subtly indicated that underneath he is as tough as is necessary.

Even, however, with Alleyn we do not really get deep down. Ngaio Marsh herself had a reticence which is perhaps peculiarly English—her parents were of firmly English stock, even though they gave their daughter the Maori name of Ngaio which means 'Reflections on the water'—and she did not allow herself to bare any souls, not her own, nor Alleyn's.

Her drawing of them is acute, perceptive, warm, but it always rests upon their outward manifestations. Perhaps in the sort of detective story she undertook to provide anything more is impossible. She certainly believed this herself. 'The more deeply and honestly,' she wrote in her autobiography, 'one examines one's characters the more disquieting becomes the skulduggery that one is obliged to practise.'

But what can be done on the surface and just below it, Ngaio Marsh did. Her writing is as good as any to be found in crime fiction. Let me end with one sentence from *Surfeit of Lampreys* that shows it. Roberta is arriving by boat in London. She looks out at the other ships at anchor in the early morning light. 'Stewards,' she says, 'pallid in their undervests, leant out of portholes to stare.' There is an artist in words.

First edition Boston: Little, Brown, 1940
First UK edition London: Collins, 1941 as *Death of a Peer*

29
ELLERY QUEEN
Calamity Town

One day in 1928, in the full flush of the puzzle detective-story's triumph on both sides of the Atlantic, two young New Yorkers, cousins, decided to enter a mystery-novel contest. They sent in their entry, *The Roman Hat Mystery*, under the pseudonym Ellery Queen. It won. But then the sponsoring magazine was taken over by another firm which gave the prize to another entry. Nothing daunted, the two cousins went on to write one detective story after another, all of the utmost ingenuity.

By 1942, however, they felt the time had come to do more than just propose games to their readers. *Calamity Town* does propose such a game, and it will be a clever reader even today who beats Ellery Queen at it. But on page after page one finds in it the fresh phrases, the truth-touching observations, the felicities that mark out a book as doing the work of the true novel, explaining the world to the world.

Take one phrase with that extra of life in it: 'It was a temptation ... to crunch the crisp dry corpses of the leaves underfoot.' 'Corpses' gives that extra to a simple description of the glories of the Fall, and it does something more. It is one of the hundreds of touches whereby Ellery Queen conducts the mystery story against a counterpoint of the changing year, a nine months' pilgrimage from late summer into the Fall; on into snow-sheeted Winter; through Spring, when ancient cemetery trees sprout 'with sly fertility'; and finally to Summer again.

But it is not only nature that Ellery Queen can describe so well. He sees into hearts. There is 'a woman trying to hold on to her world as it growled and heaved about her.' There is the silent suspect 'bowed, three-quarters dead, pickled in some strange formaldehyde of his own manufacture.' There is, on a lighter note, a whole letter written by a live-wire woman journalist to her boss that gets the tone exactly right all the way. Or there is observation of a more general kind in the picture of small-town gossip-mongers streaming 'up and down the Hill like trekking ants, pausing . . . to pick up some luscious leaf-crumb and bear it triumphantly down into the town.'

The splendidly puzzling mystery, whose developments are described with such truth, has as its starting point a situation which can hardly fail to grip the most jaded reader. In the small mid-American town of Wrightsville, Jim Haight, an outsider, is found to have written three letters laying out the course of his new and rich wife's fatal illness *before she dies*. When his visiting sister dies in her place on the exact appointed day Jim is arrested. But did he do it? And if not, what possible explanation can there be?

There is an explanation—and almost without saying—it takes a Great Detective to hit on it. Ellery Queen, detective and novelist hero of the books written pseudonymously by the cousins Ellery Queen, is such a detective. He is for a time as baffled as we are. But then, he says, 'Something's been annoying me for weeks. Flying around in my skull. Can't catch it . . .'

A few pages later, as Ellery walks down 'the eye-studded corridor in the County jail, a cell exploded in his brain with a great and disproportionate amount of light' and he actually stops dead in his tracks. But still the full revelation eludes him, until, near the end, 'a formless something took possession of his mind in a little leap, like a struck spark.' This is the leap between rational thought and intuition. A few moments later Ellery sits there 'pale and growing perceptibly paler', with the answer fully in his mind.

The Great Detective has performed the magic which it is his myth-formed lot to perform, a magic expressed as the solution to a trivial puzzle. But here it is also the solution to an enigma of the human character, and, beyond that, it is a symbol of the magic reconciliation of opposing forces into something above either.

First edition Boston: Little, Brown, 1942
First UK edition London: Gollancz, 1942

30

CYRIL HARE
Tragedy at Law

Tragedy at Law is a book with three outstanding virtues. Rather than a who-done-it? it is a when-will-he? From the very start it looks likely that Mr Justice Barber, the Judge we see going from English town to English town 'on circuit', is going to come to a sticky end. But in fact it is not until almost the final pages that the dagger gets thrust between his shoulders. The book is also a first-rate 'backgrounder', one of those detective stories half of whose attraction lies in the setting in which the crime takes place, in this case the legal world in general and circuit life in particular. And, finally, the book contrives in those last pages to be a beautifully unguessable murder story.

Cyril Hare managed the 'when-will-he?' aspect in masterly fashion. Time and again, as you stay hooked to his story waiting for what you expect to happen, he contrives to make you believe it must be 'Now', and each time, with nice plausibility, it turns out to be 'Later'.

The unpleasant yet not wholly unsympathetic Mr Justice Barber receives threatening notes of growing immediacy. Yet no one strikes. A box of chocolates—the Judge is greedy—arrives and the experienced reader says 'Aha'. But the Judge's wife has taken a chocolate too, spits it out and briskly removes the just-sucked sweetie from between the judicial jaws. Later it seems that a mysterious stranger has invaded the Judge's lodgings and turned on the gas tap in his bedroom. But again he is rescued.

So it goes on until, on page 253 out of a total of 290, the dagger is thrust at last. And in the final explanations, each past incident is decently accounted for. But, more than this, the incidents occur among people you not only believe in as likely human beings, but whom you also get to know in more than a little depth. This is perhaps a fourth virtue of the book, though it is so bound up with the fine portrayal of legal life that it is hard to separate the two. The book is at the same time a depiction of an interesting social group and a novel of manners, told with delightful sparkle.

The manners are those of the legal profession, from the Judge at its height to such lowly figures as the Judge's butler who accompanies him on his journeying from court to court and from trial to trial. One of these, a murder trial described in some detail, is ingeniously made to have a share in the plot and to add to the possible motives when the Judge, by tough courtroom tactics, ensures a guilty verdict—to the fury of the defending barrister Francis Pettigrew, who had once been in love with the Judge's wife.

Pettigrew, a splendid study of a man who has shown tremendous promise but who for a dozen different reasons has failed to fulfil that promise, is in fact to become the book's amateur detective, who just beats the official one, Inspector Mallett, used by Hare in earlier books. (In later books, indeed, Pettigrew goes on to solve a case or two himself.) He is a character one can fully believe in, and one with whom it is easy to identify and to sympathise.

Of the legal background, smoothly and amusingly woven in, the novelist of courtroom comedy Henry Cecil (a Judge himself, as was Cyril Hare under his own name), has said: 'This book is acknowledged by many lawyers to be the classic detective story with a legal background . . . written with a master's hand and wit of a very high order.'

Concerning the central murder, I am inclined to say little. With a book that starts with a corpse it is perhaps as pleasurable to watch the author's cunning hand knowing the identity of the murderer as it is to take the author on at the guessing game, but with this ingeniously compressed puzzle that exercise would be pointless.

Suffice it to say that, though the solution depends upon a nice point of English law, the clue to it is firmly placed earlier in the tale, albeit placed with enough cunning to put most readers off the scent. And, though the space Cyril Hare allowed himself between murder and solution is minimal, he contrived with fine ingenuity to present in it three, or even four, suspects for the guessing reader to choose among.

First edition London: Faber and Faber, 1942
First US edition New York: Harcourt, Brace, 1943

31
RAYMOND CHANDLER
The High Window

I do not suppose many critics, asked to choose two of Raymond Chandler's seven novels to include among the hundred best crime and mystery stories, would select *The High Window*. They would say with Jerry Speir, author of one of the half-dozen books about Chandler's art, that it 'is two stories that are insufficiently woven together ... and the crucial bridge between the two stories is never adequately realised.' I have made *The High Window* one of my choices precisely because of this plot weakness, however, though I don't feel it comes over as weakly as Mr Speir thinks.

The point I want to make is that Chandler's books depend very little on plot. Whereas one reads a Golden Age whodunit solely for plot, one reads Chandler for the characters and, even more, for the background.

So here it is: the Southern California of rich and nasty people, and poor and nasty people, that one greedily allows to linger on the tongue. We get it from the very first paragraphs, with their description of a large, tasteless house in wealth-oozing Pasadena which has inside 'a stained-glass window about the size of a tennis court.'

We get such nasty rich as Mrs Elizabeth Bright Murdock, the house's widowed owner, with her 'pewter-coloured hair set in a ruthless permanent, a hard beak and large moist eyes with the sympathetic expression of wet stones.' And nasty indeed Chandler's 'insufficient' plot shows her to be. Nasty, and believable. Chandler digs deep.

And we get the nasty poor, though of necessity they are not as deeply seen into as Mrs Murdock, since they are encountered more briefly during the hunt which Philip Marlowe, the crusader down mean streets, carries out on behalf of Mrs Murdock for a rare coin called the Brasher, or Brashear doubloon. (Chandler wanted to call the book *The Brashear Doubloon* but his publisher feared the public would pronounce it 'brassiere'—dear, innocent days of long ago.)

There are vigorous and exciting portraits of these nasty poor, such as the old coin-dealer, Elisha Morningstar, an 'elderly party in a dark grey suit with high lapels and too many buttons down the front ... Fuzz grew out of his ears, far enough to catch a moth ... A Hoover collar which no decent laundry would have allowed on the premises nudged his adam's apple and a black string tie poked a small hard knot out of the bottom of the collar, like a mouse getting ready to come out of a mousehole.'

Chandler's portraits, whether in depth or in vigorous outline, are designed, however, to do more than show us typical Southern Californians. They reflect the theme of self-condemnation, something which obsessed Chandler. He wrote to his publisher about the book that he 'seemed to have to get the thing out of my system', and this obsessive need is what powers the book, turning it from a routine 'hard-boiled' story into something hauntingly memorable.

In that same letter Chandler also said that he was afraid the book would not be a commercial success since it had 'no likeable characters.' But Marlowe, at least, is deeply likeable, as generations of eager readers have proved. He has two attractive sides to his nature, one boldly there for all to see, the other a little less conspicuous. The first is the tough man; in Chandler's own words in his famous plea for his kind of writing, 'The Simple Art of Murder', he is a man 'with rude wit, a lively sense of the grotesque, a disgust for sham, and a contempt for pettiness,' a man well able to look after himself when threatened by such people as the gun-toting Vannier in *The High Window* or the fist-ready hold-up man, Hench.

But the other side shows a softer, hidden, human Marlowe; something that comes out particularly in the closing pages when he takes Merle, Mrs Murdock's totally mixed-up secretary, back to her parents in Wichita, Kansas, and as he leaves, seeing her contentedly rolling pie-crust, thinks of himself: 'I had a funny feeling ... as though I had written a poem and it was very good and I had lost it and would never remember it again.'

First edition New York: Knopf, 1942
First UK edition London: Hamish Hamilton, 1943

32

CHRISTIANNA BRAND
Green for Danger

Green for Danger was perhaps the last golden crown of the Golden Age detective story. It is a splendidly worked-out detection puzzle, as good as any in the field. It also has substantial characters in acknowledgement of the gradual move in detective fiction away from mere mechanical figures and towards characters who evince the darknesses of real life; in effect, the move from the detective story to the crime novel. The characters are seen, I hazard, with as much depth as possible in a book that offers the full enjoyments of the pure detective story.

Their creator was constrained, however, by not being at liberty to tell us all that is going on in the mind of the one of her closed circle of six suspects who actually committed the murder. So although the characters are seen with what one might call outward penetration, and with delightfully warm vivacity, they are never truly seen from within.

I myself am particularly conscious of the sheer skill with which the characters are presented under these conditions from having, many years later, attempted as a sort of serious pastiche a detective story in the full classical style, *The Murder of the Maharajah*. I found I could present my characters with just the same amount of outward penetration that Miss Brand adopted but not a half-inch more (and I managed much less champagne vivacity, I fear).

Certainly my plot in the book, set appropriately in the year 1930, the mid-point of detection's Golden Age, was not a patch on Miss Brand's in *Green for Danger*. I did not (alas, I was not passionate enough about it) fit every piece together with the utmost scrupulousness, as various correspondents over the years have pointed out to me. Occasionally I failed to reject something that did not quite hang together. Christianna Brand, on the other hand, was ready to jig endlessly with her pieces, to reject and replace until there was not a single gap that a reader would detect.

Indeed she has compared herself to a mechanic attempting to manufacture some machine. She sees herself as poking a finger among all the little bits and pieces of metal in front of her, discarding and rearranging until the machine is there and will work. It is not, she has said, like putting together a jigsaw puzzle—that favourite analogy of Golden Age detective-story writers—because one knows with a jigsaw that all the pieces are there in the box and will at last fit together to make the picture. In something related to life, however, there will be pieces that have to be discarded, and presumably pieces that have to be put on the lathe of reason and fashioned to provide that last vital cog or ratchet.

Then, Miss Brand goes on to say, once the sorting has been done you begin to tell the story, and your troubles begin all over again. But whatever troubles she experienced as, at the height of the Blitz, she sat writing this story with a tin hat on her head, nothing of them appears in the final product. *Green for Danger* tells an unswerving story. Little Inspector Cockrill probes away at the mysterious deaths that have occurred at the military hospital in which the book is set, in the middle of that same Blitz during which its author wrote. And the reader hangs on to the coat-tails of the Inspector's disreputable mackintosh every step of the way.

Or rather gets swept every step of the way by Miss Brand's cleverness and gusto. The gusto, that warm outward penetration of personality, makes the book a very fine example incidentally of what the good romantic novel can be, something rosily warm yet never ridiculous. The cleverness lies in the fearsome problem Miss Brand set herself. She undertook to provide six suspects, each of whom could in a simple mechanical way have committed not one but two or even three murders, each of whom had a credible motive, gradually revealed, and each of whom had to be kept equally likeable the whole book through.

She succeeded. No wonder when Will Cuppy reviewed *Green for Danger* in the *New York Herald Tribune*, he said that it was 'a whooper-dooper of a detective tale.' It is.

First edition London: Dodd, Mead, 1944
First UK edition London: Bodley Head, 1945

33
MICHAEL INNES
Appleby's End

With his very first book, *Death at the President's Lodging* (in America and in paperback *Seven Suspects*), Michael Innes, otherwise Dr J.I.M. Stewart, Oxford don and novelist, was praised for having brought something new to crime fiction, the donnish detective story. That judgment was reinforced with publication of his second book, *Hamlet, Revenge!*.

It has subsequently been challenged, with the suggestion that Innes' contribution was neither altogether innovatory nor of any real importance in the development of crime fiction. I certainly quarrel with the latter part of that put-down.

The donnish story, more interesting for its asides than for its crime, may not have brought new realism to crime fiction, but it did make a distinct advance. It showed that the form of the detective story, painfully arrived at during the 1920s and 1930s, could be used to do more than merely provide puzzle games for the puzzle-minded. Together with contributions from other writers, it showed that the classical detective-story could be used to carry more or less whatever an author wished to heap on to its sturdy frame.

I have chosen *Appleby's End* because it illustrates this hypothesis to the full. It is also an enormously amusing book, even for readers who do not share the wide-ranging erudition of its author and so are bound to miss some of what the critic Michele Slung has felicitously called 'the piquant spirit of enlightened pedantry' with which it is written.

What Innes made the dear old formula whodunit carry was, indeed, a great fluffed-up featherbed of academic jokes and literary allusions, in short 'donnishness' or, often 'cultivated reverie,' to use the words of Innes's hero Inspector Appleby; (later to become Sir John, retired Scotland Yard Commissioner). Appleby says he has a weakness for cultivated reverie, and so he has, though perhaps it is also a strength.

Certainly the book begins (and I hope it puts no readers off) with such an extended reverie, inspired by a slow, slow train journey into the snow-covered depths of the English countryside. It takes in Hardy's poetry, the Great Exhibition of 1851, the artist De Chirico, the god Pan, the rape not of any sexploitation-story victim but of Prosperpine, whose fate was simply to be snatched up by the god Pluto, as well as Flaubert's *Madame Bovary* and yet more.

But Innes underpins such prolonged academic musings—prolonged, interesting and funny—with a decidedly strong, if extraordinarily odd detection plot. I reveal little if I say that in the end it is found that no murder has been committed. It is the strength of this plot, always proposing some new riddle (such as the apparent coincidence of Appleby leaving his train at a station called Appleby's End, or the substitution for a real cow of a huge marble one), which keeps the book dancing forward.

And Appleby himself is very much worth having. He is one of the breed of 'noble' detectives, parallel to Ngaio Marsh's Alleyn and to the later Mr Campion of Margery Allingham. He is not a very likely figure as a working Scotland Yard officer. He seems seldom, if ever, to consider such things as fingerprints. But his manners are notably good (though in this book he is not always very pleasant to his local colleague, Inspector Multow).

But, above all, he is a quoter. You often feel that he is more concerned to cap a literary or classical allusion than to clap the bracelets on a murderer. He is, to use the word much bandied about in *Appleby's End*, 'booksy,' and much of the pleasure in following him through his cases comes from the feeling that one might know as much as he does of the highways and byways of the world of books if only one had had time to read a little more.

To Appleby one could well apply the words which Michael Innes, writing under his own name in the novella *The Man Who Wrote Detective Stories*, employs to describe that hero: 'He loved tumbling out scraps of poetry from a ragbag collection in his mind—and particularly in absurd and extravagant contexts.' In *Appleby's End* our sleuth is whirled up and down, round and round, in as fantastical a situation as anyone could wish—and all the while out tumble the scraps of poetry.

First edition London: Gollancz, 1945
First US edition New York: Dodd, Mead, 1945

34

ELIZABETH FERRARS
Murder Among Friends

From the very first words of Elizabeth Ferrars' *Murder Among Friends* (known as *Cheat the Hangman*, by E.X. Ferrars, in the United States) you realise that the hunt you are embarking on with the author is not simply for the identity of a murderer. It is a hunt for a much more elusive quarry: for a person. 'Alice often tried to remember her first impression of Janet Markland,' she writes. 'What had she seen, what had she felt?' And almost the last words of the book, spoken in fact by the murderer, whose tracking down has provided only the superficial storyline, are: 'So there you are, Alice—now you know the whole thing. Now you know all about Janet Markland, don't you?'

Another departure from the classical Golden Age detective-story is also apparent. There is no Great Detective in pursuit solely of a worthy opponent. There is only Alice, very much an ordinary woman, if one gifted with somewhat more than average intelligence, a nicely sharp wit on occasion, an enviable persist-ence and perhaps more than the common share of curiosity about other people which it is not unjust to call 'feminine.'

It is these qualities that enable this wife and mother, who happens to meet the woman Janet Markland in London one evening towards the end of World War II—an incidental pleasure of the book is the casual descriptive touches of wartime life in England—to trust her instinct and doubt that Janet could possibly have committed murder. Despite heavy circumstantial evidence, and even blurted words that might constitute a confes-sion, Alice pursues her doubts to a conclusion. But it is an ordinary conclusion.

The 'method' this detective, hardly even a detective in the most amateur sense of the word, uses to track down the real murderer is to question as many people as she can about this unknown Janet Markland, who is apparently the epitome of level-headedness as a successful literary agent, and to find out what made her what she really was. During the course of her hesitant inquiries she comes across facts of life likely among a somewhat bohemian set of people. It is a mark of the realism Elizabeth Ferrars achieved that her regular publishers declined the book on the grounds that detective stories could not be this seamy.

The book, in fact, makes only one concession to the classical detective story: one proper, old-fashioned clue. It is enough to enable Ferrars to use the form of the detective story eventually to lay out for our benefit and pleasure a fully plausible human being. And along the way she presents us, in less depth but by no means superficially, with a whole gathering of people bound by that curious tie we call friendship.

A curious tie? Well, when you come to think about it, or when Elizabeth Ferrars directs your attention to it, you see that it is. Friends are, we say, friends; people we like and have liked for a long time. Really? Listen to non-detective Alice: 'Alice ... thought that he and Cecily must be the sort of old friends who in their hearts have always disliked one another, yet who feel in that very dislike a kind of security with one another.' A hit scored, I think, by that hard-working feminine curiosity about what really makes the people we come across tick.

So Elizabeth Ferrars, while not neglecting to provide that simple who-done-it tug which in the past had been shown to be so effective, uses the form of the detective story to put before her readers something more fascinating, the mystery of the human personality. She wrote, in fact, not a detective story but a detective novel.

And perhaps the most remarkable thing about the book is that it was written as long ago as 1946. It might have been thought then that the Golden Age detective-story, that essentially simple delight, was still in its full glory. But 1946, in fact, marked a definite ending of that phase in crime literature, though of course Golden Age-type books are still being written some forty years after *Murder Among Friends*. Quietly and without any fanfare, and indeed much in the way of informed critical comment, Elizabeth Ferrars, together with other writers such as Dorothy L. Sayers, had begun to give us a whole new sort of crime fiction.

First edition London: Collins, 1946

First US edition New York: Doubleday, 1946
as *Cheat the Hangman*

35

HELEN EUSTIS
The Horizontal Man

American crime writing has been hailed frequently for its willingness to go down the mean streets. A less frequently acknowledged, though perhaps a greater, contribution to the art is its willingness to go down the mean streets of the mind. American willingness to admit to emotion, often in contrast to the typically British distrust of the overt expression of feelings, has produced in crime fiction John Franklin Bardin, Cornell Woolrich, Jim Thompson and perhaps especially this book, one of the only two crime novels Helen Eustis wrote. (The second, *The Fool Killer*, is only three-quarters of a crime novel, a hybrid aimed simultaneously at a juvenile and an adult readership.)

The Horizontal Man is a mystery, and a thoroughly puzzling one, set essentially in the minds of its characters, although its nominal setting is an exclusive girls college, Hollymount, in Connecticut. Perhaps now, in the late 1980s, its solution (which has been compared for its startling unexpectedness to Agatha Christie's for *The Murder of Roger Ackroyd*) will be more apparent to readers acquainted with the many accounts of extraordinary personality disorders than it was back in 1946. But even if you get a hazy glimpse of the eventual outcome at a quite early stage there is still enormous pleasure to be got out of watching how Helen Eustis prepares for that topsy-turvying denouement.

In *The Horizontal Man* we enter in greater or lesser degree into the minds of a selection of people working or studying at Hollymount. There is the fiercely shy and self-distrusting student, Molly Morrison, in the grip of a thought-annihilating crush on the murder victim, the handsome Irish lecturer and poet, Kevin Boyle. There is—equally disturbed—the distinguished author suffering from total writer's block and slowly recovering from a nervous breakdown, George Hungerford. There is the fish-out-of-water young English-studies lecturer, Leonard Marks, caught between memories of a thunderous preacher grandfather and the unquenchable stirrings of sexuality. There is even the genuinely charming college president, Lucien Bainbridge, shakily dependent on his secretary and on the college psychiatrist.

All are more or less inadequate people, and Helen Eustis understands them down to the very bottom of their minds. Set against them are a clutch of people able to cope. They are the vertical men, and women, as opposed to the horizontal of the W.H. Auden verse from which Miss Eustis took her title:

> Let us honour if we can
> The vertical man
> Though we value none
> But the horizontal one.

Chief among the book's vertical men is the psychiatrist who eventually solves the mystery, Dr Julian Forstmann. Miss Eustis keeps this hero sleuth on the right side of being too upright and omniscient—just. He echoes perhaps her faith in the vast revolution that began with Sigmund Freud, a Sherlock Holmes of the dark places of the psyche.

But he is not alone in his verticality. There is the earth-mother figure of the sexually experienced, flamboyant Dr Freda Cramm, another lecturer, fighting her way at last to emotional stability. And there is a delightful portrait of the podgy, rootedly commonsensical editor of the college magazine, Kate Innes (a coded acknowledgement here, possibly, to the sensible heroine of Mary Roberts Rinehart's *The Circular Staircase*). In her, Miss Eustis is able to give full reign to a robust humour which contrasts splendidly with the dark areas into which her main story leads her.

The book, indeed, can be seen as the story of people striving to find the reasonable answer amid the seas of unreason which swirl around them, and we follow their struggles with passionate interest and hope. The book is a song, if you like, to the human ability—washed over by the strange inner events arising from our sexuality—to reach, or strive for, verticality out of the swamps of the bed-bound horizontal.

First edition New York: Harper, 1946
First UK edition London: Hamish Hamilton, 1947

36
EDMUND CRISPIN
The Moving Toyshop

The novels of 'Edmund Crispin' (Bruce Montgomery, composer, who died in 1978) are unique for their successful blending of high comedy and crime in the form of the intricate Golden Age detection plot. Of them all—and there are only nine, written, with one final exception, between 1944 and 1951—*The Moving Toyshop* is perhaps the best example, and a perennial delight.

Its comedy, as in all the Crispin books, is highly individual, a froth of bubbling spirits. It is to be found at its peak in a scene in which Crispin's detective, Professor Fen, in pursuit of a witness invades a massive choir and orchestra rehearsal in the sedate atmosphere of university Oxford where Fen holds the (non-existent) office of Professor of English Language and Literature. (The book is, of course, a sparkling example of the donnish detective story.)

Passing off his companion pursuer as the eminent German composer Hindemith, Fen hacks out a path through the orchestra ('the second horn, a sandy, undersized man, went quite out of tune with indignation'), while the amateur 300-strong chorus roar out the words of the poet Holderlin set to Brahms music: 'Blindly, blindly, from one dread hour to another.'

Balked of his prey by the massed ranks of the singers, Fen joins them, neither tunefully nor accurately, with 'We STAAAAAY not, but WAAAAnder. We grief-laden mortals, Grieee-EEEF-laden mortals' until, as his quarry slips out, he follows to hear the conductor say venomously, 'Now that the English Faculty has left us, we will go back to the letter L.' The scene stays in the mind to be revived, generally with unstoppable giggles, whenever anything reminds one of it.

Crispin devised for the book a plot exactly complementing its quality of bizarreness, a bizarreness arising (almost always legitimately) from the story itself, the high frivolity with which he describes scenes like the interrupted rehearsal. The involuted complications he contrives do not, as in most detective stories, detract from the whole. Indeed, they positively aid it.

The word to describe *The Moving Toyshop* is 'rococo'. It possesses in splendid abundance the ebullient charm of the works of art thus labelled. It is alive with flourishes. Its mainspring, the actual disappearance of a toyshop visited in midnight Oxford, has all the right fancifulness, and at the end it is explained with perfect plausibility. Here and there one even gets touches comparable to the rococo artists' trick of putting a swirl of drapery outside the picture frame, as when Fen pauses during a check in the chase to start 'making up titles for Crispin.'

It is all, of course, wildly artificial. But, however much we may as readers look for truth in writing, there are times when its very opposite, sheer fancy, truly farcical exaggeration, can overwhelm one with pleasure. *The Moving Toyshop* abounds with circumstances extraordinary beyond the bounds of expectation. Coincidences pop up like rabbits in a field. But so high-spirited is the whole that we cheerfully co-operate with the author.

Almost all classical detective stories, in fact, strain the bounds of credibility, if only in assembling so many people wanting to make away with the victim. Mostly they rely on a secret pact with the reader to gloss over this, as John Dickson Carr pointed out in his famous defence of the locked-room mystery. Crispin, however, positively delights in open complicity with his readers. 'After all,' Professor Fen says at one point to the poet who discovered the body in the disappearing toyshop, 'it's a somewhat unusual business, isn't it?'

'So unusual,' Crispin makes the poet boldly reply, 'that no one in his senses would invent it.'

As might be expected with a book written in such a rush of high spirits, and by an author scarcely more than an undergraduate, *The Moving Toyshop* has, alas, scenes that do not quite come off. It has its *longueurs*. But there is no reason why each and every one of the hundred best crime books should be perfect from first page to last, and the virtues of the book well outweigh these small failures.

First edition London: Gollancz, 1946
First US edition Philadelphia: Lippincott, 1946

37

FREDRIC BROWN

The Fabulous Clipjoint

There are certain books that are not among the all-time classics but which yet deserve to be read, as long as there are readers with eyes in their heads. Two of Fredric Brown's fall, to my mind, into this special class: his most popular book, *The Screaming Mimi*, though it is flawed, and *The Fabulous Clipjoint*.

Yet I doubt if, in Britain at least, *The Fabulous Clipjoint* has many readers. In Britain, Brown is known chiefly as a writer of science fiction. Even in his native America he is not, fifteen years after his death, much commented on. There are various possible reasons for this neglect. It is even perhaps something to do with his name. 'Brown' is desperately forgettable. Only one Brown is at all known in British literature—John, a nineteenth-century Scottish essayist—and in America there is, besides the enormously prolific crime-merchant Carter Brown, only one: Charles Brockden Brown, ignored predecessor of Edgar Allan Poe as a gothic novelist.

Other reasons for Fredric Brown's comparative neglect may be more valid. He suffers from having written in two modes, crime and science fiction. Lumpen John Public finds it hard to believe that anyone can be good at two things. But yet more telling is that Brown's books were frequently seen merely as pulp fiction. They were, indeed, often presented in paperback as just that, with cheap and lurid covers. No wonder Mickey Spillane, writer of brutish pulp *in excelsis*, called Brown his 'favourite writer of all time.' Pretty well the kiss of death.

Even a sympathetic American critic like Newton Baird has described Brown's books as 'easy-to-read entertainment' with the implication that they are easy to forget, too. Easy reading they are, but they stay in the mind. Brown's writing is a model of pure straightforwardness. His sentences are never long and very seldom complex. To the unthinking, they may seem simply to be laying down the information he wants to put over. Yet the people he puts before his readers are by no means simple.

Nor is what he has to say. *The Fabulous Clipjoint*, with its iron-grip story, its direct writing, its click-into-place plot, is beyond all these a splendid mingling of the realistic and the romantic. The romantic comes in the book's narrator hero, the young Ed Hunter. Brown catches him at just the right age, a boy just nudging into manhood. He is capable of doing what a man can do, even to going to bed with a gangster's moll, but he is also fired with the dreamy hopes of youth.

He is an earlier Holden Caulfield, of J.D. Salinger's *Catcher in the Rye*; earlier by just four years, a looker-on who is hearteningly alert for all adult phoniness. He is a later Jim Hawkins, of R.L. Stevenson's *Treasure Island*, another book I put into the category of non-masterpieces that deserve to be read for ever.

Like Jim Hawkins, Ed is seeking something of large importance, the identity of the man who killed his father rather than a lost treasure. Ed, though prey to fear like Jim, can rise to a heroism, or a toughness, he did not know he possessed, as when he helps to break down the crooked bar-owner Kaufman in a blaze of inspiration when he uses his forefinger as a gun barrel. And, like Jim again, he can bravely but stupidly disobey orders as when, in place of single-handedly re-capturing the ship *Hispaniola*, he single-handedly tackles the floozie, Claire Raymond.

The reality of *The Fabulous Clipjoint* that mingles so memorably with the romance comes from its setting, Chicago, seen in all its unvarnished brutality and squalor. 'Guys who take ten-cent beds or two-bit partitioned rooms in flophouses and in the morning somebody shakes them to wake them up, and the guy's stiff, and the clerk goes quickly through his pockets to see if he's got two bits or four bits or a dollar left, and then he phones for the city to come and get him out. That's Chicago.'

Fredric Brown described Chicago as it was, coolly and with no hectic exaggeration. This is the mark of the real writer. Nor is that all he did with this sleazy city. In the final charged pages we learn what the book's title means. Chicago, we are told, is the clipjoint, the club that takes you for as much as you let it. But it is a fabulous clipjoint. Its squalor can be lit by a light that comes from no earthly source.

First edition New York: Dutton, 1947
First UK edition London: Boardman, 1949

38

JOSEPHINE TEY

The Franchise Affair

One way of selecting the best hundred crime books would be to ask a computer which had been most read. Frankly, a few of the titles that might show in little icy green letters I would never for a moment consider. But one which, to judge from its being reprinted time and again over the forty years since its publication, would come high on the computer list also comes high on mine. It is *The Franchise Affair*.

I chose it despite the fact that it goes clean against an axiom of detective fiction to which I usually give full assent: that there must be a murder to lend weight to what otherwise would be intolerably trivial. *The Franchise Affair* is simply an account of how a fifteen-year-old girl, Betty Kane, accuses two respectable ladies, Miss Marion Sharpe and her elderly mother, of kidnapping her and attempting to force her to work for them as a maidservant—servants still lingered precariously at that time in middle-class British homes—by starving and whipping her into submission. Are they really guilty? A quiet local lawyer, Robert Blair, sets out against the odds to prove they are not.

Just that. Yet I have no difficulty in putting the book into my list, for the simple reason that it is extremely well written, in an unemphatic manner, while being an account of a crime (though not necessarily the crime of kidnap) told primarily to entertain. I may add I am backed in this judgment by the great and good Howard Haycraft, author of that comprehensive 1941 survey *Murder for Pleasure*. Asked in the late 1950s by Julian Symons what post-war writers he would now admit to his pantheon, Mr Haycraft would name only Josephine Tey.

So what exactly is it about *The Franchise Affair* that is so good? A small plus is that it is simultaneously two things. It is a truly gripping story; you really put yourself emotionally into the shoes and the mind of Robert Blair as, setting aside a huge weight of circumstantial evidence, he does his ordinary best to solve the mystery. And it is also a likely explanation of one of the great

85

historical crime puzzles, the mystery of the abduction of one Elizabeth Canning in eighteenth-century England. There is, in consequence, a sort of double pleasure in reaching Miss Tey's double solution. (The same mystery also provided the basis for the American writer Lillian de la Torre's 1945 novel, *Elizabeth is Missing*.)

But the major reason for the book's excellence is the charge that Josephine Tey (real name: Elizabeth Mackintosh) succeeded in putting into it. As you read it you feel, almost at once, that here is a writer set on saying something she believes worth saying. What it is she has to tell us, at a deeper level than solving the mystery of Elizabeth Canning or of solving the mystery she herself has contrived of Betty Kane, is what people are truly like. She wants to show us, convincingly and in depth, a group of real human beings.

So we get Robert Blair, solicitor, already in early middle age set in his ways, who yet, seeing the tea-tray brought to him each day at ten minutes to four precisely—two digestive biscuits on Tuesdays, Thursdays and Saturdays, two *petit beurres* on Mondays, Wednesdays and Fridays—feels an odd sensation in his chest, an alien doubt about whether this is all.

We get, too, Marion Sharpe, gypsyish in looks, strong-wristed golfer, impecunious gentlewoman, whose life till her mother inherited that odd house The Franchise was helping in lady-like businesses, 'Lampshades . . . or flowers, or bric-a-brac,'; and her mother, a wonderfully sharp-tongued old lady, totally independent, scorning her 'reduced circumstances' and most of the people around her. A fine, unusual, believable character-portrait.

The story that embraces these people may seem slow, but it is a necessary slowness. It enables Miss Tey to build up not just the people but their true and proper surroundings, their little, telling everyday circumstances, till at last you have to remind yourself as you read that these are people only actually alive as black marks on white paper.

First edition London: Peter Davies, 1948
First US edition New York: Macmillan, 1948

39

JOHN FRANKLIN BARDIN
Devil Take the Blue-Tail Fly

Romantic boots are big. It takes, in the wide field of crime fiction as in other wider fields, a writer who is no mean strider to wear them. John Franklin Bardin marches in them unfalteringly—indeed, even the publishing history of this book is romantic.

It was written in 1948, the successor to two other crime novels of equal romantic intensity written in the two preceding years, *The Deadly Percheron* and *The Last of Philip Banter*. These were published in America, Bardin's native country and the setting of each of them, but *Devil Take the Blue-Tail Fly*, though equally set in America, failed to find a publisher there. It was issued only in England, by the crime-devoted Victor Gollancz, who took it, unrevised, from the office of a literary agent. Though written within a span of six weeks, the book shows little sign of needing any re-working. Another sign of the true romantic.

Nor was that the end of the book's romantic history. It met with some success in Britain, was lapped up by readers as discriminating and diverse as the novelist Kingsley Amis, the politician Denis Healey, the poet-lawyer Roy Fuller and the writer of crime comedy Edmund Crispin. But with the years it became almost completely forgotten, as did its author.

In the 1970s Julian Symons, then editing the Penguin crime list, attempted to get in touch with Bardin, only to find that neither his publishers nor his agents had had any communication from him for years. Eventually Symons did track him down to Chicago, where he was editing a lawyers' magazine, and Bardin agreed with enthusiasm to the re-publication of all three of these astonishing books.

They were ahead of their time. It is this, I think, that accounts for the almost bottomless pit into which they fell and out of which they emerged, almost by a miracle, to take their place among the high points of crime fiction. They were ahead of their time because Bardin chose to explore, not the then extremely popular fringes of experience described in science fiction, but the fringes of experience found by voyaging in exactly the opposite direction. Inwards. Into the mysterious depths of the mind.

In 1976, when all three books came out again, readers who had heard of brain-washing, of the effects of LSD and of the work of the newest schools of psychology were better prepared to accept the strange, hallucinatory world that John Franklin Bardin, especially in *Devil Take the Blue-Tail Fly*, led them into. Bardin wanted in this book and the two former ones, as he said in a short comment in the encyclopaedic *Twentieth Century Crime and Mystery Writers* (1980), to warn a reader 'of the mines of his own emotions'.

So in *Devil Take the Blue-Tail Fly* (its extraordinary but altogether appropriate title is taken from a blacks' song of the mid-nineteenth century sung by one of the characters, an ironic little tale of a 'massa' killed when his horse is stung), we live in the mind of Ellen, a concert harpsichordist who has suffered a breakdown, received electric-shock therapy, been released. But she finds herself at last wholly taken over by a wicked *alter ego* named Nelle, eventually to the point where she contrives the death of her husband.

Her story is told with an almost overwhelming intensity of feeling, and in prose to match. There is, too, a wonderfully orchestrated long, slow rise to the climax; from the opening paragraphs, in which we live inside Ellen's head on the day she is to be released from the mental home and wakes to a feeling of pure joy, to the almost final words, 'she did not have to close her eyes to hear those screams. Their piercing ululation filled her ears whether she waked or slept, banishing music for ever.'

First edition London: Gollancz, 1948
First US edition New York: Macfadden, 1967

40

MARGERY ALLINGHAM
More Work for the Undertaker

Each time I read *More Work for the Undertaker*—and I am inclined to re-read it quite frequently—I find myself thinking 'surely there can't be a crime story more burstingly alive.' Margery Allingham had, supremely, the gift of energy. It infuses all her books giving them, in the cookbook expression, a rich consistency. Her best stories, and *More Work for the Undertaker* is certainly one of those, give us worlds stamped with her particular outlook, richly romantic yet springing undeniably from the actual world in which she lived.

She had energy of observation. She takes, time and again, simple, ordinary objects and transforms them almost into living people. 'On the desk,' we read here, 'the telephone squatted patiently'; or we have the police detective, the tough, vivid Charlie Luke, ringing for the landlady in the private room of a pub, thumping 'the hump-backed bell on the table.'

She had energy of characterisation. Here is the local doctor, seen through Charlie Luke's eyes: 'A tallish old boy—well, not so very old, fifty-five—married to a shrew. Overworked. Over-conscientious. Comes out of his flat nagged to a rag in the mornings and goes down to his surgery—room with a shop front like a laundry ... stooping. Back like a camel. Loose trousers, poking at the seat as if God were holding him up by the centre buttons. Head stuck out like a tortoise, waving slightly. Worried eyes. Good chap. Kind. Not as bright as some (no time for it) but professional. Professional gent.'

She had moral energy. Her earliest books were simply detective yarns, swingeingly told. But with the years she began to see that this sort of thing could be used—cried out to be used—to convey her deepest thoughts about the world and the people in it. World War II, during which her crime muse fell silent, advanced this belief by a great bound, as this, her second post-war book, shows.

The development is reflected in her view of her customary

hero, Mr Campion. Originally he was no more than a version of Baroness Orczy's Scarlet Pimpernel, the silly ass who in reality is a lot more—a member, for one thing, of the Royal family (though the exact connection is never specified). But by the time she reached *More Work for the Undertaker* he had become a pair of observing eyes (her own) and a quietly confident commentating voice. 'There were new lines on his over-thin face and with their appearance some of the old misleading vacancy of expression had vanished.' And now he looks on the people Margery Allingham has him encounter with penetration, penetrating sympathy or penetrating judgment.

And Margery Allingham also had energy of idea. The plot of *More Work for the Undertaker*, an affair of domestic murder in a house occupied by the oddest of families, the Palinodes, and of large-scale criminal activity centring, with equal oddity, on the funeral parlour of Jas Bowels & Son, 'Courtesy, Sympathy, Comfort in transit,' is a splendidly vigorous, sweeping conception. And, as well, it allowed Margery Allingham to display to the full her energy of invention over names. There are the Palinodes and Jas Bowels, minor figures like Police Sergeant Picot and Detective Officer Corkerdale or the forensic expert Sir Doberman (we never hear his surname), as well as the phone-bugging expert Thos T. Knapp and the bank clerk Oliver Drudge, known as Clot; not to mention such coinages from past books as the police Commissioner, Stanislaus Oates, and Mr Campion's faithful, obese and vulgar manservant, Magersfontein Lugg.

Humour and humanity, excitement and complexity, characters that are at once larger than life and rooted firmly in life, with a whiff of the Great Detective of past days (Mr Campion declines the Governorship of some important British colony so that he can pursue the case)—they are all there in *More Work for the Undertaker*, a marvellously rich stockpot of a book.

First edition London: Heinemann, 1948 (revised: 1964)
First US edition New York: Doubleday, 1949

41
SIMENON
My Friend Maigret

If one was constrained to place the hundred best crime books in order of precedence—something, of course, impossible—I might very well put one of the three Simenon books I have chosen in the pole position. If only because I see Simenon as the inventor of the story in which the detective is seen as *writer*. Almost always he arranges a book so that his Maigret comes to a hitherto unknown area of life and discovers, bit by bit, its essence. At which point the identity of a murderer, or an unlikely killer's reason, becomes plain.

So it is in *My Friend Maigret*. A small-time crook who has been heard boasting of 'my friend, Maigret' is murdered on the island of Porquerolles off the Mediterranean coast, and Maigret is sent to investigate. With him there goes one Inspector Pyke, of Scotland Yard, there to observe the methods of Maigret (who boasts of having no method). It is Pyke's presence, handled with delightfully teasing humour and more than a little subtlety, that makes this book particularly useful for watching Maigret at work.

At work. It might seem that one is watching him permanently at leisure. Because this is the methodless method of Maigret. He does what a writer does when a subject or setting sends through him the tingle that betokens that here is something that will enable him to explore some sector of life.

So here Maigret, or Simenon, explores the people who have come to rest on this sun-soaked, highly individual island. And how does Maigret begin? By resenting the details the local inspector tries to thrust on him, 'for in actual fact he was no longer interested in anything.' Later that first day, when Inspector Lechat inquires 'Will you be doing your interrogations at the town hall?', Maigret all but retorts 'What interrogations?' Facts are not what he seeks. Instead he longs to soak up impressions, and is a little ashamed of doing so with Pyke, British and correct (only less so than Maigret believes), at his elbow.

In the end, yielding to moral blackmail, Maigret does conduct some formal interrogations, although 'it was the island which interested him at the moment, not such and such a person in particular', and he has about the island thoughts still extremely nebulous. After the questioning session he is described as gazing at Pyke with large, sleepy eyes. 'He had a feeling that it was all futile, that he ought to have tackled it differently. For example, he would have liked to have been on the square, in the sunshine, smoking his pipe and watching . . .'.

But before long, finding Pyke less stiff-upper-lipped than he had expected, he goes out into the square, sleepily with his pipe. And 'he sensed something. He sensed a whole heap of things, as he always did at the start of a case, but he couldn't have said in what form this mist of ideas would sooner or later resolve itself.' The author is not yet ready to write.

Gradually, though, as Maigret begins to get the feel of the island's lost-land indolence and sun-and-wine-soaked irresponsibility, things germane to the murder begin to rise up from his subconscious. He realises the significance of something he has been told about the victim, that he had hoped 'to make a packet.'

Then he begins to see how certain people may be involved, and he moves into action, if only slowly. He phones Paris. 'What do I want to know exactly?', he says, echoing his subordinate's inquiry. 'I've no preconceived ideas.' But he is beginning to see what must have happened, now that the island atmosphere is firm in his mind and he has 'the feeling that he had been taking this walk daily for a very long time.'

Now he questions particular suspects, though in no very intensive way, looking at one of them 'dreamily, heavily, like a person whose thoughts were far away.' But very soon these thoughts crystallise. The answer becomes clear (we have had a clue or two decently put before us), and a brutal arrest is made. The methodless method of Maigret is once more vindicated.

First edition London: Hamish Hamilton, 1956
First US edition New York: Doubleday, 1957
as *The Methods of Maigret*
(Originally *Mon Ami Maigret*: Paris, 1949)

42

W.R. BURNETT

The Asphalt Jungle

The Asphalt Jungle has two claims for inclusion in the roll-call of the hundred best crime books. First, it is extremely well written, in terse, forward-moving American prose with depth and resonance. Second, it is the first great example of the Caper Novel, the story of some major crime told for itself in all the necessary detail. As such its successors have been legion, particularly in crime fiction's sister art, the crime film.

The caper novel is more, however, than a simple description of a major crime. It is a statement in miniature, and in terms of crime, of what happened to American society in the second half of the twentieth century, and what has been reflected in societies all over the Western world. It marks the age of collective action, as opposed to earlier ages of individual action. *The Asphalt Jungle*, in this light, is the story of the collision and the interaction between two collective organisations, the gang gathered for the caper and the police force there to frustrate it.

As a caper novel, the book sees through many eyes its story of the robbing of a half-million-dollar haul from Pelletier and Co, the biggest jewellers in the state, with a luxurious store in the middle of what Burnett calls 'the City', which is to all intents and purposes Chicago.

These eyes include the hard-bitten journalist Lou Farbstein, who like the Greek philosopher Diogenes had 'been looking out for an honest man for a long time, and had begun to feel that the flame in his lantern would splutter out before he found him.' Then there is 'Doc' Riemenschneider, the brains behind the caper; Louis Bellini, 'better known as the Schemer', crook and devoted father; and Emmerich, the boyish fifty-year-old lawyer who stakes the crime, who 'looked and talked and breathed money.' And—a key figure—there is Dix, the out-of-work heavy from the rural South, a figure ultimately of black romance, well characterised by David Wingrove in his introduction to a collection of Burnett novels as 'a fallen Adam with the taste of straw still in his mouth and the taint of the City in his nostrils.'

All are drawn with honesty and insight. We see them for what they are, and we cannot help sympathising with them a little. Crooks, too, Burnett shows us, are human beings. And they live in an unlovely world. If Burnett is sparing of his characters, he is unsparing of the city they live in. Here is the Police Commissioner describing it: 'You say the bunco squad works with the con men. You say the police are taking a fortune from syndicated prostitution—and rousting around and making their arrest records from the unsyndicated and lone-wolf prostitutes. You say the racket squad allows big-time racket men to live here for a consideration, and then kicks around and persecutes the little local boys . . .'.

I quote at some length because the speech gives a glimpse of Burnett's grasp of the low life of his day. He was at one time a desk clerk in the Northmere Hotel in Chicago, a haunt of the city's notorious gangsters. He was also one of the first on the scene of the St Valentine's Day massacre. But, as I have said, beneath the easy use of gangster talk there lies always something deeper.

It is not without relevance that *The Asphalt Jungle*, this seemingly tough-guy tale in the pulp fiction tradition, is preceded by a quotation from the philosopher and psychologist, William James (brother of Henry, the mandarin novelist): 'Man, biologically considered . . . is the most formidable of all beasts of prey, and, indeed, the only one that preys systematically on its own species.' Parallel that with Burnett's casual reference to Diogenes, already quoted, and you can see that he knew that, while in writing crime fiction the primary aim is to entertain, a writer can also use it to make his comment on his times and on the human condition.

First edition New York: Knopf, 1949
First UK edition London: Macdonald, 1950

43

MICHAEL GILBERT
Smallbone Deceased

Smallbone Deceased is in the classical tradition of the detective story, and a fine example of that art. It lacks that Golden Age staple, the Great Detective and even the Nearly Great Detective. But this only emphasises its difference from books written in Britain in the 1920s, 1930s and 1940s. *Smallbone Deceased* is clearly a late flowering of the classic art. One of its incidental pleasures comes from its depiction of Britain's immediate post-war years, with an electricity cut playing a notable part in the establishing of alibis.

The plot is in every way as good as those of Agatha Christie at her best: as neatly dovetailed, as inherently complex yet retaining a decent credibility, and as full of cunningly-suggested red herrings (I faithfully followed one while re-reading before writing this, having forgotten who was the eventual murderer). Its background—the workings, lightly exaggerated, of a firm of ultra-respectable London solicitors—is every bit as amusing and informative as that of Dorothy L. Sayers' *Murder Must Advertise*.

The book also has the additional pleasure of style. It is written in a manner delightfully urbane and warmly humorous; in the tradition, say, of Fielding and Surtees. One example: 'John had by now reached that well-defined stage in intoxication when every topic becomes the subject of exposition and generalisation, when sequences of thought range themselves in the speaker's mind, strewn about with flowery metaphor and garlanded in chains of pellucid logic; airborne flights of oratory to which the only obstacle is a certain difficulty with the palatal consonants.'

There you have precise observation (oh dear yes, I have been there in my day) seized on and fixed in fine, deliberately mannered prose ('pellucid', 'intoxication', 'palatal consonants'). And this tone is maintained throughout the book, lowered a little for the necessary passages of exposition and of action, and raised a little more for the scenes of comedy (which may contain a neatly-planted clue).

But there is something more, the something that marks the work out as that late flowering, subtly-different example of the detective story. It is marked by well-judged injections of realism.

You see it in Michael Gilbert's concern over the realities of a police investigation. A lawyer himself, his awareness of the legal aspects of the case and, more important, the necessity of producing well-attested evidence at a trial was what perhaps led him to go to some lengths, in what is a detective story and not a police procedural novel, to show the actualities of an investigation of murder. The book is peppered with descriptions of actual police work, though they are presented with great neatness and economy, and they are also generally made to push forward the progress of the story.

A second injection of realism—apart from the realistic description of life in a solicitors' office of the standing of Horniman Birley and Graine (allowing for some well-judged exaggeration)—comes in passages such as a scene with the Yard pathologist who describes the murder method, garotting. I quote: 'The photograph ... looked, at first blink, like an aerial view of the Grand Canyon of Colorado. There were innumerable fissile crevices running in from either side towards the centre, the gulfs and gullies, the potholes and pockmarks of the surrounding terrain; and there down the middle, as if ruled off by a draughtsman, was the deep, steep-sided indenture of the canyon itself, and far down at the bottom the dark line of the stream. "Effect of picture-wire on the human neck," said Dr Bland. "Two hundred magnifications".'

These touches of realism make you feel this ingenious tale is a good deal more closely related to real life than your average detective story. But note again the style of it: that nice alliteration of 'gulfs' and 'gullies', of 'potholes' and 'pockmarks'. It keeps the book in its proper realm, as a story set at a decent distance from the full ignominies of human existence.

First edition London: Hodder and Stoughton, 1950
First US edition New York: Harper, 1950

44

SIMENON

The Stain on the Snow

Simenon wrote three kinds of novel. In tandem with his Maigret stories he wrote books he called 'hard' novels, into which he saw himself as putting yet more effort, yet more psychological capital. And these 'hard' novels can be divided into those that are crime fiction and those that are not, though with almost all of the former sort there is doubt about whether they can truly be said to come under the crime fiction remit or whether they are novels, like Dostoievski's *Crime and Punishment*, that have a murder at their heart but have no hint of entertainment about them. It is a grey area.

However, I believe *The Stain on the Snow* does fall within the crime category, where it ranks among the highest. It is, to put it bluntly, quite superbly written.

Published in France in 1950 (though not translated into English until 1953), it is set during World War II in an area occupied by the Germans, though this locale is deliberately somewhat obscured, and made in effect more universal, by there being no direct references to the nationality of the German troops (they are called simply 'the Occupiers'), while the inhabitants of the unnamed city in which most of the action takes place are given Germanic or even Anglo-Saxon names. For instance, the hero, through whose eyes we see the whole, is called Frank.

I have said 'hero'. But Frank is not at all what is usually thought of as a hero-figure. He seems at first totally obnoxious. Aged eighteen, he is seen in the opening pages coolly setting about killing his first man, a fat sergeant from among the Occupiers for whom he bears not the shadow of a grudge. The only half-motive he has for sticking a knife in the man's ribs is that he will get possession of a gun, but that is clearly shown as being a secondary consideration. Frank simply feels that the time has come to take the step of killing, just as earlier in life he had taken the step of losing his virginity.

The world Simenon shows us, through Frank, is thus the

world without morality. It is a world for which a city under prolonged enemy occupation is the ideal setting. Everywhere there is corruption, spurred on by the need to keep alive, with food appallingly short, and with the bitter cold of winter made more terrible by the almost complete absence of fuel. You are lost, unless you have entered the world of the unmoral, as has Frank's mother, who in their small apartment conducts a brothel frequented by black marketeers, officers of the Occupiers and a few privileged inhabitants of the city whom she finds useful. In her cellar under the apartment block she has two tons of coal.

But Simenon is not concerned simply to paint for us a picture of the man, or rather boy, entirely without moral sense. He aims to show how conscience at last manifests itself even in such starved soil, even in someone as morally benighted as Frank—who, later in the book, calmly shoots an old woman who had been notably kind to him, when he was boarded out with her in a village near the city, because he wants to secure her collection of antique watches to bribe a General of the Occupiers.

Simenon wants to show us how, even in the forcedly arid soil that Frank represents, he has admitted into his bleak inner world the love of a girl whom he had arranged for a fellow black-marketeer to rape. Simenon wants us to realise, in the words of the rape victim's almost saintly father, at the end of the book that 'It's a tough job to be a human being.'

So the bleak book—and bleak it is with both the moral climate and the physical one evoked in a marvellously unmechanical manner—is in the end a message of hope, even if it is a terribly difficult hope. I doubt whether it is possible for the crime novel to rise to greater heights than it does in Simenon's hands here.

First edition New York: Prentice-Hall, 1950
First UK edition London: Routledge, 1953
(Originally *La Neige Etait Sale:* Paris, 1948)

45

JOSEPHINE TEY

The Daughter of Time

The Daughter of Time is generally seen as a sort of sport in crime fiction, the only example of a detective story that upsets the verdict of history on a double murder committed on the orders of a reigning monarch. If this were actually so, the book, being as well-written as it is, might deserve a place on the honour roll as a curiosity.

But, in fact, the book is not exactly this. It is more. And I have put it on this, my honour roll, because of what I see it as being: not simply an ingenious and plausible reversal of the story of the Princes in the Tower, and how their wicked uncle, Richard III, had them put to death. Nor just the dramatic revelation, backed by not a little logic, common sense and research, that the boys (who were not so much princes as the illegitimate sons of a king) were killed on the orders not of Richard III but of Henry VII, the man who wrested the crown from Richard at the Battle of Bosworth. No, *The Daughter of Time* is a crime novel, a story with murder at its centre, written with the purpose of making readers think about truth—'the daughter of Time', as an old proverb has it—and how truth can be twisted.

The book does indeed do what most commentators say it does: it takes Miss Tey's detective, Chief Inspector Alan Grant, puts him in hospital recovering from a spinal injury, and gets him interested in Richard III and soon determined to account for discrepancies in the records of the murders. Miss Tey contrives with splendid skill to make a story out of this, and to tell it splendidly.

She was confronted with the problem of all conventional, classical whodunits: that they have a static situation, a murder committed by an unknown who has contrived to hide how it was done, which must yet be told in an ongoing way. It needs really only one starburst of inspiration by the detective to see how the murder was done and end the book. So great pains must be taken to spin out the situation, like a ball of hot sugar, till it makes a long strand for readers to gobble their way along.

Miss Tey, by adroitly delaying the facts Grant needs to build up his case against Henry VII, contrives just such a long-spun sugar thread. It begins with Grant's first reliance on a single postcard reproduction of a contemporary portrait of Richard, showing no villain but a fine and interesting face; it goes on with Grant, not implausibly, having at first just a couple of child's history books at his disposal ('But the king won no profit from this wicked deed'), and at last reaches a final twist when it seems Grant's whole new theory is in danger of falling to pieces.

At the risk of somewhat spoiling the story I must state what this last twist is: it is the discovery by a young American researcher helping Grant that the whole astounding theory had been written about at intervals over the past 350 years. Because *this* is what *The Daughter of Time* is actually about: the fact that truth can not only be twisted but that it will tend to stay twisted, whatever truth-tellers may do. Indeed, my own 1950s multi-volume encyclopedia bears this out nicely by writing of Richard III in terms almost as simplistic as the child's history already quoted.

The prime example of this persistence of error, which Grant at first seems to mention only as a similar instance, is a confrontation in 1910 at a place called Tonypandy between striking Welsh miners and bullet-firing soldiers, whereas in sober fact the confrontation was with police armed only with rolled-up mackintoshes. But, Grant says, it is still widely believed in 1950 that miners were killed. His researcher produces a similar case, the so-called Boston Massacre when British troops were supposed to have mown down countless innocent civilians, although in fact there was only a minor incident with a total of four casualties.

So 'Tonypandy' becomes a key word in the book, and Miss Tey finds example after example of this process whereby truth, daughter of Time, is traduced. It makes a fine novel, lurking behind a fine crime story, with an innocent suspect cleared against all odds and the true murderer revealed.

First edition London: Peter Davies, 1951
First US edition New York: Macmillan, 1952

46
HILLARY WAUGH
Last Seen Wearing . . .

Some time in 1950 an American crime writer, Hillary Waugh, who had three books to his credit featuring a toughie called Sheridan Wesley, happened to pick up a book of factual crime cases. It was much the usual sort of thing, aiming to grab readers by offering gruesome or sexy details. But Waugh was struck by the tone of its writing: flat, detail-crammed and unmistakably dealing with real events. He wondered if he could transfer that tone to a fiction story and thus give it something special, something not offered by all other writers of crime fiction.

The book he wrote to try out this theory was *Last Seen Wearing . . .*, and it took him two years to get it published. Yet it is now acknowledged not only as a pioneer volume in the category of police procedural novels, but as a classic of the sub-genre. Other books, in retrospect, proved to be police procedurals predating *Last Seen Wearing . . .*, notably those by Lawrence Treat beginning with one called *V as in Victim*; but it was Waugh's book which, despite its initial unsuccess arising from that new approach, eventually gained recognition for this kind of crime story.

Deservedly so. Waugh did catch to a T that tone he had been impressed by in his chance-read volume of true-crime cases. He hits with deadly accuracy the note struck by a non-fiction writer, usually some sort of journalist, desperately concerned to convince readers that nothing in his pages is made up (though quite frequently things are). The result is always a proliferation of unnecessary detail. Anything goes in, provided it has been seen, once, by that journalistic eye.

Waugh used just that sort of detail—detail that a practising fiction writer would always attempt to discard as slowing up progress. But, in this case, facts like these did not have that effect, since each one contributes to the air of realism. Many years later, in an essay on the American police procedural he wrote for a volume called *Whodunit* that I edited, Waugh explained that, in fact, realism cannot truly be attained in this sort of book, since almost all police work is actually dull routine, as well as depending on the efforts of many people and having its crimes solved more often than not by someone coming in from the street with the vital information.

But he did produce an air of realism in *Last Seen Wearing*. . . . Example: 'She led the way into a large combination study and parlour . . . lined with neutral shade of wallpaper on which clipper ships sat.' What on earth have those clipper ships to do with the disappearance of a girl student from her room at Parker College, Bristol, Massachusetts? Nothing. What a reader would be wanting to know at this point in the book is whether the girl's house-mother, whose parlour we are entering, will be able to throw any light on that disappearance. But the flat description of the wall and its paper has its foreseen effect. It adds, as it were secretly, to the air of reality.

Take in with this trick of the caught tone a good uncluttered story, and you have another ingredient giving *Last Seen Wearing* . . . its classic standing. There are no sub-plots. Nothing takes away from the single problem Waugh presents, first as a how-did-it-happen? in place of a who-done-it?, and later as a will-police-work-nail-the-murderer?. There is, too, one good old-fashioned clue for a reader to miss. Or for the police in the book, and the astute reader, to hit on. It comes in the missing girl's diary. I say no more.

Finally, the crime, when it is found to *be* a crime, is shown as nothing like the diabolically clever affairs that tested Hercule Poirot or Sherlock Holmes. It proves to be a spur-of-the-moment murder, just the sort of thing that occurs in real life, and which is generally either never solved, or solved within hours of the discovery of the body. It is Hillary Waugh's achievement that out of this he spins a story that keeps its suspense from the first page to the last.

First edition New York: Doubleday, 1952
First UK edition London: Gollancz, 1953

47

MARGERY ALLINGHAM

The Tiger in the Smoke

The Tiger in the Smoke is one of the peaks of crime fiction. It is a
mystery story. It is a story of suspense. But, too, it is a story so
powerful, so onwardly rushing, that it can carry on its tumbling,
tossing waters a great many weighty objects—and ultimately the
weightiest of considerations, good and evil. But before those it
sweeps you onwards, riding massive tree-trunks of atmosphere
and boulders of fine characterisation.

The atmosphere put richly before you is that of a certain
section of the huge metropolis of London, in certain weather
conditions and at a certain time in its long history. That time is
the period immediately after World War II, and remnants of that
gigantic conflict abound, from the very opening puzzle of
whether a dimly-glimpsed man is someone reported missing
believed dead but now claiming, or hinting, that he is still alive
down to odd little pieces of the social history of those days that
have a new interest now.

But those are mere trivia, little sticks borne along on the flood.
What has more weight is the weather: fog, London fog as for a
century or more it had existed (though now with Clean Air
legislation it is a thing of the past). Fog is marvellously evoked,
but it also plays a major part as a symbol of the shrouded
mystery in which the earlier events occur. The second sentence
of the whole book runs: 'The fog was like a saffron blanket
soaked in ice-water.' And the last but one chapter opens: 'In the
morning, when the sun was shining through the newly-cleaned
windows . . . as blandly as if no such thing as a London fog had
ever existed . . .' and one knows then that the mystery is on the
point of being cleared up.

The final ingredient of this atmosphere is the area of London
itself, the then 'square mile of vice' round Paddington Station,
the evil core of the huge city referred to in slang as 'The Smoke,'
depicted with a power that is exaggeration not exaggerated. 'To
the west the Park dripped wretchedly and to the north the great

railway terminus slammed and banged and exploded hollowly about its affairs. Between lay winding miles of butter-coloured stucco in every conceivable state of repair.'

So much for atmosphere. But, standing out from this vivid, almost hallucinatory background, are the people. And they are drawn with as much vividness, and with yet more insight. There is, for instance, a mere incidental character, Mrs Gollie, the pub manager's wife, coming to give evidence 'as if she was hastening to the scene of some terrible disaster, or perhaps merely going on the stage.' And listen to the way she talks: 'I saw him, you see, and, I mean to say, you want to know, don't you?'

Then there is, hovering as always in the later Allingham books, Mr Campion, 'easiest of men to overlook or underestimate.' But, bulking larger, there is Canon Avril, the embodiment of good, who 'asked so little of life that its frugal bounty amazed and delighted him.' It is not easy to portray a wholly good person. Even Charles Dickens was apt to smear them over with a thick sauce of sentimentality. But Margery Allingham succeeds altogether with Avril.

As she succeeds, at the other end of the spectrum, with Jack Havoc, the tiger in the Smoke, the escaped prisoner whose first murder victim is found when the fog is at its thickest 'rolling up from the river dense as a featherbed', hanging between street lamps 'in blinding and abominable folds.' Havoc is a believer in 'the Science of Luck' with his 'I'm one of the lucky ones ... I watch for every opportunity and I never do the soft thing.' That is his ruthless creed, the principle of evil, and Margery Allingham makes one believe in it and in him, if at the end she finds in his character just the smallest glint of 'the soft thing.' It reflects, surely, her belief that good exists in every man, woman and child. And that reinforces our hope that this is indeed so.

First edition London: Chatto and Windus, 1952
First US edition New York: Doubleday, 1952

48

JOHN BINGHAM
Five Roundabouts to Heaven

John Bingham brought to crime fiction something new. He approached the genre with what might be called psychological realpolitik. Instead of presenting a world where in the end justice is done and the murderer brought to light, as in the classical detective story and even, in principle, in the private-eye story, Bingham showed people as being moved this way and that by the inexorable facts of life and by opportunistic grabbing at what seems any quick way out of a particular dilemma.

This much was apparent in his first novel, *My Name Is Michael Sibley*, famous for the unpleasant reality of the investigating officers who land the innocent hero in a cell, and notable for the fact that its murder is never solved. In *Five Roundabouts to Heaven* this revolutionary attitude to crime fiction (since often copied) is developed even more.

The book recounts in a series of flashbacks, most skilfully laid out, how it comes about that Philip Bartels, a traveller for a wine firm and an averagely sympathetic man, murders the wife he once loved and for whom he still feels the deepest pity. Its narrator-hero, who tells the story in the first person, is the man who coolly manipulates its events. But, although he shows himself as a realist to the point of cynicism, his attitude is not shared by the author. Instead he lays it out as being simply what happens in life.

In doing so he shows very considerable understanding of the way people—cynics or believers—arrive at the actions they undertake. He illustrates not what should happen in logic but what does happen through the curious mixture of logic and emotions—often contradictory emotions—that are the actual workings of our minds. To read the passages where John Bingham does this most clearly is to recognise, with a stimulating shock, what has gone on in one's own head.

The book has other virtues as well. The descriptive writing is of a high standard. Take this account of a cheap hotel-room

Bartels briefly occupies: 'the mass-produced furniture, the linoleum-covered floor with the narrow strip of carpet by the bed, the window-panes of frosted glass so that you could not see out of them, and the one harsh electric-light bulb hanging from the middle of the ceiling.' Sadly accurate, but also locating the unsuccessful Bartels for us and arousing sympathy for him, a sympathy that will give a grimly cutting edge to the subsequent story of his downfall at the hands of the narrator.

Bingham, too, can raise his essentially squalid tale to a height where he can be seen to ponder the ancient verities and ultimate simplicities of the human situation. Towards the book's climax he allows Bartels, driving fast towards his home (along a road with five roundabouts) hoping to be in time to unset the fatal trap he has laid for the wife he has not the courage to leave, to reflect on sin and virtue. Sin, he thinks, is not simple. Virtue is simple, but not easy. Sin, he realises, is tortuous and twisted, involving not only straight lies but lies within lies, the ever-present need to be on the watch. But on the other hand virtue, though not in the least tortuous, is very hard to live up to.

On a lower level this book, like its predecessor, shows the supposed guardians and protectors of virtue, the police, as in fact tyrants, here on a small scale where in *My Name is Michael Sibley* they put the hero in jeopardy of his life. For Philip Bartels they are just one more wretched obstacle as he drives along the road with five roundabouts and is stopped because his car's rear light is out. He rectifies this with a bang of his hand. But his troubles have scarcely begun. 'You were, of course, committing an offence, sir,' says one of the officers, taking out his notebook with play-acting ponderousness. So the power game is played out in miniature, as Bartels seethes with an impatience he must conceal.

Finally, the book is lit by flashes of dark humour, a little shocking yet invigoratingly delightful. They extend to an 'Author's Note' postscript, where Bingham says the poison he has written of has been given a fictitious name 'in the public interest', and adds: 'The main purpose in mentioning this is to save discontented husbands the trouble of searching fruitlessly through medical books.'

First edition London: Gollancz, 1953

First US edition New York: Dodd, Mead, 1953 as *The Tender Poisoner*

49

RAYMOND CHANDLER
The Long Goodbye

The Long Goodbye was Raymond Chandler's last great attempt
to write the sort of crime novel he believed could and should be
written. *Playback*, which comes after it, is more of a despairing
last kick. And what Chandler thought could be done was, in his
own words in a letter to a friend, to find 'a means of expression
which might remain on the level of unintellectual thinking and
yet acquire the power to say things which are usually said only
with a literary air.'

How well he kept his balance on that desperate tightrope is
something that can be judged only in the individual gawping of
each watcher below. But *The Long Goodbye* is certainly Chandler's most daring walk from one end of the swaying rope to the
other.

And, as the book into which he put his fondest hopes, it is not
surprising that he also put a great deal of himself. In fact, he put
himself in three times. First, of course, there is Marlowe, his hero
and mouthpiece. Marlowe is his ideal of himself, an ideal he was
able to regard simultaneously with pride and a wry acknowledgement of how he might look a fool. There is a revealing
moment when Marlowe first meets the gangster, Mendy Menen-
dez, who promptly labels him 'Tarzan on a big red scooter.' In
other words, an idealised hero with an incongruous child-like
simplicity about him.

But Chandler also appears as the writer Roger Wade, drink-
sodden author of 'fat sex and swordplay historical novels',
money-making bestsellers, as Chandler was the hard-drinking
author of 'hard-boiled' crime stories that made a lot of money. In
other words, he could not help wondering, fearing and doubting
whether his great enterprise of saying things usually said only in
literary terms was not a great chimera after all.

Then there is the third Chandler: Terry Lennox, drunk and (it
is gradually revealed) war hero. Chandler laid no claim to being a
war hero, but he was, though reluctant to talk about it, a war

victim, one of the many whose whole lives were deeply affected by the experiences of World War I; the politican and later Prime Minister, Harold Macmillan, is a prime example. Chandler, who had dual British/American nationality, joined the Canadian Army in 1917 and was the sole survivor in his unit of an artillery bombardment in 1918, eventually writing, in a single short story, of being 'alone in a universe of brutal noise' under a night sky 'white and blind and diseased like a world gone leprous.'

This traumatic experience came in what was seen as 'a war to end wars'. Imagine then the impact World War II must have made on this sensitive, even shrinking man. And he made his creation, the scarred Terry Lennox, a commando who was captured and tortured. 'It wasn't any fun with those Nazi doctors,' he says once in a terse aside.

So Chandler asks 'Why?' Why does humankind produce the phenomenon of Nazism? Why, the book demands again and again, do things have to be the way they are? Why, Marlowe asks himself, does he go on being a private eye? Why does he do one thing rather than another?

Of course, the story of the book also asks why. Why does Lennox, apparently, commit suicide? Why is there something iffy about the whole situation? And all the questions are asked in the language that Chandler evolved for asking such questions within the private-eye story.

So we get the famous put-downs. I choose one at random. Marlowe is visiting an ultra-chic investigation agency that has a hundred grey-suited employees; a boss, Colonel Carne, with 'as much charm as a pair of steel puddler's underpants'; and a receptionist who has 'an iron smile and eyes that could count the money in your hip wallet.' She rebukes Marlowe with 'We are very particular about details here. Colonel Carne says you never know when the most trivial fact may turn out to be vital.' And Marlow ripostes 'Or the other way around.' She doesn't get it.

So, yes, for one reader at least *The Last Goodbye* achieves Chandler's aim. It says something—it says a very great deal—in a way wholly remote from the literary novel.

First edition London: Hamish Hamilton, 1953
First US edition Boston: Houghton Mifflin, 1953

50

GUY CULLINGFORD
Post Mortem

Guy Cullingford's *Post Mortem* is perhaps the most unlikely among my choices of the hundred best crime and mystery books. So I was somewhat reassured, when preparing to write about it, to come across Mary Groff's assessment in that monumental, and pretty magnificent tome *Twentieth Century Crime and Mystery Writers*. 'If Guy Cullingford has a fault,' she wrote, 'it is perhaps that all the characterisations are so entertaining that one can lose sight of the crime and the victim.'

Certainly, the characterisations in *Post Mortem* are extremely entertaining, but in this case I think it unlikely that one will lose sight of crime and victim since the latter is—a brilliant stroke—a ghost, who both narrates the story and acts as the book's sleuth. The idea is splendid in its simplicity, something that once done could never be repeated, and enormously entertaining in itself. What fun is had with the notion of mere ghostness. Here is the narrator-spirit describing his former parlourmaid serving dinner: 'I stood in front of the sideboard ... but my presence had no effect on Jenkins at all. She reached right through me for her dishes without turning a hair.'

All along, too, there is a delicious undertow of quietly witty sniping at the deserving targets set up by life in general. It begins in the book's opening words: 'I am a writer and a moderately successful one—though far indeed from being the cornerstone of a crime club or the pillar of a popular publishing concern.' The darts are quietly planted.

That wit, hardly seeming to be there until you pay full attention, is what makes Guy Cullingford for me one of the pleasantest female companions to sit next to at the dinners of the Detection Club in London. Yes, female companions. Because, for reasons unknown, Constance Lindsay Taylor, after her first book (*Murder With Relish*, published in 1948) where she used an ambiguous initial to conceal her sex, chose always to write under her decidedly male pseudonym.

Entertaining characterisation is, I suppose, what makes *Post Mortem*, for all that it is comparatively little-known, one of the classics of crime. Some more examples would include snippets of the narrator's pre-death assessments of his grown-up children, who, he has come to suspect, harbour designs on his life. There is his elder son, who at twenty-seven is still undecided about a job: 'The only thing that would settle Julian's career for him would be a full-scale war, and that solution seems a little harsh on the rest of us.' Or his brother: 'Robert is now nearly twenty-one, and takes himself more seriously than he will do when he is twice that age.' And finally: 'As for my daughter, Juliet, I imagine that had she been anything but the dim echo of her mother, I might have cared for her more. But I have seen it done once already, only better.'

But Guy Cullingford's delightful malice comes to a peak with the give-away things her narrator says of himself (as well as his assessments of his children turning out to be largely wrong). He ponders, for instance, over 'the true attitude of a father to his sons, as opposed to the conventional one' which turns out to be, baldly, 'I have never felt the slightest shade of affection for either of my boys since they turned three years of age.'

It is another stroke of brilliance to have made this central figure so utterly unlikeable, and yet to force us to see the events of his post-mortem quest for the identity of his murderer sympathetically, through his eyes.

What enabled 'Guy Cullingford' to bring off this feat is the quality of her writing. Time and again, right up until the final deliciously ambiguous twist in the tail, she produces the small but different phrase to describe what it is she wants us to see or feel. Unashamedly I quote once again: 'Suspicions ... are as unreliable as ferrets which are apt to pursue their underground activities in empty, profitless burrows.'

Such fresh and telling phrases are the salt which has kept this book, a third of a century after its publication, from showing any signs of time's mildew.

First edition London: Hammond, Hammond, 1953
First US edition Philadelphia: Lippincott, 1953

51

SHELLEY SMITH

The Party at No. 5

have chosen *The Party at No. 5* (or *The Cellar at No. 5*, as it is
alled in America) firstly, of course, because it is an extremely
good book, one that I am happy to see among the 'best hundred'.
But I have also had in mind that it is an example, (necessarily
are) of the best sort of novel written by English women writers
of the time, with an added virtue in the tension of its crime plot.

The writers I have in mind are such as Rosamund Lehmann,
Elizabeth Bowen (though she was Anglo-Irish), Olivia Manning
or Elizabeth Taylor, a distinguished 'school'. Mary McCarthy is,
perhaps, the nearest American equivalent. It is their gifts of
perceptive character-study—mostly feminine—psychological insight and keen social observation (albeit of limited layers of
ociety) combined for the most part with quiet coolness of style
hat I see in this book.

But to Shelley Smith's perceptions about its 'heroine', the
ageing Mrs Rampage in her big London house yearning over her
araway married daughter and cherishing her motley collection
of beautiful and valuable objects, and about the woman who is
hrust on her, the widowed Mrs Roach, pious and self-centred,
he has added a story of frightening power.

For two-thirds of the book we read only of the struggle,
conducted genteelly under the surface with just occasional out-
breaks of vituperation, between the two ladies. Great stress is
aid, rightly, on the ladylikeness of each of the combatants, a
actor that takes nothing from the intensity of their battle. At its
limax, perhaps inevitably, a killing occurs, and from there on
he book takes on something of the horror story—the quiet
horror story—until it reaches its ordained, justice-filled end.

Shelley Smith conducts the slow-burn struggle that is the main
interest with superb timing. First one contestant seems assured of
victory, then the other. And each battle in this war is on a larger,
more involving scale. At each victory for one side or the other
ou think, 'Well, that must be that', but each time Shelley Smith

produces an entirely plausible reversal. It is a long duel fought with half-expressed feelings and, as an occasional illuminating firework, the forced downright lie by which one or other of the embattled pair seeks to gain an ultimate result. But that result, in the end, is achieved only with the descending poker striking the frail skull.

Equally, Shelley Smith allows her readers to discover the depths of her two protagonists only little by little. At first one is all sympathy for Mrs Ramage, alone in her big house, not finding on this, her birthday, a letter from her daughter; exclaiming aloud of herself with attractive derision, 'Poor old Mum'; and swinging an instant later into a more cheerful mood when she sees that the day is going to be fine, and immediately believing that the letter (which we are already convinced will never come) will tumble through the letter-box with the second post.

In the same way, the portrait we first get of her opponent-to-be, Mrs Roach, seems wholly sympathetic. We see her through the eyes of Mrs Ramage's carelessly do-gooding niece. She judges her 'to be the wife of a vicar in some provincial town. She had just that look of utterly respectable and unseductive attractiveness which is to be found nowhere else in the world; the look of simple goodness.'

But before all is done 'the look of simple goodness' is shown to conceal an iron determination to secure her own comforts, a tendency to unambiguous theft coupled with regular church-going and a vein of remorseless cruelty. On the other side of the battle line, Mrs Rampage is shown, too, to be a mass of unlovely traits, colossal meanness coupled with a darting extravagance in the purchase of 'pretty things', a sprawling vulgarity and a complete lack of sympathy for any underling she feels has betrayed her.

Yet by the time all this is revealed about our two lady wrestlers (wrestlers with words, looks and sulks, be it understood), we find we are committed to them. Shelley Smith has caught us in her trap. We are forced to understand two people with hardly a redeeming feature between them. And we have been engrossed in a struggle culminating in one fatal blow.

First edition London: Collins, 1954
First US edition New York: Harper, 1954 as *The Cellar at No. 5*

52

PATRICIA HIGHSMITH
The Talented Mr Ripley

Tom glanced behind him and saw the man coming out of the Green Cage heading his way.' Thus, bang in the middle, with a whiff of unease, begins Patricia Highsmith's saga about Tom Ripley, running eventually to four major books, though she cannot have known when she wrote those mysteriously edgy words what lay in the far distance. But she did know, indeed, what lay immediately ahead; Tom Ripley—we learn his surname almost at once when he imagines a police hand on his shoulder and the words 'Tom Ripley, you're under arrest'—is going to be a creature of his age, the era that the poet W.H. Auden called the Age of Anxiety.

Very soon, too, we get in the book a typical Ripley action. He asks himself whether he should go into a bar near the Green Cage, where his mysterious pursuer apparently spotted him, or whether he should contrive safely to hide himself in a dark doorway on Park Avenue. He plumps, almost unhesitatingly, for the riskier alternative. And he turns out to be lucky. His pursuer is only a worried father ready to finance a trip to Europe for Tom so that he can contact his stay-away son. 'Something always turned up. That was Tom's philosophy.' An echo here of Dickens' Mr Micawber with his 'in case anything turns up.' But Dickens, while exulting in Mr Micawber, disapproves of him. Patricia Highsmith exults in Tom Ripley, in a more wry fashion, and by no means disapproves.

Tom Ripley is a thief, and before the book is done a double murderer, whom we like—or, at least, cannot help sympathising with. Others recoil. I well remember a meeting of the judges for the Crime Writers' Association's Gold Dagger award where one of our number announced that if we chose *Ripley's Game* for the prize she would resign.

In later books in the Ripley saga it becomes clear—just—what it is that makes some of us like Tom so much. In these books we are briefly shown sides of his character that are fundamentally admirable, his genuine love of art and his true appreciation of the fruits of the earth, especially if deliciously cooked. Or there is his love for the beautiful French wife he later acquires, and the simple affection he feels for his friends, and his real interest in the earth-loving pursuit of gardening. But here, on his first appearance, almost all we have to make us go along with him is his charm, a quality hard to portray from the outside, and yet harder from the inside.

Perhaps, though, another quality that attracts us to Tom, with a sort of awed admiration, is his willingness to take risks. We have already glimpsed it in the opening pages of this first Ripley book. Soon we get a yet more telling example, when Tom deliberately puts at hazard his trip to Europe, which will get him out of the way of the police, by giving a different name for the advertising agency where he has just claimed, falsely, that he works.

Tom lives, then, in a world of dizzying chance. And so Patricia Highsmith wants to tell us, do we all. But she shows us this frightening, wrong world in no spirit of railing criticism nor even with the relished cynicism many another author would wallow in. All she says is: this is the way things are. One could produce a booming roll-call of great names that have said much the same thing: Kierkegaard (Tom quotes him once in a later novel), Gide with his famous *acte gratuit*, Sartre, and even Henry James (Tom's adventures in Europe are a modern re-telling of many of the James novels). But the Ripley books are altogether less solemn than these heavyweights. And deliberately so. Patricia Highsmith, for all her unblinking stare at the terrors of our time, never forgets that her aim is to write not a novel but a crime novel, that she wants first of all to entertain.

She treats us, then, time and again to spurts of idiosyncratic, throwaway, deadpan humour. I find them very funny. They are perhaps the final touch that makes the Ripley books in general and *The Talented Mr Ripley* in particular novels that are wonderfully, insanely readable.

First edition New York: Coward-McCann, 1955
First UK edition London: Cresset Press, 1957

53
MARGARET MILLAR
Beast in View

Margaret Millar is surely one of late twentieth-century crime fiction's best writers, in the sense that the actual writing in her books, the prose, is of superb quality. On almost every page of this one there is some description, whether of a physical thing or a mental state, that sends a sharp ray of extra meaning into the reader's mind. We talk of those vellum sheets the monks of old used to decorate with enamel-bright colours as illuminated manuscripts: Margaret Millar's images produce illuminated pages.

I could fill all the space at my disposal with examples. Here are just a few. First, the 'hero' of the book, Paul Blackshear, fifty-year-old, semi-retired, a successful stockbroker: 'Blackshear made a wry grimace as he pictured himself in the role of . . . reluctant rescuer, a tired, detached, balding knight in Harris tweeds.' Or there is the maidservant who is owed 'back wages in civility as well as cash.' Just two extra words about that civility, and a relationship between employer and employee is thrown into sharp light. One last instance: a mother learning apparently harsh truths about her daughter. 'Mrs Merrick's plump face was like rising dough.' Phrases as simply telling as this come only from the white heat of a fine creative mind.

But it is the use to which Mrs Millar puts her strongly imagined words that makes this book so exceptional. She is concerned with laying down a truth, or truths, about the people with whom she fills her pages. There is Miss Clarvoe, the central character, the thirty-year-old perpetual spinster living like a recluse in a private suite in a second-rank hotel in Hollywood, oblivious of the pulsing life that goes on all round her, a life etched in rapidly and effectively by Mrs Millar with a few overheard banal words from the room next to Miss Clarvoe's suite. There is her brother, the pathetic homosexual, seen with a compassion that takes nothing away from his unlikeability. There is their foolish widowed mother, looking like 'a starved sparrow preserved in ice.' Each of them is put before us in a white revealing light, revealing and understanding.

But the book is by no means a series of portraits, however compelling. It is a story, a swiftly moving, grabbing story, that begins with Miss Clarvoe receiving a telephone call that seems to come from a mad woman, and tells of how Paul Blackshear, appealed to, sets out to track down the caller—and finds in the last pages a figure of evil more desperate than in his worst moments he has been able to imagine.

Mrs Millar can take us to the beast-core in the human beings she shows us. Other writers, chiefly of horror fiction, often set out to portray evil, and almost always their desire to give us a happy *frisson* leads them to laying on the adjectives, piling up the effects. Not Mrs Millar. Truths about what can happen to human beings are what she is aiming to find. They are the beasts she has in view. And she has the toughness of mind to be able to portray them as they are, neither turning away in fear (as most of us are apt to do when confronted with the worst man can do to man) nor overpainting in a desperate effort to convince readers of something not fully grasped by the writer.

Yet—again—the book is not a study of a disturbed mind, whether treated as factual description or fictional reconstruction. *Beast in View* is crime fiction. It is, despite the hard truths it tells, entertainment. And nowhere is this more apparent than in the final grand trick Mrs Millar plays on us readers, as if we were puppets in the hands of an Agatha Christie. The book is a study in madness, and it is also a splendid conjuring trick, with no cheating. The main clue is there in its opening pages, neatly placed before us and neatly glossed over while our eyes are made to focus on something else.

So, a rare feat: a book that is simultaneously a whodunit game and a deep and compassionate study of the dark places of the human psyche.

First edition New York: Random House, 1955
First UK edition London: Gollancz, 1955

116

54

JOHN CREASEY

Gideon's Week

One day in 1954 or thereabouts a London police inspector who happened to be a neighbour of the extremely prolific author John Creasey—he of the twenty-five pseudonyms ranging from Margaret Cooke to Tex Reilly—challenged him with 'Why don't you show us as we are?' Next year, under the pseudonym of J.J. Marric, Creasey produced the first of what was to be a long stream of stories featuring Gideon of the Yard. And, save perhaps that, Creasey being a nice chap, the books do not dwell on the worser side of the Metropolitan Police, they do show the force and its workings as they are. Or, certainly, as they were at the time of writing.

Gideon's Week opens with George Gideon—name well chosen to say 'a good man'—just promoted to Commander and in charge of the Criminal Investigation Department at Scotland Yard. Straight away we get those little details of the running of the Yard that contribute to give the book, and all the saga, that aura of authenticity which is so quietly fascinating.

'One of the advantages of his new rank,' Marric/Creasey writes, 'was the fact that parking space was always left for him.' And we register, without stopping to notice, that you have to have attained that high a rank to get this unacknowledged privilege. Perhaps we also register, again without particularly noticing, that the detail is given us in very ordinary language. There is that intrusive and unnecessary 'the fact that'. Creasey was no master of gem-hard, economical prose. But what he has to tell us he tells in a plain workmanlike style, never laden with the dazzling adjectives more pretentious writers attempt.

'Gideon's first mentor in the Criminal Investigation Department had been fond of saying that the burden of proof was the heaviest burden the Yard had to carry,' Creasey writes at the book's very start, nicely planting a little moral that is to pop up later with added force. And then he, in the voice of George Gideon, comments: 'Trite but true.' You could apply that label

117

to the whole book. And it is not as derogatory as you might think. There is a certain triteness, yes, but there is also a great deal of simple, detailed truth. And it has a powerful cumulative effect.

So, as we read, we get these true little details slipped in without fuss, such as Gideon noticing that the door of the office he shares with Chief Inspector Lemaitre is open by an inch as he approaches. This is one of the countless tiny pieces of what might be called 'secret etiquette' that Creasey handles so well. The door is just open so that Lemaitre will get a moment's warning of the arrival of his boss and can greet him in the correctly accepted manner.

It all adds to the authenticity of this multiple portrait of a great police organisation at work. You get it in other ways, too, bearing perhaps more directly on criminal investigation. There is Gideon's observation, for instance, that a spell of really cold weather means fewer burglaries, since breaking and entering is made more hazardous by slippery ice and frozen fingers. And, equally, that when (as in the climax here) a major raid is carried out on some area suspected of harbouring a dangerous man, the minor crooks will slip off into neighbouring districts depleted of their full quota of officers, with burglary in mind.

So as the routines are described and varying excitements arise we get, first, a portrait of a police force shown 'as we are', and then a portrait of a senior police officer, if not warts and all with at least a minor wart or two left. It is a portrait that is probably fairly near the mark for more than a few senior policemen in Britain at any one time, men who are conscientious, tough enough when they have to be—'there was a hard streak in Gideon; had there not been he would never have reached his position'—not at all intellectual but decidedly shrewd, and, above all, despite the newspapers' eagerly seized-on stories of corruption and chicanery, decent and honest and determined to get at the truth.

First edition London: Hodder and Stoughton, 1956
First US edition New York: Harper, 1956

55

STANLEY ELLIN
Mystery Stories

Mystery Stories is a dull title for a book which critic Julian Symons has called 'the finest collection of stories in the crime form published in the past half-century', a judgement I am happy to concur with. But that title, though dull, does say exactly what the contents of the book are—mystery stories, that and no more. 'These are short stories, for God's sake,' Ellin wrote in his introduction, years later, to a complete collection of his tales up to 1979; 'not some great overblown kapok-stuffed novel.' Each one, he went on, was a story, and it was short. There you have him and them: modest, cheerful, unpretentious, seeing just what's what—and author eventually of crime novels notably unkapok-stuffed and notably saying what short stories cannot.

What was what in the 1956 collection was a handful of short stories of the very first quality, led off by Ellin's first published story, 'The Specialty of the House', which won the annual contest run by *Ellery Queen's Mystery Magazine*, as did no fewer than six immediate successors. But, though that now-classic tale was Ellin's first to be published, it was by no means the first he wrote. He learnt his craft long and hard and in silence, if not in a silence he wished for.

He began that learning process, he has said, at the age of three. He was ill, and his father read to him Beatrix Potter's immortal tale *Peter Rabbit*. And then read it again, and again, at the infant Ellin's demand until the budding writer had it word perfect in his head. He had recognised, he said, 'the true magic.' It was something in the course of his growing-up that he recognised from time to time again; in Hemingway's contributions to the magazines that came into the Ellin home, in Faulkner, in Scott Fitzgerald and in Ring Lardner. On the family bookshelves he discovered Mark Twain, Kipling, Poe, Stevenson and finally de Maupassant, 'the true magic again.'

It was not until his late college days, however, that he tried to produce the true magic himself, though through all his childhood he had been, he admits, 'an incorrigible daydreamer.' But those early daydreams did not seem to produce the right stuff, and it was only after many years and a period of failing interest that at the age of thirty and the insistence of his wife he had one last attempt. During this he conceived an idea 'so outrageous' that even as he wrote he told himself that this way lies oblivion. The outrageous idea, which I will not divulge to anyone who has not read the story (no one who has will have forgotten it) was the notion for 'The Specialty of the House'—the story that gave the British edition of this first collection its title.

But the book contains nine other stories hardly less good. 'The Moment of Decision' is a tale about a conjuror, Raymond the Magician, a flabbergasting riddle piece that could be preferred without causing offence to 'The Specialty of the House'. 'The Cat's-Paw' is a story that evokes comparison with Doyle's masterpiece 'The Red-headed League'. 'The House Party' is a fantasy—Ellin has said that one of the attractions of crime fiction for him is its infinite diversity of theme and treatment—which won the Mystery Writers of America's Edgar award for its year. 'Broker's Special' is a splendid crime-on-the-lines tale, one of the sub-sub-genre of railway mysteries. 'The Orderly World of Mr Appleby' is a fine example of the 'perfect murder' sub-sub-genre.

Yet you could hardly do better than to pick out from the bunch 'The Best of Everything', a story about a young man in a very prestigious office who, consumed with envy for his idle fellow-employees gifted with the inherited aplomb of Money, Family and School, arrives at a way of acquiring the outward air of all these (and the boss's daughter to boot) only to meet with a fearful and beautifully logical comeuppance. Told with a marvellous tone of what might be called tough deflation—'It is also necessary to come riding in golden armor, mounted on a blooded horse, and bearing orchestra seats to the best musical comedy in town'—and flipping in its murder in the same easy manner: 'after considerable choked protest and thrashing around, Charlie Peace lay dead.' It has a plot and a punch, reverberating long in the mind, to rival that classic story by Ellin's hero de Maupassant 'The Necklace.'

First edition New York: Simon and Schuster, 1956
First UK edition London: Boardman, 1957
Later issued as *The Speciality of the House, and other stories*

56

SIMENON

Maigret in Court

Some of Simenon's Maigret novels are, I suppose, less successful than others, though what he does is always remarkable. So I have chosen *Maigret in Court* from among a host of other possibilities because it gives as good a portrait as any of Simenon's extraordinary detective.

It covers more or less the whole life of the man, referring to his childhood when he was an altar-boy serving Mass in the country church where he was brought up, and to his coming retirement at the mandatory age of fifty-five when he envisages himself back in the countryside sitting in a corner of a café playing *belote*, a card game for which there seems to be no foreign equivalent and which thus emphasises Maigret's intense Frenchness (though his creator was Belgian), and equally his bred-in-the-bone affinity with the *bourgeoisie*.

But over and above this, the opening scene of the book, a court hearing, gives us a picture of Maigret the believer in the subtleties and complexities of life. We get it from his stifled angry reactions to the various formulas of the legal process and its necessarily gross simplifications. Even though Maigret has accustomed himself to falling in with the conventions, to the extent of wearing an overcoat and carrying a hat in the court even though its building is actually connected directly with police headquarters, sometimes when faced with a particularly hidebound magistrate he clenches his fists in impotence at the way the rigidities of procedure have prevented the full truth appearing. It is that full truth which he feels is indispensable in judging anyone's actions.

And, of course, it is the full truth of a man's actions, or a woman's, that Simenon is dedicated to producing for us through his invented personage, Maigret. Maigret is very different from the archetypal Great Detective of British crime fiction or the archetypal private-eye of American. The typical British Great Detective solves mysteries by standing back, observing and pondering. 'You see but you do not observe,' Sherlock Holmes rebukes Dr Watson, while Poirot, that most British of Belgians, refers everything to his little grey cells. Raymond Chandler's Marlowe and his host of successors, on the other hand, solve their cases by going in two-fisted.

Maigret does neither of these things. He may to some small extent exercise logical deduction, as here, where he works out that because there is the victim's blood on the sleeve of a suspect's Sunday suit it means, not that he was the killer, but that someone deliberately borrowed the suit. In other books he is shown, too, behaving in a typical Great Detective manner by going into a trance of some sort (once in bed dully fighting off a heavy cold), and then combining the rational and the imaginative to solve the apparently unsolvable. Very occasionally, even, he is tough with a suspect in a faint reflection of the American way of detection.

But far outshining these approaches is his customary manner of dealing with his cases: by understanding. As I put it earlier, he is the detective as author. Here he strives to get into the mind, not as it happens of the actual killer but of the suspect he has arrested at the insistence of the Examining Magistrate, and whom he contrives to get freed in a court scene that might come from a Perry Mason drama, except that Maigret on the stand produces not crude facts but a subtle analysis of the accused's background.

So, with Maigret, we come to understand at a profound level one human being, the suspect Gaston Meurant, who eventually comes to shoot the man who had callously murdered the victims of the crime he himself was originally arraigned for. And Maigret lets him do it. He acts, in a phrase Simenon used about him at the outset of his career, as a Mender of Destinies, a putter-right of the injustices of an imperfect and hidebound world. A high task for a high priest of detection.

First UK edition London: Hamish Hamilton, 1961
(Originally *Maigret aux Assizes*: Paris, 1960)

57

MICHAEL INNES
The New Sonia Wayward

This book is an unashamed personal favourite of mine, but it does have other claims to inclusion in the Grand Order of the Hundred Best. It is a fine example of the work of Michael Innes, *not* featuring urbane, quotation-imbued Appleby. It is, too, as a contemporary reviewer enthused, 'wonderfully written.' And it is funny—to my mind very funny, though I realise that what I find hilarious may to another be merely mildly risible.

But a book whose very title, *The New Sonia Wayward*, is a pun and a pun rooted in the very heart of its plot must have more than a little going for it. The New Sonia Wayward is, in fact, both the new novel supposedly written by Sonia Wayward, bestselling romantic novelist, as well as the lady who eventually comes to take her place. In the very first page the first Sonia dies of a sudden stroke while at sea in the small craft owned by her husband, Colonel Ffolliot Petticate, who, after a moment's bewilderment, eats the chops she was cooking when her sudden demise occurred, consumes most of a bottle of whisky and is then inspired to give her the burial at sea which he feels in his capacity as master of the vessel he is entitled to perform. First joke.

Joke the second comes in the heading to the first chapter, 'Colonel Petticate at Sea', another neat pun. Plot development the second comes with Petticate's resolve that Sonia's literary output, on which he has depended for the finer things in life, must go on. At once Michael Innes has at his command a fruitful and delicious source of light irony.

Petticate now visits Sonia's publisher with a view to finding out more about books he has hitherto given scant attention. The publisher, Ambrose Wedge, is interested to hear about the new Wayward, one-third already written. 'It builds up suspense?' he asks. 'Oh, most decidedly,' Petticate replies: 'I've been spending quite a lot of time wondering what's going to happen next.' And, as he continues the book himself, all sorts of nice small surprises follow, little petards of words exploded.

But Michael Innes does more than this. The late, great Margery Allingham once gave me a rough formula for crime fiction: 'a surprise every ten pages and a shock every twenty.' And, if not at these precise intervals, Innes does provide some splendid shocks. On the very train back to his comfortable country house from his interview with Wedge, the Colonel is faced with a woman looking exactly like his truly dead wife. A *volte-face* that is neatly resolved, and later used in the plot to great effect. A similar trick is played two-thirds of the way through when Petticate, now being blackmailed by his odious servants, Mr and Mrs Hennwife, believes he has riposted by causing an ancient barn to collapse on them fatally, and then is greeted by the smooth Hennwife with the words 'You rang, sir?'

The timing is immaculate. And its effect is enhanced by that being precisely the right thing for Hennwife to say. Innes, in fact, fills the book with characters, not of depth, but of tremendous coloration. Too many to single out, except perhaps to look for a moment at Ambrose Wedge, publisher and man of splendidly elaborated meanness, down to tapping his cigar 'against an ashtray thoughtfully donated to his impoverished enterprise by a firm of mineral-water manufacturers.' A neat joke by an author against publishers in general, and a swift addition to a brightly-coloured picture.

Innes is, in short, a magician with words, a relishing magician. Look how cleverly he ameliorates any harshness that his beauti-fully-crafted plot leads him into. The woman who becomes the new Sonia Wayward is referred to as possibly 'an elderly harlot,'—not, note, an ancient whore nor anything more graphic. Similarly, Petticate's sexual tastes are wrapped up in the finely melliflous phrase 'a man not without intermittent inclinations to venery.' The effect is exactly the same as Agatha Christie killing off a victim with 'a neat hole in the middle of the forehead.' It allows a story of crime to be told as a long, marvellously sustained joke, peppered, too, with jokelets in abundance.

Oh, and by the way—though I am resolute that this is a crime story, when you look back at it you will see that no crime was actually committed.

First edition London: Gollancz, 1960
First US edition New York: Dodd, Mead, 1960
as *The Case of Sonia Wayward*

58

NICOLAS FREELING
Gun Before Butter

It cannot be expected that one particular assessor of fiction should be equally sympathetic to every manifestation in the field under consideration. So let me confess at once that I don't much like the work of Nicolas Freeling. But that work has been much praised by reviewers, critics and literary historians whose judgments I respect, so I have little hesitation in including *Gun Before Butter*, one of Freeling's output that has been much singled out, in this assembly.

Freeling as a writer showers the unprotected reader with opinions. Often these are contradictory—witness his simultaneous trumpeting and blasting of the city of Amsterdam in the opening pages here—and always they are expressed in the starkest terms. He seems to set out, much of the time through the mouth of his detective Van der Valk, to shock—which is something different from being naturally shocking. He appears to delight in the unusualness of the opinions he holds.

He is, too, infuriatingly knowing, a trait displaying what seems to me a similar attitude to his lambasting of his readers with his opinionated views. For example, he frequently allows Van der Valk to think or speak in untranslated French. A word or two of simple French whose meaning is obvious is, of course, not out of place in crime fiction, as witness Agatha Christie having Hercule Poirot fall into his natural Belgian French when it is simple, and keep to English when the thought is complex. But Freeling does precisely the opposite.

Then, too, Freeling will expect every reader to pick up quite abstruse cultural references, as when he describes a girl by saying simply she has 'a Sisley look.' Or referring, maddeningly, to an orchestral conductor just as 'Erich', leaving the reader to wonder for three-quarters of the book just who is meant until Freeling deigns to throw in a 'Kleiber'. Nor are these casually-dropped references always at the high cultural level which, it might be argued, Freeling has some right to expect of readers of intelligent crime fiction. In one instance at least we are asked to recognise 'Captain Haddock', but surely it is too much to expect every reader to know the Tintin comic-strip books.

Yet, set against these irritating tricks, Freeling does have virtues of a high order. The very opinions which often make me boil with rage can be expressed with a telling sharpness that delights. I barked with laughter when I read that Van der Valk had said 'that Dutch was a language for farm-girls to call chickens in.' I recognised a deflating pithiness worthy almost of Raymond Chandler in the description of a senior detective in the political police as being 'as self-important as an advertising agency' or another of a woman hotel-owner 'about as tender . . . and gentle as a footballer's right boot.'

Alongside this sharpness there is its opposite: sympathy. As when Van der Valk first sees the corpse of the murdered man central to the book's story, 'a man who, until a few hours ago was an alert, breathing human being, with his own vivid eyes and ears and nose, with his public life and his private life and his own inner, secret life. And now he lies like a sack.' Or there is the lyrical, loving description—too long to quote—of the woodland cottage that was the dead man's hidden retreat.

Freeling possesses a strongly developed power of seeing into that which lies below, often that 'inner, secret life.' Indeed, this is what *Gun Before Butter* is about. It is more, much more, than a thriller centred round the unusual and very European business of the smuggling of butter between Holland, where it was cheap, and Belgium, where it was twice the price. It is more, too, than a vehicle for expressing the author's cranky notions. The book is designed to present a portrait-in-depth of one curious, odd, fiercely independent girl, Lucienne Englebert, daughter of a famous conductor and by choice a petrol-pump girl, a deliberate drop-out. And in a long section in which Van der Valk does not even figure, we get the final revelation of how she came to be what she eventually was, and why the book's murder was committed.

Because this is what Freeling is above all: a writer of the why-done-it. And perhaps, despite his every irritating mannerism, as good a one as any.

First edition London: Gollancz, 1963

First US edition New York: Harper, 1964 as *A Question of Loyalty*

59

DOROTHY B. HUGHES

The Expendable Man

The Expendable Man, a late addition to the thirteen crime stories Dorothy B. Hughes wrote with great success in one prolific spell between 1940 and 1952, is one of the great trick novels of crime fiction. Yet to call it that is to belittle it. Its trick is no clever, superimposed bit of literary legerdemain: it is integral to the whole conception of the book.

So much so that I have little hesitation in giving Ms Hughes' trick away here and now, even though that may to an extent spoil the book's first impact for those who have yet to read it. But as with Agatha Christie (whose tricks were literary legerdemain, and most delightfully so), there is as much pleasure to be got out of watching the cunning hand preparing the firework surprise as there is in innocently reading the book and being rocked back when the surprise comes.

You are rocked back by Ms Hughes some fifty pages into her story, and I can certify that the effect is truly rocking. You even read past the vital word, just one word in a sentence of swift dialogue, before you realise what it has said, and what a new and different light it casts on everything you have read up to that moment. Till then you are engrossed—Ms Hughes is a fine storyteller—in an account of a young American intern doctor driving his parents' white Cadillac between Los Angeles, where his hospital is, and Phoenix, Arizona, where his well-off parents live and his sister is about to get married. He stops in a stretch of desert highway and picks up a young, feckless girl wanting a lift.

So far, so fine. Vivid descriptions of the landscape—Ms Hughes began her writing career with a volume of poetry—and a nice study of the girl, a fluent liar and apparently ready at the drop of a scarf to use a little moral blackmail to extend that lift all the way to her destination, also in Phoenix. The young man, one begins to feel, is perhaps a little paranoid about the dangers of giving a girl on her own a lift, and is even a little bit of a prig.

Then comes Ms Hughes' bombshell. Let me quote the piece of

dialogue entire. It is spoken by an unpleasant, macho police detective named Venner, questioning the hero, Dr Densmore, after a girl resembling the one to whom he gave the lift has been found dead. 'We got a tip,' he says. 'Right after that report went out on the radio. This guy says a nigger doctor driving a big white Cadillac brought Bonnie Lee to Phoenix.'

A nigger doctor. The words slip by, then pull you up sharp. When I first read the book I stopped and went back and combed through the pages to see if I had missed something. But, no. There is no explicit statement that Dr Densmore, successful intern at a great Los Angeles hospital and acme of all that is middle class, is actually black. But there are clues, placed with all the craft of an Agatha Christie.

A girl that Hugh Densmore—and what cunning in that Christian name—sets his eye on before the wedding is described as having a beautiful sand-brown complexion. 'Ah yes, a sun-lover,' one says at the time. But, of course, she too is a black. Then a swimming-pool at the motel where Hugh stays is described. 'Across the green was a tropical blue pool with clusters of sky-tall palm trees bending over it. Hot-pink umbrellas shaded white tables.' How inviting, one thinks as one reads; how well described, even. And one wonders just fleetingly why Hugh, who is hot and ragged, does not go out and take a cooling dip. It is only after one has read that one word 'nigger' that one realises he was avoiding possible unpleasantness he might be subjected to in largely white Phoenix, Arizona, in the mid-1960s.

And after that one speech of Detective Venner's, in an adroitly-plotted succession of events keeping up the suspense right to the last pages, one sees Hugh in a new light. No longer is he a mite priggish, no longer unnecessarily uptight. Instead he becomes one of those heroes one does not merely ride along with during the progress of a story, but a person one identifies with, palpitatingly. And in doing so one gets a fearsome insight into man's inhumanity to man, racist-view up; into what can make one person see another as 'expendable'; and, more, into man's decency to man. A fine achievement, through a literary trick.

First edition London: Deutsch, 1964
First US edition New York: Ransom, 1963

60

JIM THOMPSON

Pop. 1280

The great merit of the novels of Jim Thompson is that they are completely without good taste, and of them perhaps *Pop. 1280* (the title refers to the population of a small town in an imaginary Potts County in deepest America) has the least good taste of all.

A few examples. The hero, Nick Corey, the seemingly weakly-corrupt sheriff of Potts County, eventually shoots one of his tormentors and then kicks him. 'You might think,' he comments, 'it wasn't real nice to kick a dying man, and maybe it wasn't. But I'd been wanting to kick him for a long time, and it just never had seemed safe till now.'

Sex, naturally, plays a large part in this tissue of bad taste. A favourite quote of mine comes from Rosa, Nick's wife, who after telling him that she is not going to say what she had in mind because she is 'a decent woman', promptly goes on: 'If I wasn't ... I'd heist a leg and pee in your ear until it washed out that stinking pile of crap you call brains.'

Or there is the humour of bodily functions with Nick in reflective mood as he sits idly at his desk, having of course no law-keeping to do amid the prevailing corruption. 'I found a long hair sticking out of my nose, and I jerked it out and looked at it, and it didn't look particularly interesting. I dropped it on to the floor, wonderin' if falling hair from fellas' noses was noted along with fallin' sparrows.' I spare you the remainder of Nick's reverie, which goes from the lavatorial to the masturbatory in the same vein of easy humour.

But note that casual reference to the falling sparrows of the Bible. It shows that behind the lavatory humour and behind the story of crime and corruption, Jim Thompson had a more serious purpose, or a deeper and darker vision of life. And, as Nick Corey's story progresses we find that the flicked-in reference to the New Testament grows monstrously until we hear Nick saying, 'I'm the saviour himself, Christ on the cross, come right here to Potts County, because God knows I was needed here.'

While a little earlier Nick philosophises that 'a heck of a lot of things are bound to go wrong in a world as big as this one. And if there's any answer to why it's that way—and there ain't always—why, it's probably not just one answer by itself, but thousands of answers.' And, of course, why a heck of a lot of things are bound to go wrong is the question that the great novels equally confront, though for the most part (one might except Rabelais) they do not do it with such ebullient lack of good taste.

Nick, despite his unlovely manners and willingness to kick a dying man, is not an entirely callous creature. He feels, as he says, 'sorry for people.' But, he goes on, 'When you're sorry for someone you want to help them, and when it sinks in on you that you can't, that there's too god-danged many of them . . .' There he breaks off, unable to say what he wants to do in a world where nothing can be done.

Because it is a bleak view of life that Jim Thompson is concerned to present, through the foul-talking mouth of Nick Corey. 'What else is there to do,' he asks, 'but laugh and joke . . . how else can you bear up under the unbearable?'

A bleak, bleak view. And I think were this all, I would say a book like *Pop. 1280* deserved the oblivion it nearly fell into. It was first published in America as a paperback in 1964, and did not appear in Britain until 1983, when it came out in a fine hardback edition together with three other Thompson novels and an excellent introduction by Nick Kimberley.

But its bleak view has two redeeming features. There is, first, those bad-taste jokes. They bring gusts of optimistic laughter through the grey, grim prospect. And, second, there is the writing itself. That someone can look at the world and see it in its most corrupt and impossible-of-remedy aspect, and can then put it down in words which convey to the full the meaning of that vision is in itself a major cause for optimism.

It makes the book that brings it off one worthy of preservation, not merely in the vaults of the British Library or the Library of Congress, but in the minds of many readers.

First edition New York: Fawcett, 1964
First UK edition London: Zomba, 1983

61
MIGNON G. EBERHART
R.S.V.P. Murder

Mignon G. Eberhart, or, as she was known in Britain, M.G. Eberhart, is important in crime fiction as heir and successor to Mary Roberts Rinehart. After a trial period producing what might be called nurse-and-doctor detection, she found her true *métier* in a well-judged mixture of suspense, seen from the point of view of a female heroine, and mystery. She became, in fact, a star writer in the 1st. pers. sing. fem. tradition.

She has some fifty titles to her credit, and, as with some other authors in this selection, it was not easy to pick one of her books from the others as being above her customary level of high competence. I eventually chose *R.S.V.P. Murder* because in many ways it shows M.G. Eberhart at her most typical.

To begin with it is partly set on the Riviera, and not a few of the Eberhart books have similarly exotic locales as their starting points (*Five Passengers from Lisbon, Message from Hongkong*). Then its characters are chosen from among the wealthy, an ingredient necessary to lend a proper air of romance, giving the reader something to aspire to or dream of. And, finally, *R.S.V.P. Murder* is an excellent example of the way an atmosphere of suspense can be built up out of dozens of tiny hints and vague intimations. M.G. Eberhart frequently uses glancing references to characters' eyes, for instance; state just once that someone's eyes are 'cold', and for the rest of the book suspicion lingers that he or she must be the person behind mysterious events.

The mysterious events in *R.S.V.P. Murder* are cunningly chosen, and cunningly worked out. At its start on the Promenade des Anglais in fashionable Nice, the young American heroine, whose father has just died leaving her a moneyless orphan, learns that he is not the impeccably upright man she had always believed him to be. A trial lawyer famed for his successes, he has sent in his dying days five letters to people whose secrets he had learnt, hinting in finely roundabout ways that after his death they should send his daughter large cash contributions, since she will

131

have come into possession of his confidential diary. But Fran, our heroine, has no notion to whom these near-blackmail letters, possibly putting her life in danger, have been sent. The book tells the story of how she unearths the recipients one by one, hunts for the missing diary—and discovers love.

The discovery of love and a loved one is, of course, a mandatory element in 1st. pers. sing. fem. writing. It is a style that is often mocked, a close relative to the 'Had I But Known' school where heroines step into the utmost danger at the dictate of nothing more than the author's need to produce a suspenseful situation—such as the point in *R.S.V.P. Murder* where Fran thinks 'My careful reasoning, my plan for a sensible approach . . . everything in fact that was sensible at all disappeared.'

But this is an isolated moment where the worst excesses are just a hairsbreadth away. For all the rest of the book M.G. Eberhart plays with us, her readers, with high adroitness. Which is what we—male as well as female, I dare claim—really like. The situations of peril here, as elsewhere in M.G. Eberhart's work, are made credible because the heroine to whom they happen is a believable, middle-of-the-road character and her thoughts are brought to us at that moment of danger.

It is only fair to add that, as a writer of English prose, M.G. Eberhart is not among the greats, though her writing is always perfectly serviceable. But the best writing is not a necessary ingredient of the best crime fiction (though it's nice when you get it); there are many other factors that take an author to crime's heights. M.G. Eberhart possessed them. She could create an atmosphere of true suspense. She could devise a plot of real ingenuity. She could produce characters with enough reality about them to lift what might have been merely mechanical into the realm of engrossing fiction.

First edition New York: Random House, 1965
First UK edition London: Collins, 1966

62

JULIAN SYMONS

The Man Who Killed Himself

Julian Symons in his book about Edgar Allan Poe, *The Tell-tale Heart*, distinguished between two Poes, Logical Poe and Visionary Poe. He was perhaps the better able to see this divide in Poe because it corresponds to a division in his own crime fiction. His crime books come, broadly speaking, in two modes, the ingenious and the perceptive. For this collection I have chosen one of each. *The Man Who Killed Himself* is my example of Symons the ingenious.

Except that it isn't only this. If I had wanted ingenuity and nothing more, I suppose I would have selected *The Plot Against Roger Rider*. But this book, which has more to it than the wonderfully ingenious, is one that has impressed me to a greater extent. It shows—and I derive great pleasure from this—Symons the philosopher, the student of human nature in depth, as well as Symons the laugh-aloud creator of comic situations.

But first the ingenuity, which is also a hands-rubbing delight. *The Man Who Killed Himself* is at the outset the story of timid, suburban Arthur Brownjohn, and in the opening pages we get a description of suburban life of a fierce accuracy that almost scorches the page. But the first half of the book also contains the parallel story of Major Easonby Mellon, vigorous and dicey owner of a matrimonial agency. And soon we learn that Arthur Brownjohn and Easonby Mellon are actually one and the same person.

Which brings us to the first hints of the deeper layers, as Arthur contrives that Easonby Mellon shall patently murder the bullying wife he daily resents. Masks and fantasies: they are a staple of the Symons *œuvre*. Time and again they recur, and Symons himself has said, in an introduction to an omnibus collection of his novels, that what absorbs him most is 'the violence behind respectable faces.'

But part at least of *The Man Who Killed Himself* is that straightforward satire on suburban life, and satire, however

133

fierce, is always in the mode of comedy. Thus we get delightfully cool humour when, in flash-back, Arthur's proposal to well-off but lumpen Clare is accepted with alacrity, and he feels 'as if he had put his head inside the jaws of an apparently stuffed alligator and had found them decisively snapped together.' Or there is the moment of the actual murder, when Arthur in his richly-suited, bewigged Easonby Mellon disguise enters his own house, revolver at the ready in his pocket, only for Clare to say 'What are you doing in those ridiculous clothes, and that—' She finds it impossible actually to name his transforming wig, and simply commands 'Take it off immediately.' I have heard Julian Symons read this passage to an audience in Berlin, and it brought the house down.

Ingenuity (and there is a great deal more of it in the final ramifications), laugh-aloud humour and speculation about man's fascination for masks and his need for them—but on top of all that something more: Symons the philosopher.

The Man Who Killed Himself is a crime story that continues to put us in the murderer's shoes *after* his successful crime. In doing so it shows us that the crime was successful only in the most limited, mechanical sense. Because Arthur Brownjohn, free at last and established in the home of his choice, finds that 'in any meaningful sense, he did not exist.' His being had been created, he realises, in large part out of his reactions to others. In his hated suburban home he had played with model racing cars in the attic, not because it was what he himself wanted to do but as a reaction to the bullying which Clare had meted out. We—all of us, Symons says—need an experience of the Other.

So when, in the book's penultimate ironic jab, the detectives who have satisfied themselves that Easonby Mellon was responsible for Clare's death 'prove' that Arthur used Easonby Mellon as a hired killer, he simply goes mad. He has been defeated by his own ingenuity. Then we come to the final irony of all. Arthur is in Broadmoor Criminal Lunatic Asylum, and the book's very last words are 'He ate voraciously, grew fat and seemed quite happy.'

The crime story turned definitively into the crime novel.

First edition London: Collins, 1967
First US edition New York: Harper, 1967

63

EMMA LATHEN
Murder Against the Grain

The novels, written jointly by Mary Latsis and Martha Henissart under the name Emma Lathen (work it out), are among the most amusing crime stories in the canon—and the most informative. They opened their account in 1961 with *Banking on Death*, a book that introduced the world of Wall Street to crime writing, as well as their perennial hero, John Putnam Thatcher, senior vice-president of the Sloan Guaranty Trust. At once they showed that they not only knew about banking and office procedures, but that they had the ability to make them crisply clear to the most unfinancial of readers.

Murder Against the Grain was the sixth Thatcher case, and, if ever Emma Lathen had needed to get into her stride—and she hardly did—by her sixth book she certainly knew all there was to know about telling a story, about handing to readers on a plate a fascinating world about which most of them knew nothing, and finally about how to spice the whole with humour without ever making any part of the dish too hot to savour.

Each of the Lathen books has considered a different aspect of the world of finance and its meshing with the world of industry, commerce or entertainment. John Putnam Thatcher, Emma Lathen says in this book, 'was always willing to learn about the ways in which money was made.' Plainly, this also goes for the two ladies who make up Miss Lathen, and indeed Mary Latsis was an economist and Martha Henissart had a career in corporate finance and banking, but they are more than interested themselves: they have the power to interest us too.

The area of financial complications made clear, and amusing, in *Murder Against the Grain* was the early trading treaty between the U.S.A. and the U.S.S.R., under which surplus American wheat was shipped to Russia. Emma Lathen ingeniously conceived of a major crime this might give rise to: the cheating of the Sloan out of 985,000 dollars (not for Lathen the crudity of a million dollars, not the first-joke humour of

999,999). Then, yet more ingeniously, murder was added, since it is a curious fact that to hold readers in an entertainment novel it must feature a crime of this ultimate importance.

Then, subject laid down and plot arrived at, Emma Lathen proceeds briskly and pointedly to sketch out characters by the dozen and to tell the story. And bouncingly told it is, much assisted by the particular brand of Lathen humour, all the more remarkable for its unique stamp when you consider that it is the product of two minds, each writing alternate chapters. But two minds do provide two terminals between which sparks can fly.

The humour is, to my mind, of an oddly British cast. It relies frequently on a tone of light exaggeration, as in the description of a meeting of the Sloan investment committee being interrupted by a secretary. The meeting is one whose 'solemn deliberations were sacrosanct', and it took Miss Turvin, the secretary, 'several days before she could think of the whole thing without shuddering.' This is the method favoured by as dyed-in-the-wool English a writer as P.G. Wodehouse.

In handling character a similar rather British deflation is used, and with splendid timing. Whether it is the flurry of solemn editorial comment from around the world that forms the prologue (and neatly introduces a complex subject), with each editorialist pompously taking a diametrically opposite view from his predecessor, or whether it is a simple hire-car driver loosing off about bigwigs taking a liner trip as 'so many bums ready to sit in the sun for a week and relax from the heavy partying', only for us to be reminded that the liner is to plough across the Atlantic in March, the device is the same. Deflation. The comment is sharp, but also amusing.

Yet if the basic method seems British—and this may account for British readers lapping up Miss Lathen—it is always Americanised, always that much sharper. But it is always fun, too, and this in the end is the great contribution Emma Lathen has made to crime fiction: a bubbling and overwhelming sense of fun.

First edition New York: Macmillan, 1967
First UK edition London: Gollancz, 1967

64
MAJ SJÖWALL AND PER WAHLÖÖ
Roseanna

Once upon a time crime fiction was the simple detective story, a game between the writer and the reader. Then, gradually, writers realised that the format could be used to do what straight novels do, to say things about life. The culmination of this movement came perhaps in the ten novels a pair of Swedish Communist writers, Maj Sjöwall and Per Wahlöö, produced between 1967 and 1976.

The ten books were planned as an assault on Swedish society, and by implication on all Western society. The authors, according to an essay Per Wahlöö wrote when the series had just begun, aimed to start with one or two seemingly innocuous stories and then, having established a sympathetic hero, Inspector Martin Beck, and a group of colleagues around him, bit by bit to introduce more and more direct criticism of the Swedish state and the Swedish way of life. The first book was *Roseanna*.

I have chosen it in preference to the others—they are all of a high standard—because it is the one of the ten that most clearly stays within the bounds of crime fiction, although one of the later ones, *The Locked Room*, does contain a John-Dickson-Carr-type puzzle, and a good one. But it also carries a heavy load of direct social criticism, and may be said to have crossed the mine-strewn border between crime fiction and pure fiction (or, rather, impure didactic fiction).

Roseanna, however, can be read almost without reservation as a simple police procedural story. Its authors certainly provided it with a plot worthy of the best in this sub-genre. The body of a girl is discovered when a dredger goes to work at the mouth of a ship canal somewhere in Sweden. Nothing is known of the girl, not even her name, and nor does it appear that anything will come to light. No similar person is on any of the Swedish lists of missing persons, nor on those of neighbouring countries. So even to discover who the victim is seems an impossibility, and to find who murdered her an impossibility of impossibilities.

But Martin Beck and a colleague from the town where the body was found become possessed by a sullen determination not to be beaten by these circumstances. And eventually news comes from distant America that the description they have furnished worldwide fits one Roseanna McGraw, who set out on a lone tour of Europe and never returned.

So the hunt for her killer can begin. Eventually, Martin Beck realises that on a tourist boat like the one Roseanna had been aboard, people take photographs by the dozen, then, after much solid police work getting hold of them, hundreds of such photographs are examined by him and his colleagues, and at last they find some shots of Roseanna accompanied by a man.

Their task is, of course, by no means over then. They succeed eventually in identifying the man, and Martin Beck questions him. He admits that he talked to Roseanna, but there appears to be no other evidence against him. Beck, however, is convinced he is the killer and, again after a good deal of time has passed, he succeeds—though nearly failing—in using a policewoman to trap his man and at last get a confession.

A fine example of the police procedural, and one that sticks closely to what seems like actual police work. But, even in this first of the authors' ten purpose-filled books, the aim of the whole can be seen. It comes in what might appear to be excessive description. We are told, for instance, the population figure of the small town where Roseanna's body was found. We are given Martin Beck's career from the age of twenty-one, and a good deal about his inability to sleep, his tendency to indigestion, his limping marriage. Together, these and a hundred other seemingly irrelevant facts put the story of the hunt for Roseanna's killer into a wider, deeper perspective.

Chance, too, is allowed to play a bigger role than most storytellers, those shapers of events to their own ends, would allow. This, once more, introduces an element of outside reality. So, as one puts the book down, one is apt to think: a good story, and interesting, but also, in the words of the newspaper advertisement, 'all human life is there'.

First edition New York: Pantheon, 1967
First UK edition London: Gollancz, 1968

65

GEORGE SIMS

The Last Best Friend

A crime novel that is about a man changing is a rarity indeed. Many books in the *genre* are set within a time-lapse of only a day or two, which is quite appropriate for their purposes. But occasionally a crime story is made to last over enough time to show how a character can start as a limited man or woman and end as something more. Mary Roberts Rinehart's *The Circular Staircase* was one such. *The Last Best Friend*, though essentially it takes place over quite a short span of time, is also of this kind.

You believe in Ned Balfour, London dealer in autograph letters and manuscripts, when you meet him, hedonistically on holiday with a luscious girl called Bunty. You follow him in the quest he embarks on when he gets, first, a curious, worrying cable—'Vital I have your advice on terrible decision'—from an old friend, Sammy Weiss, and then when he hears Sammy has died, apparently throwing himself from the tenth storey of a block of flats, although he has a morbid fear of heights, acrophobia. Sammy has met what the poet Southey called 'the last best friend,' death. So for this account of Sammy's last friend's doubting hunt for whoever might, despite the lack of all evidence, have killed him, George Sims has his punning title.

In a subtle weaving of suspense and that old infallible whodunit tug we go with Ned here and there through a London George Sims seems to know in its every peculiar corner, in search of the truth. And as we go we meet the various people who might be able to give Ned a clue, as all the while he wonders whether in fact he has set out on a wild-goose chase.

The possible providers of confirmatory clues are a fascinating varied bunch, and all quiveringly alive. Each is made clear to us with sympathy, and in depth. There is Max Weber, the high-powered art-dealer, protected by defensive layers of assistants, all of a pattern, 'quiet, discreet, very polite and, underneath, as tough as old boots.' Weber himself has a face 'as calm as Buster Keaton's, but restlessness, impatience, unfulfilled desires showed in his blue-grey eyes.' Next there is Howard Garratt, owner of a gallery in the seedy Seven Dials area as tatty as Max Weber's is opulently discreet; possibly an Old Etonian, a sponger with 'a puny rachitic physique.' And then there is Leo Spiegl, flamboyant, jokey, 'said to have attended a summer sale at Christie's in a Hawaiian shirt and Bermuda shorts', who yet when his store of quips and insults is expended can be relied upon for sober truth.

So the search goes on, leading Ned into active danger just when he is about to give up, from which he extricates himself by using his fists. Sims is particularly good at describing fighting, bringing to such passages the exactitude of the poet he was in his early days. No biff, bam, wham for him, but 'a very short punch, using the youth's momentum to provide the power.'

But this exactitude, which extends to all the visual aspects of life that Sims describes, is simultaneously his triumph and something like his downfall. He cannot resist a hundred and one touches of precise description: 'a sunbleached rosewood table,' 'a charmingly coloured Cantazala majolica reproduction of the Madonna and Child by della Robbia,' 'lily-covered water now frequented only by fat carp and golden orphe and green whirring dragon-flies.'

All such peripheral elaborations show up Sims as an amateur writer (his main interest was his antiquarian bookselling business), an assessment intended not at all disparagingly. He can, on occasion (but not here) fearsomely break the rules as only an amateur can, as when in *The End of the Web* he interests the reader engrossingly in an apparent hero whom he arbitrarily kills off on Page 50.

Amateurism can spoil marvellously promising material, but here it hardly does. Perhaps one or two of the curious London locations are a little over-described, but mostly we benefit from the amateur's love of things; after all, 'lover' is what 'amateur' means. So we get all those vibrantly alive people, all those odd, quirky settings brought sparklingly to life, and above all we get that intense interest in the hero that makes him a man who has convincingly changed, a man we seem to know in the flesh and to the depths.

First edition London: Gollancz, 1967
First US edition New York: Stein, 1968

66
PETER DICKINSON
The Glass-sided Ants' Nest

My unpaid assistant critic in this gathering of crime greats, O.F. Time (Old Father, as we affectionately call him), tells me that I was a little unfair to this book when I reviewed it in *The Times* on its first appearance. (It was called then *Skin Deep*, as some wiseacre at Dickinson's publishers had pronounced that no book with insects in the title ever did well.) Now, getting on for twenty years later, I find I am left with a strong, abiding memory of that first reading, surely the best praise.

My memory is, first, of its extraordinary setting. In the attics of a row of curiously-built London houses, Peter Dickinson postulated that there lives intact a small primitive New Guinea tribe. Here are its women members mourning the murder victim as the attic door is opened: 'The caged smells weltered out ... rugby changing rooms, burnt tyres, Italian restaurants, meths, cheap talcum ... They wore jerseys and woollen skirts, but they didn't sit English—they squatted on the floor boards in attitudes which spoke of bare breasts and coarse cotton prints knotted at the waist. *Tikaru mindi kmava itaki jissu.*'

These last chanted words are in a language Peter Dickinson created for the purpose. A manifestation of the extraordinary, forceful imagination that has been his chief gift to crime fiction. In another book, *Sleep and His Brother*, he imagined a group of child victims of a disease which turned them into sleepily charming psychic sensitives; my wife was so convinced by this invention that she hurried to examine our children for the telltale symptom. Dickinson once told me, indeed, that his method of work was to create whatever he needed as facts for his story and to do the research afterwards, a system which puts to utter shame the majority of us who have painfully to hunt out a preliminary mass of facts to feed our imaginations.

Not for nothing has Dickinson said of his crime writing that he thinks of it as science fiction with the science left out. But he also prides himself on writing 'proper detective stories, with

141

clues and solutions.' In *The Glass-sided Ants' Nest*, partly over-shaded by that extraordinary background, there are just such clues, as well as a solution both hard to guess and logical. It is in another book, *One Foot in the Grave*, that a proper clue is cunningly presented in the form of a piece of jam-roll pudding.

In this book, though it is the first, Dickinson has a proper series detective as well, Superintendent Jimmy Pibble. And, as one might expect, he is as odd a detective as could be, for all that he is a Scotland Yard officer and pays due attention to the routines of police work. Despite, as we learn, early promise as a detective and considerable intelligence (it would have been hard for Peter Dickinson, a scintillatingly intelligent man, not to have created a sleuth with more than an ordinary grasp of logic and the facts of life), despite even being known as 'a copper's copper,' Pibble is doomed from the start. He is always given the assignments that are bound to bring condemnation in place of kudos. He is also unfashionably unsexy and, perhaps even worse, no asserter of his rights.

In this book he also fills an odd role. Unlike other series heroes, he is the chief psychological interest of the whole, because, beneath the rich layers of fantasy, we have here a study of a particular, and almost peculiar, mentality: the man who is haunted not by a ghost from the past but by, so to speak, a ghost from the future. From the outset Jimmy Pibble, not untough policeman, fears a certain sort of individual. He calls him, indeed, 'his destined Adversary', and as soon as he meets him—he is a fairly ordinary man, a hail-fellow-well-met ex-Air Force type—'his innards cringed.'

A large part of the book, then, is a subtle study of this relationship, perhaps more usual than is generally thought. And, since this is coupled with a first-rate plot, splendidly effective writing and that memorably extraordinary setting, it is little wonder that this first novel walked away with the Crime Writers' Association Gold Dagger award for its year. Dickinson's next book, *A Pride of Heroes* gained the same prize in the following year, a hitherto unique feat.

First edition London: Hodder and Stoughton, 1968, as *Skin Deep*
First US edition New York: Harper and Row, 1968
Later published as *The Glass-sided Ants' Nest*

67

HELEN McCLOY
Mr Splitfoot

Mr Splitfoot is a novel that shows just what can be done with the seemingly simple form of the classical detective story; the sort of book which Helen McCloy herself has said, in a comment on her own work in *Twentieth Century Crime and Mystery Writers*, is 'fun to write and fun to read.' It has all the classic ingredients, 'a detective who appears in each book,' I am quoting again, 'a startling or puzzling beginning followed by twists and turns in the plot, including hidden clues to the murderer, and a surprise ending.'

The detective here is Dr Basil Willing (he does not, in fact, appear in all the McCloy novels, but he does feature in many), the first psychiatrist sleuth actually to employ psychological knowledge in solving crimes. In this story he uses, among other things, the simple fact that it is almost impossible for the human brain to locate the origin of a sound without some accompanying visual assistance. He is not perhaps one of the Great Detectives, lacking that magnification of character that seems to be necessary, but he is Helen McCloy's eyes and voice, and this is much.

A puzzling beginning. We are in the shoes of an adolescent girl prowling through an empty house with intent. Intent to do what? Helen McCloy cunningly keeps us in suspense about that, but almost at once comes Twist No. 1, a voice snapping out 'Caught you!', and this leads instantly onwards. Helen McCloy is telling a story, with all the storyteller's art.

So much for the twists and turns she talked about. Hidden clues are there, too, fairly placed for any reader wanting the fun element. And the surprise ending is the classic revelation of the murderer as the person you simultaneously least suspected and had most reason to suspect. But all this is merely the framework of the book, the fun that makes it a pleasure to read.

Behind it and interwoven with it there is a good deal more, and it is this more that makes the book, with some others of the McCloy *œuvre* if full justice were to be done, one to hang, as it were, in the National Gallery of Crime Fiction.

Take the title, to begin with. Mr Splitfoot is an old New England soubriquet for the Devil, and the book ingeniously makes use of an old custom, the saying of 'Mr Splitfoot, do as I do' with the mysterious repeating answer that sometimes comes, as an essential part of the plot. But Mr Splitfoot, as Basil Willing (or Helen McCloy) points out is, also a symbol for the two sides of our nature, a parallel, as Willing again points out, to Stevenson's famous Dr Jekyll and Mr Hyde.

The book is threaded through with other references to great writers of the past, such as quoting the sixteenth-century French essayist Montaigne on the various selves that lurk in each one of us. It is a reference which brings to mind the little-known poem of Arthur Conan Doyle's that I mentioned earlier, 'The Inner Room', in which he speaks of 'the motley company' inside his head including the one 'whose black soul shrinks away from a lawyer-ridden day and has thoughts he dare not say, half avowed.' Sherlock Holmes, too, is a figure Helen McCloy acknowledges in the course of her narrative.

There are also comments culled from something deeper than wide reading, culled from a thoughtful experience of life. They may be as slight as a chance reflection on 'the ancient hills' surrounding the snowbound house in the remote Catskills where the murders take place. Or it may be a sharp comment on contemporary sloppy thinking, as in Willing's thoughts about the twentieth-century convention that allots more sympathy to the perpetrator of a crime than to its victim, 'an inverted sentimentality as mechanical as the sentimentality from which it derived.' There's a slap for you.

Or it may be flashes of that intuitive insight I like to call wisdom. It is this that makes Willing think about one of the suspects, 'He must be resigned to success, and perhaps that was harder to bear in old age. Failure can console itself with so many ifs ... But there are no consolations for success.' It is finally, I believe, this sort of wisdom that makes of what seems at first glance to be 'only a detective story' something memorable.

First edition New York: Dodd, Mead, 1968

First UK edition London: Gollancz, 1969

68

NICHOLAS BLAKE
The Private Wound

Thirty years after Nicholas Blake had written *The Beast Must Die* and shortly after, flying under his true colours as Cecil Day-Lewis, he had been made Poet Laureate, he produced what was to be his last crime novel, *The Private Wound*. The years between had, to be frank, seen somewhat of a decline in his art. There is a whiff of the potboiler—the merest whiff perhaps— about some of his output then. But with this book all was massively changed.

Gone is Blake's familiar sleuth, Nigel Strangeways, and gone with him is all the fanciful apparatus of literary references, puns and allusions that so delighted us as we read the early books, and delighted us a little less as the years went by. Almost all that remains of the literary is the book's epigraph, a somewhat obscure but telling quotation from Shakespeare's *Two Gentlemen of Verona*, 'The private wound is deepest.' Gone as well is the mandatory unreality of the classical detective story, though Nicholas Blake contrives with tremendous literary adroitness to keep its elements—some proper clues and, certainly, a surprise final discovery.

In place of the unreality (which in its due place is entirely proper) there is a pervading reality, almost smoking off the pages. It derives partly from the book being a re-telling of an early experience of the author's, in his own words in his autobiography, 'a shameless, half-savage, inordinate affair' he had with a beautiful and unrestrained woman called in real life Billie, who is transformed in the book, where the physical setting is also transferred to a wonderfully well described West of Ireland, to Harry.

And from the very first page of *The Private Wound* one knows one is in the presence of a true writer of imaginative literature. One feels upheld in the hands of a master. Here is the throbbingly-recalled first description of Harry: 'I am lying on a bed drenched with our sweat. She is standing by the open window to cool herself in the moonlight. I see again the hour-glass figure, the sloping shoulders, the rather short legs, that disturbing groove of the spine halfway hidden by her dark red hair.'

Throughout the story of love, violence and mystery in the fateful pre-war months of 1938 this level of intensity is kept up. The tiny, revealing details are always there, matted and springy as the down on skin. Each pale wisp of hair may seem unnecessary to the body from which it grows, but together they transform that body from some metal-encased robot into something alive.

And real. That beatingly-true description of sexual aftermath is taken up in other passages that show how writing about the sexual act need not be a tissue of exaggerations or a wild swirl into indifferent poeticising. Equally, too, violence is described—plain physical violence—with that combination of detachment and commitment that is the mark of the best fiction. The book confronts man's inhumanity to man fairly and truly. It shows terrible things being done by credible human beings, fellows to us all.

In sum, we have in *The Private Wound* a good—even very good—detective story entwinedly combined with a novel that stays long in the memory; whole, sad, true and lit by the menacing flames that have sprung from Ireland's violent history and by the leaping shadows of the yet more violent future which in 1938 the whole world was shortly to see.

For some reason, perhaps connected with that tunnel of darkness into which a writer's reputation so often plunges with death (Day-Lewis died in 1972), the book has been much neglected. It fails, for instance, to secure even a mention in the assessment of Nicholas Blake in the all-embracing *Twentieth Century Crime and Mystery Writers*. But it ought to have its place, and a high one at that, in any listing of crime's hundred best books.

First edition London: Collins, 1968
First US edition New York: Harper and Row, 1968

[1969]

69

PATRICIA HIGHSMITH
The Tremor of Forgery

What is it, I have sometimes asked myself, about the books of Patricia Highsmith that makes them simply so hard to put down? A jumble of qualities, more or less linked together, is the nearest I get to an answer. I have chosen *The Tremor of Forgery* from among her books not presided over by Tom Ripley as in many ways the most characteristic, where perhaps we shall see that jumble of qualities most clearly.

The first thing to say is that the book has only the shadow of a crime: it tells us that Miss Highsmith never depends for her readability on your bizarre murder or monster hijack. Nothing so crude. But, make no mistake, just because the crime here is so tenuous this is still a crime story (though it ventures near to the pure novel's territory) and it certainly lacks nothing in tension—indeed, it pulsates with unease. There are no mysterious figures waving guns. No blood is made insistently to drip. There are, in fact, just one or two places where figures that are ambiguous rather than mysterious impinge, and there is one small episode where someone is heard wiping up what is possibly spilt blood. But that is all.

Yet the uneasiness is there from the very beginning when the narrator-hero, Howard Ingham, a fairly successful American novelist just arrived in Tunisia to look for local colour for a film script, asks in the lobby of his hotel, 'You're sure there's no letter for me?' Why, we cannot help asking ourselves, is he so anxious to get a letter? Who will it be from? What will it tell him? The tremor of unease is there.

And, more crudely, a little riddle has been put before the reader in the book's very first lines, a riddle the reader can hardly help wanting to know the answer to. This is a technical device Miss Highsmith herself recommended in a short book she wrote in her early days called *Plotting and Writing Suspense Fiction*. It should never be forgotten that, though she may appear to write in a thoroughly haphazard manner, she is as good a technician of

147

storytelling as, say, Agatha Christie.

But how different in manner. Where in an Agatha Christie all is simple and logical and laid-out bar the meaning of the clues that expose the final mystery, in Highsmith all is fuzzy, ambiguous, doubtful, except at the end when you ponder the book as a whole, its final meaning.

Fuzziness, ambiguity is, indeed, the subject of *The Tremor of Forgery*, a subject echoed by the shimmering Tunisian heat that pervades the story. 'What was possible and what wasn't?' Ingham thinks to himself towards the end; his months in Tunisia had made 'this borderline fuzzy.' In another characteristic Highsmithian phrase a little later on, she speaks of Ingham making up his mind not to write a letter to his ex-wife as 'a brinkish decision.'

The book is full of such decisions and of phrases that state something only immediately to qualify it. 'He was on an assignment to write a film script about two young people in love, or rather three.' Or 'Ingham knew the man he had hit was Abdullah. At least, he was ninety percent sure of it.' Or, 'On the other hand, what was the other hand?' A glimpse here of Patricia Highsmith's wry, teasing humour, something that glints at intervals throughout and does its share in making the whole so clawingly readable.

And, that second illustration—it is the nearest the story gets to an actual crime—shows us Ingham after he has thrown his typewriter at an intruder and does not know, never does know, whether he has killed him, or whom he has possibly killed. More unease. More readability.

More, too, of the to-and-fro indecisiveness of real life, such as one can see if one stops and analyses one's own recent behaviour in the complex, mind-battering world of today. It is a philosophy for such a world, a way of being able to look at it clearly, that is the theme behind the subject—heat-shimmering, distorting, fuzzy Tunisia—of the book. It is hardly a popular concept, or a sentimentally safe one. But does it not speak of the world that has come into existence about our ears more faithfully, more helpfully, than writing of a world constructed from outmoded conventions?

First edition New York: Doubleday, 1969
First US edition London: Heinemann, 1969

70

CHESTER HIMES
Blind Man With A Pistol

In selecting these hundred best books I have tried to avoid basing my choices on anything other than the merits of the books themselves, but in the case of Chester Himes another consideration has influenced me: his life, though the book I have chosen can stand comparison with any of its ninety-nine fellows. But Chester Himes, who was born in 1909 and died in 1984, spent seven of those years in the Ohio State Penitentiary, and so had an experience of the authentic depths. It was while he was inside that he took to reading the books of Dashiell Hammett and decided, approaching the age of fifty, that he, too, might be able to produce something of the sort if he 'told it like it is.'

The other important fact about Chester Himes as a man is that he was black. His books are so firmly imbued with the experience of being black in America, and to a small extent in France where he spent the last part of his life, that there is no getting away from the race question.

His notion of telling it like it is paid off, though not with the certainty it deserved to. His first book, written originally in French, as were all his books except this one, won for him the Grand Prix de la Littérature Policière. But subsequently, with the books going only into paperback in the English-speaking countries, he went through a bad patch. He did not deserve to. The books, especially this one, bring us a fundamentally tragic vision in terms that are often wildly funny.

And in Coffin Ed Johnson and Grave Digger Jones he created a duo of detectives fit to stand beside any in the roll of memorable sleuths. They embody, in an uncompromisingly black way, all that is best in the American private-eye tradition, though they are in fact detectives of the New York Police Department. They contrive, however, to get themselves so loosely linked to the white police high-ups of the world outside Harlem where they operate that, beyond just reporting by radio to Captain Anderson when they find a corpse, they are to all intents as much their own men as Philip Marlowe or Lew Archer. They didn't care, Himes writes, who became boss. 'We just get pissed-off with all the red tape,' Grave Digger once said. 'We want to get down to the nitty-gritty.'

So they do, to the nitty-gritty of the horrifyingly violent and macabre world of black Harlem, where they war industriously against their soul brothers on the other side of the law, as tough and violent themselves on occasion as the criminals they aim to prevent from committing worse violence. They maintain a grand unconcern with such lesser crimes as prostitution and its feeder vices like bottle peddlers, short con and steering, and as far as they are concerned 'pansies could pansy all they pleased.'

And they make jokes. The first thing to learn about whore-chasing, Coffin Ed gravely observes, 'is what to do with your money while screwing.' Simple, Grave Digger answers, feeding him: you leave what you don't need at home. And Coffin Ed comes up with the punch-line. 'And let your old lady find it? What's the difference?'

But they also make comments on the sordid surroundings they work in, like the indoor walls of an apartment block they visit in the course of a night's duty, 'covered with obscene graffiti, mammoth sexual organs, vulgar limericks, opened legs, telephone numbers, outright boasting, insidious suggestions, and impertinent or pertinent comments about the various tenants' love habits.' Grave Digger takes it all in. 'And people live here,' he says, his eyes sad.

There is worse than this, too. As the book's twin stories of grotesque and serious crime draw to an end there is an extraordinary scene in a subway train beneath teeming Harlem when a blind man gets in, believes himself to be insulted, pulls out a big .45 revolver and attempts to shoot a 'fat, yellow preacher' who has tried to calm him with 'Peace, man, God don't know no colour.' And pandemonium follows as the blind man looses off shot after shot.

It is a fearful symbol of how Chester Himes came to see life, in Harlem and elsewhere. He says in a preface that he was told this true story by a friend, and then thought 'that all unorganised violence is like a blind man with a pistol.'

First edition New York: Morrow, 1969

First UK edition London: Hodder and Stoughton, 1969

71

JOAN FLEMING

Young Man, I Think You're Dying

There are rules for writing books. Mostly unstated, and decidedly complex. Perhaps they can be summed up as one commandment: 'Thou shalt write a book in essence like all the books that have been written before thine.' If you break this commandment you can expect, as you can with the other set, to get your comeuppance, or rather godownance. But, fiction being different from the rigidities of the moral universe, on occasion a writer can break this first and greatest of the commandments and be shot up into the heaven of the hundred best crime and mystery books.

Such a writer is Joan Fleming, such a book *Young Man, I Think You're Dying*. It is the story of young Joe Bogey, a cook in a London pizza bar and part-time tearaway, and of how he eventually comes to his senses after being nearly fitted-up for a murder committed by his best friend. Or is it? Because by the end it seems that it has been the story of the best friend, a young man with the unlikely, not to say impossible, name of W. Sledge, and of how he eventually gets his comeuppance, or godownance.

So Rule No. 1 is broken: horses switched in mid-stream. And, on the side, one or two other rules are broken, such as characters being given ridiculous names though they are not meant as figures of fun. Soon there is added the (literary) crime of allowing characters to know more than they possibly could in real life, as having working-class, ill-educated W. Sledge, when reflecting on coincidence in general, cite an announcement in the prestigious obituary columns of *The Times*, that stuffiest of newspapers, of two people named Kipper dying on the same day. No doubt Miss Fleming had seen the announcement herself, but to put it into the head of W. Sledge is rule-breaking with a vengeance. It could almost be said to be deliberately designed to stop readers having that suspension of disbelief all fiction requires.

Then the words that W. Sledge and his equally unlikely named companion, Joe Bogey (names insisted on time and again) speak veer wildly between just-possible slangy talk and rather elaborate prose. Nor does Miss Fleming always get her slang right: she seems possessed of the idea, for instance, that the London slang for a policeman is 'dick'. A moment to consult a dictionary would have told her that a dick is a private-eye or even a police detective in American and English English, but never an ordinary copper or cop. Yet somehow . . .

Most of the characters we meet in the course of this changed-horses story are as unlikely as W. Sledge and Joe Bogey. There is a mysterious upper-class girl whom Joe finds sleeping on the roof of the tower block where he lives, a block called (incidentally without much reality) the Fiery Beacon. This girl, Frances, speaks mostly in a reverse of W. Sledge's style, in grammatically correct speech dotted with vulgarisms. Or there is the pizza bar's cleaning lady who is made to be, for no good reason, a genteel person called Mrs James Trelawny, and who gives the bar, Miss Fleming writes, 'more than a taint of an English seaside tea-room.' Is it likely such a person would have such a job? No, it is not.

Yet somehow Joan Fleming gets away with it all. To the extent, indeed, of winning the Crime Writers' Association Gold Dagger, a prize that has particular value from being awarded by a jury of critics. Why did they consider this book better than any others before them? The answer, I think, is that it spills over with demonic, maniacal energy. Joan Fleming grabs her unlikely characters, her less-than-likely way with their speech, her cavalier treatment of readers' expectations about storyline and, by sheer exuberance, makes them all cohere into something unique.

At the end you are left with the impression, hard indeed to forget, of a mad whirling world that has been subjected to an intense and intensely moral scrutiny, a scrutiny about as powerful as a poised car-crusher about to descend.

First edition London: Collins, 1970
First US edition New York: Putnam, 1970

72

MARGARET MILLAR
Beyond This Point Are Monsters

There is no settling the point of precedency between a louse and a flea, said the great Dr Samuel Johnson when asked whether Derrick or Smart was the better poet. Similarly, to my mind, there is no settling precedence between a lion and an elephant. I might have chosen *How Like An Angel* as my second example of the work of Margaret Millar. Or I might have plumped for *A Stranger in My Grave*, with its classic opening mystery of the gravestone marked with the name of a living person. But my wavering finger has alighted on a book as good as either of these, *Beyond This Point Are Monsters*.

One reason for choosing it is that its title and the key passage from which it is taken exemplify one of Mrs Millar's greatest virtues, her recognition of the abysses in the human psyche that may lie behind the most ordinary-seeming individuals. The title is taken from a warning at the edge of a reproduced medieval map once owned by Robert Osborne, the young married man who disappeared one night a year before the book opens. Robert, as a boy, had copied those words to make a notice for the door of his room.

'The world of Robert's map,' his mother tells Devon, the girl he married and the book's heroine, 'was nice and flat and simple. It had areas for people and areas for monsters. What a shock it is to discover the world is round and the areas merge and nothing separates the monsters and ourselves.' The book is, on the one hand, an exploration and a recognition of the monstrous parts of the human mind, but, on the other—and this is what singles out Mrs Millar as better than many of the best—she also explores and recognises the angel part of us.

In this book she does so chiefly through her imaginatively sympathetic portraits of the Mexicans who work the Southern California ranch-farm once owned by Robert Osborne. She sees into their minds with rare empathy and apparent effortlessness.

There is, for example, fourteen-year-old Jaime. 'He lay now

on his stomach in the back of the station wagon, gnawing his right thumbnail and wondering if the kids at school knew where he was and what he had to do'—to testify at the hearing to establish that Robert Osborne is dead—'Maybe they were already blowing it up into something wild like he was a friend of the fuzz. Word like that could put a guy down for the rest of his life.'

Or there is another witness: Carla Lopez, an eighteen-year-old divorcing mother entirely gripped by the conviction that she has had a jinx on her ever since she was born. 'If I did a rain dance there'd probably be a year's drought.' A nice example of the darts of humour that add to a story full of hinted darkness.

They are signs of the sheer good writing that Mrs Millar rises to, and which take to heights a book with already an excellent plot, keeping you on your toes asking 'Is this the way of it?' or 'Is it that?', and with a fine last-paragraph-but-one twist of irony and surprise. But, to my mind at least, the prose, the actual words used, is what puts the seal on the whole.

It may sometimes, indeed, be just one actual word. 'A little hum of laughter vibrated through the courtroom and bounced gently off the walls.' That 'bounced' is what makes the merely good into the splendid.

Or there are the two owls that Devon sees at night as she sits outside and ponders the ever-darkening mystery she is caught up in, and the way the simple and almost pre-determined court hearing appears to be turning up, from burial by earth and time, facts and feelings she had never suspected the existence of. 'Both owls flew silently over her head and vanished into the tamarisk trees that ringed the reservoir. She had often heard the owls between twilight and dawn, but this was the first time she had had more than a glimpse of their faces, and it was a shock to her to discover that they didn't look like birds at all but monkeys or ugly children, accidentally winged.' A fine and vivid piece of nature watching, but also a sudden, sharp, penetrating symbol.

No wonder, reading the book before writing this, I twice laid it down and murmured aloud 'Jesus, how well she writes.'

First edition New York: Random House, 1970
First UK edition London: Gollancz, 1971

73

ED McBAIN

Sadie When She Died

Ed McBain has produced over a period of some thirty years a police procedural series, stories of the detectives of the 87th Precinct in an imaginary city, running to more than 35 books. 'The people, the places are all fictitious,' says the preface to each book; 'Only the police routine is based on established investigatory techniques.' As a matter of fact, the city can be seen to be New York turned on to its side, but—totally imagined or half-real—it matters not. There is never any difficulty in believing, while you read, that you are reading about real people.

The reason for this, I believe, is that McBain has developed to a high point the technique of providing easy reading. You whizz, for a variety of reasons, through the pages and, as you make that headlong journey, there is never time to question any of the things McBain tells you. It is for this reason that out of all the series I have chosen *Sadie When She Died* for the way it shows McBain at his swiftest.

I might, on the other hand, have picked the book that preceded this one, *Hail, Hail, the Gang's All Here*, since it uses all the varied characters McBain has invented for the series and has no fewer than fourteen different storylines to keep them all in play. But perhaps that feat, though dizzying to watch, makes the book less good than it might be.

Sadie When She Died uses a fair selection of all these multiple heroes. Chief among them is Carella, the detective whose persistent belief that in this case an intruder in the apartment of the wealthy lawyer Gerald Fletcher, who has admitted stabbing Fletcher's wife, was not in fact her murderer, provides the main story. But Bert Kling, the ever-learning, features largely too, and brings in incidentally Meyer Meyer (his father named him thus out of Jewish humour). Even the moronic street cops, Monoghan and Monroe, rate a brief, memory-jogging mention. Of McBain's major creations, only Cotton Hawes, son of the pastor, is absent.

But the book is here for its speed. First, McBain provides a tremendous puzzle-tug. It comes in the very first words when Carella, unbelievingly, hears Gerald Fletcher declare he is *'very glad she's dead.'* Only in almost the last words do we discover why.

Then there is the famous McBain joky irony. If ever he has to convey facts that are in themselves possibly somewhat boring, he adopts this breezily light tone, as in his description of the Interrogation Room where Fletcher is questioned. A neat joke about the way all criminals know about its one-way mirror gets you zoomingly past the necessary underlining of Fletcher's intransigent view of his beautiful wife's death.

The next weapon in McBain's armoury is the use of apparent pieces of real life. It may come in tiny things like giving a precise time for an event which in fictional terms needs no such accuracy: 'the call came from a physician in Riverhead at 4.37.' This is it, you feel, when you read that pinpointed time; I must hurry on to find the significance. And by the time you have found there isn't any, McBain has you on a new helter-skelter. Or it might be his famous trick of giving you a slice of 'real life' such as a purported print-out of a question-and-answer session. Partly you think, once again, 'This is extra important', and partly you read at double speed the duff parts (Q: Ten PM? A: Yes, ten PM). The McBain conjuring trick works once more.

Yet another device is similar in effect. McBain gives you the lifelike bits other writers leave out, the mundane exchanges with a receptionist before an important interview, for instance. And, because you realise that these are absolutely insignificant, you hurry, hurry, hurry. So McBain can confine his main story to, when you count them, very few pages, and you read a novel-length book with the speed of a short story, getting thrown in some nice little tales, like the interchange between Bert Kling and Meyer Meyer over the efficacy of a copper anti-bursitis bracelet.

Not only does an 87th Precinct book give you two for the price of one, or sometimes fourteen for the price of one, but each of them is faster than almost anything else on the shelves. And through that very speed McBain succeeds in leaving in your mind an impression of detective life that is hard to forget.

First edition New York: Doubleday, 1972
First UK edition London: Hamish Hamilton, 1972

74

GEORGE V. HIGGINS

The Friends of Eddie Coyle

Roughly speaking, you can divide crime fiction into two kinds: the cosy and the gritty, Christie and Chandler. But the gritty, it may be said, has a curious tendency to slide with time into cosiness. So that what set out to be gritty as thrown gravel, like Chandler's Marlowe stories, becomes eventually smooth—pickled in nostalgia, and revealing an essentially unrealistic romanticism under the surface. So, every decade or two, a new attempt has to be made to get back to true grit.

In the early 1970s that attempt was made, with startling success, by an assistant U.S. Attorney for Massachusetts, one George V. Higgins. Enraged and admiring, Norman Mailer said of *The Friends of Eddie Coyle*, 'What I can't get over is that so good a first novel was written by the fuzz.'

Where Higgins dug down to his new true grit was in the dialogue he used to do much of the telling of his story. He succeeded in getting into it a good deal more of the groping hesitations and ineffective convolutions of the talk of your less articulate criminal, or for that matter of the non-criminal, than anyone had hitherto managed. He filled these longish passages with up-to-date criminal slang and the timeless obscenities that were, at that period, not so often set down in print.

Here's a small sample, though you really need to read the whole book to get the full flavour: 'I can't understand where the fuck he is. That friend of mine, I was telling you about. He give me both his tickets. I invited my wife's nephew. I can't understand where he is. Loves hockey, that kid. I don't know how he stays in school, he's always down here, scrounging for tickets. Twenty years old. But bright kid.'

This sort of inconsequential, subcutaneously mysterious talk builds up and up, one layer following another. When you have read a page you find you have a better understanding of each of the paragraphs in it. When you come to the end of a chapter you realise you have somehow acquired more of a grasp of the contents of each of its pages. Of course, though much of the onward flow is conveyed by this oblique, salty dialogue, the whole of the book is not written in it; there are passages of pure narration that advance the action as well, written in direct uncomplicated prose that might almost be a lawyer's report.

'At five minutes of six, Dave Foley escaped from the traffic on Route 128 and parked the Charger at the Red Coach Grille in Braintree. He went into the bar and took a table in the rear corner that allowed him to watch the door and the television set above the bar. He ordered a vodka martini on the rocks with a twist.' This is a typical chapter start. And, for the most part, it is only in such seemingly dull passages that one learns of the appalling violence that threads through and through criminal life in Boston: the calm killings, the unemotional matter-of-duty maimings and beatings-up.

So the picture that emerges as you lay down the book is certainly one that makes many of the previous attempts at reality in crime fiction look over-romanticised or under-facted. But I would be misinforming you if I implied that the whole book is on these two notes, vividly complex dialogue and swift photographic reportage. One of its merits is the variety Higgins succeeded in getting into what might seem to be only alternate specimens of those two manners.

Higgins is no mean writer. Part of *The Friends of Eddie Coyle* first appeared in a literary magazine, *North American Review*, and its doing so is a clue to Higgins's ultimate aim. When I met him on a trip to England in 1986 and greeted him, open-armed, as a fellow crime-writer among a conference full of academics I received a swift rebuff. 'I'm a novelist,' he said. Or he might have said 'I'm a novelist, is all.' I contend that what emerged on to the pages in *The Friends of Eddie Coyle* was in fact a crime novel, and an important one.

First edition New York: Knopf, 1972

First UK edition London: Secker and Warburg, 1972

75

JULIAN SYMONS
The Players and the Game

f *The Man Who Killed Himself* was an example of Julian
ymons as the constructor of wonderfully clever teasers with
eriousness bobbing and weaving through, then *The Players and
he Game* shows Symons as the critic of society and life, with an
lement of playfulness still retained. The book is based on two
orrific real-life cases; the so-called Lonely Hearts murders in
America in the 1940s, for which an unlikely couple, Raymond
'ernandez and Martha Beck, joined in murder and were even-
ually found guilty of committing three and suspected of seven-
een others; and the Moors Murders in the 1960s in Britain, in
which, again, a couple united in what was called *folie à deux.*

Grim enough cases both of them, especially as children were
he victims in the latter. So how does it come about that they can
e made the basis of a mere crime novel, a piece of entertainment
iction? Julian Symons has his answers which are to my mind
onvincing on the whole.

In an essay in a book of collected reviews, *Critical Occasions*,
e says: 'To exclude realism of description and language from the
rime novel in a period when it has been accepted as normal in
ther fiction is almost to prevent its practitioners from attemp-
ing serious work.' Certainly in *The Players and the Game*
ymons felt free to state in plain terms appalling details. 'Some
our dozen incisions had been made in her body, so that by the
ime she died she must have been a mass of blood . . .'

In a little book Symons wrote some years after *Critical
Occasions*, called *The Modern Crime Story*, he elaborates his
heory in specific defence of *The Players and the Game*. 'Why
hould one use such a sordid and horrific tale?' he writes. 'Partly
ecause it actually happened. That is, it seems to me that there
hould be no subjects barred from any writer.' And he goes on,
the fact that crime fiction is so widely regarded as a form of
vriting stamped "for amusement only", makes it in my view all
he more necessary to assert and to show that it isn't true.' In

other words, there is a distinction between 'amusement' and 'entertainment'. The latter can do things other than make readers gleefully rub their hands: it can simply hold them. As such it is a legitimate weapon in the writer's armoury.

And here Symons wields that weapon both playfully and brilliantly—a term he himself, with a bob of modesty, uses of his handling of the guessing element whereby he attempts to conceal the identities of his two protagonists, who speak of themselves simply as 'Dracula' and 'Bonnie'. He does it 'by what seems to me a fairly brilliant piece of juggling with extracts from journals and other bits of trickery.' I confirm the brilliance, especially in the case of Dracula, whose identity is put before one with all the cunning boldness of the great Agatha.

But it is the seriousness that makes the book, for me, what it is, one of my top hundred. For one thing it is set to a considerable extent in the world of work, where men and women actually spend the greater part of their time, yet which few novelists tackle. Symons, who spent a dozen early years in a routine office job, did not blot out this period (as Dickens did with his blacking factory days) but instead let it enter his subconscious to emerge many years later.

More, within a story that asks, in a slightly altered form, that old tugging question 'Who done it?', *The Players and the Game* considers, it is not too much to say, a major philosophical concept on which much that is characteristic of twentieth century life is based. The book questions, albeit obliquely, the theory of conduct called Irrationalism, a theory that began with the Romantics' glorification of natural impulses and was in our time snatched up by D.H. Lawrence with his preaching of instinct, and was above all promulgated by the philosopher Nietzsche, the man said to lie behind Conan Doyle's arch-villain Moriarty.

And Nietzsche himself figures abundantly in the journal 'Dracula' keeps. Indeed, the book's last words, spoken by the unmasked figure, are: 'My name is Nietzsche Caesar. I have effected in my own person the Transvaluation of All Values. I forgive you all.' But the madman has been brought to justice.

First edition London: Collins, 1972
First US edition New York: Harper, 1972

76

STANLEY ELLIN
Mirror, Mirror on the Wall

Sex edged its way into crime fiction very slowly. In the classic puzzle-stories of the Golden Age it was hardly there at all, occasionally a remote motive in an age of difficult divorce or a final taking of the hand with a 'Darling, it's all over now.' Little more. With crime, in Raymond Chandler's words about Dashiell Hammett, being given 'back to the kind of people who commit it for reasons' something more entered in, though Hammett's Nora asking Nick in *The Thin Man* whether he got an erection while grappling with the luscious Mimi was cut out of British editions. However, after World War II, sex entered the crime world in no uncertain way. And yet...

Yet it was used, almost always, more or less only as extra titillation. Only with Stanley Ellin's *Mirror, Mirror on the Wall* did sexuality really become an integral part of a murder mystery. Ellin was always wonderfully cunning with a plot, and here he contrived a murder mystery depending entirely on the unravelling of its hero's sex life, going back to his feelings for his protective Southern belle mother and to his macho, shaggy-chested, fight-teaching father, and going on to his most adult fantasies.

But the book is still a murder mystery. It has a surprise ending that zonks you with the best. It has clues—a whopper within the first twenty pages. It goes so far as to have a message in code, just as if it was an early Sherlock Holmes case. Yet all are necessary parts of the book's 'background', which is the hero's sexuality; that and nothing more.

If that were all, *Mirror, Mirror on the Wall* would have earned its place in my list of the hundred best, but it is not all. The book is wonderfully well-written. Dialogue and narration are in sinewy, fresh-minted, no-holds-barred prose in the very best tradition of American writing.

Take the narrator's teenage son answering a somewhat embarrassed question about his sex life. 'Well, like say you're with a girl and everything is set up to ball her. Her folks are away, the lights are low, the whole *shtick*. So when do you ask her if she's on the pill? I mean, you ask too soon and she thinks that's all you've got on your mind . . .'

And there follows the narrator's reflection: 'Jesus, the romantic problems youth has today certainly are complicated by science.' A nice example of the irrepressible Ellin humour, even when the matter is murder. Humour comes even more to the fore in his portrait of the narrator's psychiatrist, Dr Joseph Ernst, 'the Shrink of Shrinks.' Dr Ernst is made classically ridiculous, almost cruelly so. 'Peter . . . Your thoughts wander, you follow them like a child following a butterfly through tall grass, coming closer and closer to the precipice. That is not good.' But, fun though Ellin makes of this figure, he also time and again gives him the last laugh vis-à-vis the hero. So you see both sides.

It is in the meshes of this prose, true, fast-moving and lithe, that there is held up the ticklish matter the book deals with (and writing about sex is still a tricky business, touching as it is bound to do on the most hidden, most sensitive aspects of each reader's nature). Ellin uses all the words, the words that are likely to offend and are generally labelled 'dirty', but held in place as they are in the web of the whole they are no longer 'dirty'. They are no longer words used for their titillating or shocking effect, as in so many cheaper crime novels, and cheaper novels of all sorts.

They are used because they are the words to say what Ellin has to say about an area of human life circumscribed entirely by his hero's feelings about his particular sexuality. The book is, if you like, the triumph of all that is good in the concept of the Permissive Society, in freedom to examine this once dark, under-wraps, huge territory. No wonder when *Mirror, Mirror on the Wall* was translated into French it won the Grand Prix du Meilleur Roman Policier Étranger.

First edition New York: Random House, 1972
First UK edition London: Cape, 1973

77

TONY HILLERMAN
Dance Hall of the Dead

Dance Hall of the Dead is an example of the so-called 'ethnic' crime story, but I have placed it in my hundred-best list not for that reason but because it is an exceptionally fine crime novel. Part of this quality, however, is of course due to the ethnic content.

The ethnic crime story is, as I see it, a crime novel which considers some aspect of life by looking at the contrast between how people live in its country of origin and how they live in some very different part of the world. Part of its appeal may be its setting in a Communist country; it may work, as my own fiction attempts to do, by being set in an Asian country; or, in the case of *Dance Hall of the Dead*, it may work by being set among the Navajo and Zuni peoples of America's New Mexico. Out of the contrast between their approach to life and that of the majority of Americans all around them, there emerges a sharper, better picture of dilemmas and difficulties common to humankind everywhere.

You get this at the very start of the book, the first short chapter of which describes a boy of fourteen out running. But this is how the opening words depict him: 'Shulawitsi, the Little Fire God, member of the Council of the Gods and Deputy of the Sun, had taped his track shoes to his feet.' There you get that contrast, as diametrically expressed as possible: the Deputy of the Sun, and the boy caught up in the contemporary adolescent fashion for running just like thousands of young Americans all around.

Tony Hillerman goes on to elaborate this contrast a little, and in doing so brings out for us the quality of boyishness common to young males the world over. He does so because he wants us to have a glowing, memorable image of this boy who at the end of the chapter is cut down by an unknown hand. That image, of universal boyishness brutally struck down, is what will fuel our interest throughout the ensuing inquiry conducted by the Navajo police officer, Lieut. Joe Leaphorn.

And we need to have our interest fuelled more strongly than it would be in a simple whodunit story, because Hillerman wants us to begin to understand the very different way of life which his Navajo characters carry in their heads. This he does, keeping our heads down in his story while feeding us with not a little information. 'In this book,' he says in an Author's Note, 'the setting is genuine ... accurately depicted to the best of my ability.' And the best of his ability is considerable.

Because, apart from everything else, Hillerman can *write*. He has the gift of calling up a whole picture, vague in background, precise in foreground, in just a few words. Here is something as simple as Joe Leaphorn smoking a cigarette as he tries to wheedle information out of a young witness: 'Leaphorn spoke thoughtfully. He exhaled a cloud of smoke. It hung blue in the still sunlight.' Reading that, there sprung up in my mind a vivid scene, and the thought was planted in me that Joe Leaphorn was a patient, skilled interrogator by any standards.

Indeed, he is more. At the climax of the book, after a long, tense action scene, he lies wounded and drugged, shot by a tranquillising dart designed for use with wild deer. And in the state of trance thus induced he does exactly what Sherlock Holmes, Dupin and all the Great Detectives do: he combines in the depths of his mind the rational process and the process of the imagination to get a notion of what lies behind all the complications and contradictions of his case.

With writing as easily read and as expressive as the short passage I have quoted, Hillerman paints for us a very different way of life from our own, be it in America or Europe, with enough of our familiar way to point the contrast. So at one moment he deals neatly with the six different law enforcement agencies caught up in the investigation, and at another he gives us a considerable exposition of the Navajo religion, central to both the story and the theme of the book, such as the idea that it takes five days for the spirit of one whose life has ended to reach a remote lake called the Dance Hall of the Dead.

First edition New York: Harper and Row, 1973
First UK edition London: Pluto, 1985

78

PETER DICKINSON

The Poison Oracle

The Poison Oracle is a book that is at once a good old-fashioned
detective puzzle and an examination of perhaps the most important problem facing Western civilisation, no less. And it is a
tribute to the crime novel, and especially to Peter Dickinson as
author, that it is possible to make this claim.

The problem which the book tackles is the whole complex of
ideas and hard brutal facts that arises from our ability to alter
through the discoveries of science the environment around us.
The jargon word for it is 'ecology': a massive subject, and an
extremely complex one. It is the great virtue of Dickinson's
deliberate, head-on confrontation that he does not answer it with
any one simple slogan. Shouting 'Greenpeace' is too easy for
him.

But perhaps the chief merit of the book is that Dickinson does
not allow his major theme to swamp his minor art. He plainly
hopes to make his readers more aware of the implications of what
is being done to their world, but he realises that they have taken
up his book expecting a crime story (though if they know
Dickinson at all they will be expecting a crime story with at least
double the customary intellectual content), and he takes a lot of
care to provide just what is expected. But, as he does so, the
questions he wants to stir up in torpid minds constantly break
through the surface.

So we get the dear, long-loved murder mystery, even if it does
have new twists. The setting, for example, though it is as
enclosed as any snow-bound old house with a body in its library,
is an oil-sheik's palace somewhere in Arabia, built upside-down;
that is, with the larger floors above the smaller for the good and
sufficient reason that this keeps out the heat better.

There is a locked-room mystery, too. Except that the room is a
locked zoo, where the sheik keeps a menagerie of apes with the
object of experimenting to see how far their intelligence can be
made to take them; the intelligence, in particular, of what might

be called the girl in the case, the remarkable chimpanzee Dinah. And in—another detectival staple—the final gathering of the suspects it is Dinah's newly-discovered ability to cope with the grammatical concept of the relative clause, as she spells out her thoughts by means of coloured shapes moved into differing combinations, that at last exposes the murderer.

There is poison. The poison of the book's slightly mysterious title is four things at once, which adds to the considerable depth of the whole. First, the poison is the actual toxic substance that kills the victim. Second, it is the thing that confirms Dinah's final accusation. Third, it is a simple and powerful symbol for the poisoning activities which civilisation is inflicting on the world it has to live on ('Soon all you fools will be dead. Cause and effect. Cause and effect. Cause and effect' are the book's last words). And, fourth, the poison is an image for the flow of words back and forth around the world, that both adds to that ill and seeks to trace its source.

The flow of words, this way and that, to which Dickinson contributes, of course. He offers no panacea. Instead he explores with words, as the true novelist should, as many aspects as he can encompass of the syndrome he has chosen to confront. He uses, then, characterisation, ranging from the sympathetic and extremely likeable Dinah, through the hero, a brilliant and fearfully naïve linguist, on through the delightful sheik, Oxford-veneered and ruthless Bedu underneath, to a handful of primitive marsh-dwellers. Each one illuminates the central dilemma from a different angle.

Nor does the fantastic background—the sheik's palace, the desert and the neighbouring marshes—fail to play a double part; half is extraordinary, put there for our amusement, and half says something through the cunning of symbolism. Ponder for a moment just one flick of description, 'the ugly noise of the lungfish adapting themselves over thousands of generations to live in an altered world.' Doesn't that make us ask ourselves 'Are we altering our world much faster than we are adapting to it?'

All this in the compass of the humble detective story.

First edition London: Hodder and Stoughton, 1974
First US edition New York: Pantheon, 1974

79
GREGORY McDONALD
Fletch

One might think that intelligence, even a considerable degree of intelligence, was mandatory for a writer of the best crime fiction. Not necessarily. To begin with, what makes a work of fiction really good is the amount its author can get from the subconscious on to the page, and intelligence there is only of use in organising the material after it has appeared. Secondly, too much intelligence can produce a book that is too complex to be read with any pleasure, and pleasure is an essential ingredient.

But occasionally a writer contrives to have intelligence spurting out of his ears and is yet still able to keep readers-to-be so much in mind as to give them a truly gripping story. Gregory McDonald is one such writer—at least in most of his output. As a measure of his intelligence, the rapid movement of a penetrating mind, one has only to read a few pages of this book, a notable début that won for him the Edgar award of the Mystery Writers of America.

Its protagonist Fletch, otherwise I.M. Fletcher, one of McDonald's perennial heroes, is a reporter, or to be more precise an in-depth investigator. We first meet him, in fact, when he is working on a story about the drug scene on a notorious California beach; tanned as any beach boy and as feckless as any drugs-dependent drifter, it only later emerges that he was awarded the Bronze Star for his services with the Marines in Vietnam, and that, with characteristic throw-away modesty, he refuses to collect it.

Fletch is, in fact, the model of the reporter as crime-fiction hero, a figure very much of our day and, to the writer, very useful as a man (sometimes a woman) even less tied to the legalities than a private-eye (whose licence is always in jeopardy) and designed even more as a penetrating machine for investigation. Implicit throughout this book is the sanctity of the press investigation. Listen to Fletch talking to his immediate editor, a former cookery columnist currently sleeping with the editor-in-chief, when she argues that the paper ought to tell the local police of his undercover assignment in their area: 'You never blow a story! To anyone, at any time, ever! Christ, I wish I didn't have to talk to you, you're such an idiot.'

And when Fletch breaks the drugs racket on the beach it is revealed, of course, that the local chief of police is the man behind it. I disclose this since, in fact, it is reasonably obvious before Fletch latches on to it, neatly though McDonald handles this aspect of his story. What is far less obvious is the other half of his tandem tale. The book opens with two-thirds of a page of rapid back-and-forth dialogue between Fletch on his beach and an unnamed man, which ends with the words 'I want you to murder me.' As intriguing a beginning for any first crime novel as you could find. Why this man with his 'black shoes tainted with sand' wants to be murdered, whether he even does, forms the main part of the book. Fletch investigates every aspect of the man's life, mostly by telephone and using the most bare-faced lies to gain the information he wants, often adopting quickly-assumed names so polysyllabic that no one is going to remember them when the call is over. Try catching 'Yahmenaraleski' on the end of a crackly line.

This sort of thing—the sheer impudence—is the charm of Fletch, the charm that keeps one glued to his progress however shocking bits of it seem, such as the fifteen-year-old druggie prostitute with whom he shares a room and her suggestion that he, too, should become a prostitute. 'You might make money, is all.'

Fletch is brilliantly clever, but comes over—cunningly enough—with one just able to follow his swift thoughts. He is delightfully perverse, upsetting one's pre-conceived notions in the nicest way. He is plainly and simply mischievous, and one squats on his shoulder revelling in the mischief. He is Fletch, magician and crime-solving reporter.

First edition Indianapolis: Bobbs-Merril, 1974
First UK edition London: Gollancz, 1976

80

P.D. JAMES
The Black Tower

Paradoxically, the one subject that the writers of the classical Golden Age detective-story could not afford to let creep into their pages was death. Real death. So Agatha Christie had the fatal shot in her final Poirot tale produce only that neat hole in the middle of the forehead. Sanitisation was the rule. All the more astonishing, then, that in *The Black Tower* P.D. James succeeded in writing a classical story of detection with its whole subject death and dying.

The book is set in a large house on the Dorset coast called Toynton Grange, which is a home for incurables: a pretty unmentionable matter for starters. As the book begins P.D. James's customary detective, Commander Adam Dalgliesh, is not macho-like raring to go on a new case but instead is lying in a hospital bed suffering from what had been diagnosed as acute leukemia, a sentence of death. But now, as the title of Chapter One puts it, he is awarded a 'Sentence of Life.'

From those very opening pages you find you are in the hands of a writer who is not going to shirk anything. When the great consultant physician approaches it is not at all romance and sentimentality à la Dr Kildare. Dressed for a fashionable wedding, P.D. James writes, the doctor could have been the groom himself, with the flower in his buttonhole and himself looking 'as if they had been brought and burnished to a peak of artificial perfection, gift wrapped in invisible foil, and immune to chance winds, frosts and ungentle fingers.'

Coming grudgingly back to life, Dalgliesh goes to Toynton Grange to visit an old clergyman friend of his father's, who has written him a mildly disturbing letter. He finds the clergyman has died, and at the big house with the ominous black tower perched above the dangerous cliffs, in which once a Victorian eccentric had walled himself up alive, he soon suspects murder.

The closed community limits the number of possible suspects in the classical form which P.D. James has delighted to read and write, and it provides her with a fine gallery of real, tormented people to portray for our pleasure and, be it said, for our enlightenment. The surrounding countryside gives her room for the descriptions she delights in, and which lend all her books an especial warm solidity. Indeed, she has said that it was walking along that breath-taking piece of coastline that put the first glimmerings of the book into her head.

On top of all this she sets us a crime puzzle absolutely in the traditional manner. It has its clues, its revealing interviews (which often cunningly reveal something other than they appear to do), its surprises and its picture of a classical detective at work, a picture to compare with Lord Peter Wimsey, Roderick Alleyn or John Appleby.

Adam Dalgliesh is one of the profound pleasures of the book. In it we see, perhaps for the first time, into the interior of a man we had been taught in his earlier cases to admire, and to stand somewhere just behind. Now we enter in. We knew him as a poet, but only as a poet seen occasionally at his publisher's parties. Now we are given an inkling, not of the poetry itself (P.D. James is too modest and too sensible to attempt that) but of the sensibility that could produce poems.

Here is Dalgliesh looking back at the first weekend he spent at Toynton Grange: 'He saw it as a series of pictures, so different from the later images of violence and death that he could almost believe his life ... had been led on two levels and at different periods of time. Those early and gentle pictures, unlike the later harsh black and white stills from some crude horror film, were suffused with colour and feeling and smell.' There, indeed, you get a hint of a poem, with both the horror film and the gentle colour-washed, scent-pervaded pictures in it. It is a poem that a man who was a true poet, besides being a proven policeman, could clearly have written. A pretty fair achievement.

First edition London: Faber and Faber, 1975
First US edition New York: Scribner, 1975

81

CELIA FREMLIN

The Long Shadow

Through a crime reviewer's hands in the course of a year there are apt to pass as many as three hundred books, give or take a few dozen, of which less than half can be got on to the pages of even the most welcoming newspaper. And of that half, how many dare the reviewer, living in a house with unexpandable walls, allow to stay on his shelves? Very, very few. Of all the books that came to me during fifteen years of reviewing for *The Times*, I find Celia Fremlin's *The Long Shadow* in one of those places of selective honour.

It might have been other books of hers. But her first, *The Hours Before Dawn*, which won the Mystery Writers of America's Edgar in 1960, was before my reviewing days, as was the much- and rightly-praised *Uncle Paul*. But I am happy that in these pages *The Long Shadow* should be my choice, for it is a book that is not only splendidly enjoyable on every page, but it also carries—essential cargo—a fine ballast of truth. Its story of a newly-widowed woman who becomes caught up, inexplicably it seems, by mysterious warnings and messages, unfolds with brilliant ingenuity. Always the mystery seems on the point of being explained, and each time, with complete plausibility, the bewildered narrator Imogen is plunged yet more deeply into the inexplicable.

Any hint of the mechanical in this beautifully engineered plot is swept away by the sensitivity and perception with which Celia Fremlin puts before us the people of her book. It is seen in almost the first words. Imogen has had to explain yet once more to an acquaintance that her Classics professor husband has recently died. 'She waited,' Celia Fremlin writes, 'for the tiny recoil behind his eyes, the twitch of unease.' And one realises that in one's day, one had also been unable to restrain the tiny recoil when one has been put in the embarrassing, but common enough, predicament.

Common enough. It is one of Celia Fremlin's great virtues that she sets her books among the common experiences. One of her British publishers once said to me, delight shining in his eyes, 'You can feel the wet nappies hanging to dry brushing against your face.' And, whether they be British nappies or American diapers, the experience is a small everyday occurrence of the period of early parenthood which most of us know. But against this ordinariness—here it is new widowhood's embarrassments, but there is also the wretched seaside holiday in *Uncle Paul*, or the domestic jangle of metal coat-hangers in *The Spider-Orchid*—Celia Fremlin sets terror.

What she aims to do, she has said, is to put a plot that is exciting or terrifying against a background that is domestic, very ordinary, humdrum. It is an aim she succeeds in carrying out to the utmost in *The Long Shadow*. By that method of hers she is able to explore her characters, caught in the searchlight of the unexpected, to a deeper degree than she ever could if she wrote the sort of women's novel full of acute observation which, without the crime or the looming possibility of a crime, her books might be.

Yet there is one other quality that needs to be added. Almost surprisingly, in view of the unease she succeeds in transferring from her heroine to us her readers, Celia Fremlin is also, and quite frequently, sharply funny. Here is Imogen's stepson advising her on what sort of students she might take as lodgers. 'I'd choose Depressions rather than Anxiety States ... From the point of view of a landlady, Depressions are good because they lie in bed till midday and don't eat breakfast. Whereas Anxiety States want grapefruit—All-Bran—the lot.'

Through all this there is Celia Fremlin's excellent writing. Her style is graceful, polished, pointed. Her perceptions are always acute, sometimes almost to the point of cruelty. Her insights, since they so often seem to be insights into the obscurer corners of one's own psyche, are often frightening. There is a film, a Czech one I think, whose title is *Closely Observed Trains*. Celia Fremlin's book might well bear the label *Closely Observed Strains*.

First edition London: Gollancz, 1975
First US edition New York: Doubleday, 1976

82
COLIN WATSON
The Naked Nuns

There are only a very few crime stories that are pleasurable because they view the baser parts of our nature not with the cosinesses of a typical Agatha Christie or the romanticised realism of Raymond Chandler, but as hilarious farce. The books which Colin Watson set in the imaginary English provincial town of Flaxborough clearly come into this category, and *The Naked Nuns* is one of his best.

From its very title you get a whiff of the contents within. 'Naked': the word tells you that sex in its grosser aspects will rear its head. 'Nuns': the word indicates, surely, that though the matter will appear on the surface to be well into the area of pornography, somehow an air of frivolity will deflate any over-excited notions.

So, from the book's second sparkling chapter—the first has briefly established the plot—the frivolous, the fireworkily farcical appears. It is a most cunningly drawn-out expectation scene, taking place in a lady's bedroom. 'The Deputy Town Clerk of Flaxborough,' it begins, 'stared down reflectively upon the satin nightdress case of Mrs Sophie Hatch . . . and wondered whether he had been wise, after all, to accept her invitation.' Whether you are re-reading the book and know that the invitation will turn out merely to be to watch the working of Mrs Hatch's darkness-operated curtain-closing apparatus, or whether the closing paragraph of the chapter which reveals this comes as a surprise, you will hardly be able to read it without constant chuckles of pleasure.

They may be chuckles at the comically tension-mounting suspense. They may be chuckles at the sexual innuendoes. Or they may be chuckles at Colin Watson's scalpel-sharp exposure of middle-class pretensions, deadly accurate as regards British provincial life, but applying equally to the same sort of materialistic snobbery anywhere. The décor of Mrs Hatch's bedroom, the mother-of-pearl vinyl wallcovering, the café-au-lait fitted carpet, the dressing-table made to look like a white piano, its keys operating little drawers for cosmetics and its mirror etched with music notes, the midnight-blue padded ceiling and the vast water-bed, 'a round, lung-pink, be-frilled slab that wobbled with the passage of traffic like some incredibly obese ballerina', may be unique to the *nouveau riche* of the British provinces, but the equivalents are to be found wherever *nouveaux riches* exist.

And note that adjective 'lung-pink'. It brings one to a stop with a wince of dismay before one accepts Watson's wittily jaundiced view of his characters. He is an expert in saying the unsayable. So we have in this opening scene, for instance, a character chuckling 'with the aid of some spare phlegm.' The mention of what is generally by common consent unmentioned sends an unsparing searchlight beam on to the pretentiousness of the people portrayed.

So, with similar bedroom and lavatory jokes, all carried off by a simple delight in their existence, Watson's story unfolds until at last his astute and modestly sane Inspector Purbright unravels a reasonably tortuous plot with the revelation that the naked nuns of the title are simply misprinted Vatican postage stamps of considerable value.

But Watson does not reach this point without there having taken place a 'Medieval Banquet' organised for American tourists at the Floradora Club (which masks a cheerful brothel, each girl named after a flower), where 'capons' are served by waitresses dressed as Nell Gwyn, their bosomy charms disguising the ill-cooked chickens they hand round. As one who has seen the actual thing on one unforgotten occasion, I can vouch for the dreadful accuracy of Watson's account.

It is this accuracy, this telling it how it was with only the smallest exaggeration, that accounts for the solidity of Watson's Flaxborough saga, a work that eventually extended to twelve hilarious volumes. It is hilarity backed by a certain truth. So that in the end Watson created in his imaginary Flaxborough a place it is not preposterous to compare with the creation of Arnold Bennett in his classic Five Towns novels, or even perhaps with William Faulkner's Yoknapatawa County.

First edition London: Eyre Methuen, 1975
First US edition New York: Putnam, 1975

83

ROSS MACDONALD
The Blue Hammer

Ross Macdonald once wrote that he had found to his pleasure that the two best private detectives he knew personally much resembled his own fictional detective, Lew Archer, in their intelligent humaneness, their interest in other people rather than themselves, and the toughness of mind that enabled them to face with open eyes all human weaknesses, including their own. Then he added a little extra: 'Both of them dearly love to tell a story.'

It is this telling of a story, often unremarked upon because it is so unexpected, that is, I think, the chief merit of the Lew Archer novels; books that have been hailed by the critic William Goldman in the *New York Times Book Review* as 'the finest series of detective novels ever written by an American.' And, in many ways, Macdonald's last book, *The Blue Hammer*, though it is probably less well-known than the *The Moving Target* (which has been filmed) or *The Underground Man*, is the peak of his achievement.

The story Macdonald tells in *The Blue Hammer* is of Archer's quest for an answer to the mystery of the disappearance some thirty years earlier of the young painter, Richard Chantrey. It begins with him being asked to find a Chantrey painting missing from the house of a typically high-rich California couple, Jack and Ruth Biemeyer. Before the quest has carried him very far it has brought about a murder, and another follows. By the end Archer has discovered the killer as well as taking to bed the funky newspaper reporter, Betty Jo Siddon, kidnapped in the course of his complex investigation.

It is a short passage describing Betty Jo lying beside Archer at dawn that gives the book its curious title. 'After a while I could see the steady blue pulse in her temple, the beating of the silent hammer which meant that she was alive. I hoped that the blue hammer would never stop.' From which we see that the book is a paean of praise to life, to the continuing future, even to its farthest romantic reach of defying death for ever.

Set against this wide-eyed optimism are the dead, the dying and the lookers-back to a dead past. As is almost always the case with Ross Macdonald, the mainspring here goes back to tremendous and terrible events that occurred when the rich and aged people Archer meets were young and mostly bad. So his investigation takes him away from the California Macdonald describes so well to an Arizona he describes almost as well and to past events there. Towards the end, as Archer begins to understand, he says 'I felt the thirty-two-year case was completing a long curve back to its source.' That element of time, of people having a history, is what makes the Archer stories dense with lived life.

Part of their strength comes from the particular identification, too, that Macdonald made with Archer. At the start, he has written, Archer was created 'from the inside out.' He himself was not Archer, 'but Archer was me.' Later, and notably here, Macdonald feels that he threw off the strong influence of Raymond Chandler and developed Archer away from being 'a fantasy projection of myself and my personal needs.' He goes on: 'Cool, I think, is the word for our mature relationship. Archer himself has what New Englanders call "weaned affections".'

It is this mature outlook that gives *The Blue Hammer* its exceptional strength. But note that however much Lew Archer is the mature and distanced Macdonald, and however much he remains the classical American private eye investigating by going in there, he is also that figure of myth, the Great Detective.

He solves this case in just that same sudden fiery fusing of disparate elements with which Dupin solved the mystery of the Rue Morgue. Let him speak for himself: 'These facts coming together in my mind gave me a kind of subterranean jolt, like an earthquake fault beginning to make its first tentative move. I was breathing quickly and my head was pounding.' The authentic revealing trance of the Great Detective.

First edition New York: Knopf, 1970
First UK edition London: Collins, 1976

AGATHA CHRISTIE
Sleeping Murder

Sleeping Murder is in many ways the most typical case of Agatha Christie's second-most-famous sleuth, Miss Marple. It was also her last case, though the book was in fact written during World War II but kept in a safe until the end of her creator's career.

We hear of Miss Marple first at second-hand, in a jocular remark of her nephew: 'She's what I should describe as a perfect Period Piece,' he says; 'Victorian to the core. All her dressing-tables have their legs swathed in chintz. She lives in a village where nothing ever happens.' A few paragraphs on (Agatha Christie is a swift storyteller) we meet the lady herself and learn that 'Her blue eyes often had a little twinkle in them.' Thus economically Agatha Christie tells us her sleuth is only outwardly an old pussy.

Soon we see her commonsensical attitude to life and a certain shrewdness that is based on simple and direct observation. The book's young heroine has been devastatingly affected at hearing in the theatre Webster's famous lines 'Cover her face. Mine eyes dazzle, she died young.' Miss Marple convinces her she had heard the words eighteen years earlier at the time she saw a dead body. 'Children are odd little creatures,' she says. 'If they are badly frightened, especially by something they don't understand, they don't talk about it.' Sound psychology, coming, one guesses, as much from Mrs Christie, mother of a daughter, as from Miss Marple. 'There was something oyster-like about Rosalind,' Agatha Christie remarks in her autobiography.

Miss Marple's armoury also encompasses the wisdom of experience, as when she advises the heroine, Gwenda, not to go into what had happened eighteen years before. Don't, she says in more or less these words, play detectives. A tricky passage for the writer of detective stories, who knows that the book is going to end abruptly in Chapter Five if Miss Marple's advice is taken to let sleeping murder lie. Adroitly handled, though; it tells us that the book is a degree more serious than the unashamedly frivolous works with which the author began. It is going to say something, a certain amount, about real people and, more, about the existence of evil.

But before we encounter this evil we glimpse Miss Marple, the charmingly sly, cajoling her doctor into insisting she needs a holiday and that the only place for it is the seaside town where Gwenda lives. And, once there, we see her, playing the elderly gossip for all she is worth, gently extracting information as she debates the merits of knitting patterns. Then about midway through the book we get a picture of Miss Marple as the feminine sleuth as opposed to the male, as opposed indeed to the unmentioned presence of Hercule Poirot. 'Gentlemen,' she says, 'always seem to be able to tabulate these things so clearly.' And we know, because we realise that Miss Marple is going to solve this case, that Poirot-like tabulation will not provide the answer. Now we are in the realm of pure intuition.

When Miss Marple, hearing a fact about the days of this long-ago murder, experiences the evil she has forecast ('There's a great deal of—well, *queerness* about—more than people imagine'), her intuition is such that she becomes physically affected to the point of looking actually ill.

But before the end Miss Marple the hard-headed is to the fore again. She says she is 'a little worried' by the way Gwenda has accepted all she has been told; 'I'm afraid I have a sadly distrustful nature.' An attitude justified in the book's brilliant *denouement* when it is revealed that a letter apparently written by the victim at a later date than the murder, a letter verified by an expert as in the same hand as a specimen of the victim's writing, does not necessarily mean the victim was alive at the later date. Quite simply, Gwenda (and everybody else) has taken the murderer's word for it that the specimen was written by the victim when both it and the letter were written by the murderer himself.

'It really is very dangerous to believe people,' Miss Marple says. 'I never have for years.' Portrait of woman as detective, and a dazzling one.

First edition London: Collins, 1976
First US edition New York: Dodd, Mead, 1976

85

DOROTHY SALISBURY DAVIS
A Death in the Life

Crime and compassion: they seem an unlikely coupling. Yet in the books of Dorothy Salisbury Davis (from which out of a by no means meagre output of decidedly varied approaches I have almost arbitrarily selected this book) the two are not only closely interwoven, but in that interweaving lies a good part of their success.

Compassion runs like a soft silver thread through almost everything that Dorothy Salisbury Davis has written. It is frequently a compassion not simply for the victim of a crime, of murder, but also for its perpetrator. She sees that, very often, the person who on the surface seems a cold-blooded killer is— scratch the skin only a little—a human being like other human beings, like those of us reading her books. Indeed, she has stated as her aim—perhaps an involuntary one—the pursuit of truth, which she sees as shining out best amid the dark excesses which, in theory, we are all capable of reaching.

I think it is not too outlandish to label this quality Woman Wisdom. It is something Dorothy Salisbury Davis shares with the best, the very best, of the crime novelists of her sex. It shows itself, paradoxically in a crime writer, as an abhorrence of violence (she once edited a volume called *Crime Without Murder*). Yet when necessary, as it is from time to time in *A Death in the Life*, she does not flinch from facing the violence that can erupt from men and women too oppressed by the stresses of modern living, of which the worser quarters of New York, her setting here, can be taken as a symbol.

Her books have been well described as being serious studies of character set against particular environments, and in *A Death in the Life* ('The Life,' for the benefit of the more innocent reader, is the profession of prostitution in the language of its American practitioners) she shows us this life, unflinchingly and even at times with warm humour, through the half-innocent, half-aware eyes of Julie Hayes, a young, footloose, upper-middle-class New

Yorker, who, almost on a whim, sets up as a fortune-teller in th
centre of one of the city's prostitute prowling-grounds.

Julie Hayes is the nearest Dorothy Salisbury Davis has bee
able to come towards creating and nurturing a running hero o
heroine. She has deplored her inabililty to do this, seeing it (no
without justice) as being a way in which a crime writer, writin
books that of their nature have difficulty in making the impact o
a powerful straight novel, can nevertheless make a memorabl
impression. She has said that, before she hit on Julie, she alway
grew tired of a central character as soon as the first situation i
which they had been involved was brought to a successfu
conclusion. But to this lack she makes one exception: 'Myself
as she puts it, making it clear that this is no joke. She is right t
do so, because what links all the books she has written is th
presence of their author, a person she has described as 'a restles
and sometimes troubled writer.' It is that troubled quality that i
her strength.

But she has other considerable weapons at her command. He
technique is first class. *A Death in the Life* is sown with quietl
swift and effective descriptions. Vividness abounds. As you rea
you feel, too, that you are in the hands of a writer who know
exactly what she is doing, and in this book what she is doing is b
no means simple and straightforward. Ambiguities run throug
it.

This is a matter for rejoicing. A book without ambiguities is, i
this complex and contradictory world, a book that is probabl
not worth more than a quick perusal. And *A Death in the Lif*
leaves its readers with a fine final ambiguity (though not abou
the actual answer to the question 'Who done it?'). John Fowle:
that most inward-looking of novelists, has spoken somewhere c
the power of the unanswered. Graham Greene is notable for th
way he allows suspense to continue after his story is tol
Raymond Chandler once suggested that the ideal mystery wa
one you would read 'if the end was missing.' *A Death in the Lif*
has all the ongoingness evoked by this trio of great names.

First edition New York: Scribner, 1976
First UK edition London: Gollancz, 1977

DOROTHY UHNAK
The Investigation

Dorothy Uhnak has three qualifications for writing a first-class crime novel. First, she was for fourteen years a policewoman in New York, spending twelve of those years as a detective moving steadily up the promotion ladder. Second, she is a woman and is impelled by a wish to show that a woman can hold her own in places usually thought of as men's worlds. Third, she can write, although in a style that is more hammer than chisel.

She began with a non-fiction account of her own early career called *Policewoman*, a book on which a popular television series was based. After leaving the police she wrote fiction, a book featuring a young woman police officer called Christie Opara. It shared the Mystery Writers of America prize for a first novel. Two other Opara books followed, each making the case for a woman detective who could be as successful as any. Then she produced a more ambitious venture, a long novel called *Law and Order* which chronicled three generations of a New York police family, the O'Malleys. The book has been hailed as deserving to become a classic of crime fiction.

I have, however, preferred its successor, *The Investigation*, as being the fruit of all that Dorothy Uhnak learned in writing *Law and Order*. Told with all her vigour of style, a prose that batters you into understanding what she wants to say, it is the story of a woman on the other side of the line dividing the so-called good (like Christie Opara) from the so-called bad. Kitty Keeler is revealed in the story as having been the beloved mistress of a Mafia boss, Alfredo Veronne, a figure who rings true indeed. But Kitty, though nominally a criminal and suspected of murdering her two children, is no black-painted villainess. Instead, she is shown convincingly as a woman. And, more, she is shown as the equivalent of Christie Opara, as a woman capable of running a business, of taking decisions, and also as a mother in the full meaning of the term. 'I never deserved any medals as the best mother of the year,' she says to her detective lover towards the end of the book as they talk about her two murdered sons, 'but when it gets down to it, who the hell does? *I did love them*. Italics Dorothy Uhnak's, typical of her sledgehammer style.

Kitty goes on to tell her lover, Detective Joe Peters, who with solid persistence has fought his way to the truth about the murder of the two boys, just what her relations with the dead Mafia boss, Alfredo Veronne, had been. 'I was of value to him, Joe. Not just my body. God, he was the only one who loved me for my brain. Yes, *loved* me. And trusted me, Joe. You know what it's like for a man like Alfredo to *trust*—completely, totally?'

This in its simplicity is *Dallas* or *Dynasty* territory, and indeed *The Investigation* became a bestseller and had a huge paperback sale. But it is a better book than this might seem to indicate (though large sales are not to be despised as an indication of the effectiveness of a book). What *The Investigation* does have, however, that is not present in the smooth surface of high-class television soap is a real acknowledgement of the appalling things men and women can do.

This is what Detective Uhnak learnt in those years as a New York cop. And when she became a writer she proved to have the gift of being able to convey these appalling things in words (no wonder that they are often heavy-handed words). It is not a gift given to every writer, not even to every writer who sets out to write about crime. But the emotional shell Dorothy Uhnak developed in her early years as a policewoman, and which she describes well in her Christie Opara books, stood her in good stead when she came to imagine events similar to the ones she had had to face in real life.

So she is able to present them to us in all their horror, but shown coolly. It is a considerable feat.

First edition London: Hodder and Stoughton, 1977
First US edition New York: Simon and Schuster, 1977

87

RUTH RENDELL

A Judgement in Stone

Reviewing *A Judgement in Stone* ten years ago I wrote 'This could become a classic among chillers.' I like to think that my prophecy has now been made good. Certainly, during all the time that has passed since 1977, whenever I have been reminded of the book a strong impression of it—of its implacable story recounted, as I said in *The Times*, 'with Vermeer-like accuracy and inevitability'—came back into my head.

Inevitability is the key word. The book treads out a path of doomed inevitability from its very first words: 'Eunice Parch-man killed the Coverdale family because she could not read or write.' The book is indeed, in one sense, a study of the potentially evil-making effects of the mischance of illiteracy, but it is more than that. It is a study of evil itself, a powerful account, sympathetic for all its relentless accuracy, of how a mass murder can happen.

It is, too, an intensely gripping story, which is achieved without the benefit of the famous who-done-it? tug. From those opening words one knows what is going to happen, who is going to be the killer and, if in outline only, who are to be the victims. But part of the pleasure, or perhaps the chill, of reading the book is to meet one by one this Coverdale family who we know are to meet their deaths. Because Ruth Rendell has drawn fine portraits of each one of them; nice, attractive, believable people with flaws in their characters, but only such flaws as we ourselves possess.

There is George Coverdale, the father, a man of good intellect and decent common sense if touched with a little pomposity. One who does not deserve to die. There is his younger second wife, Jacqueline, with whom he is devotedly in love; a touch vain, a trifle lazy in things that do not interest her, and plainly well-meaning. It is her laziness, combined with that well-meaningness, which allows her to take on Eunice Parchman as housekeeper without checking the crudely-fabricated references she has induced a blackmail victim to supply.

Then there are the two children, one from each side of the family, and equally nice in their different ways. Giles, at seventeen still at school, is a charming head-in-the-clouds swot, delightfully full of romantic notions gathered from his reading. A boy with an obviously brilliant future ahead of him—and destined, we know, to die at Eunice Parchman's hands. And Melinda, a deliciously well done portrait of young girlhood, friendly as a puppy, pretty as the proverbial picture; a young woman designed if anyone ever was for marriage and happy motherhood. Yet doomed.

That thudding note of doom sounds deeply out as one turns the pages. When George's older married daughter, pregnant, meets Eunice she feels 'as if a coldness, almost an icy breath, emanated from her.' But, preoccupied with the coming birth, she says nothing. Then Jacqueline fails to take up the false reference, just a phone call away. 'In that moment ... an invisible thread lassoed each of them, bound them to one another, related them more closely than blood.'

Stroke after warning stroke sounds out, blithely ignored by the victims-to-be, as Eunice appears to be the ideal home help at the pleasant country house. George goes for his annual check-up with the doctor and is given a mild warning about his blood pressure. At once he makes a will and shows it to Jacqueline who almost light-heartedly says that, younger than him by some years, she is likely to live on long after his death. But, adds Ruth Rendell implacably, 'she was to be a widow for only fifteen minutes.'

Finally, there is the double irony arising from the dismissal of the paragon housekeeper because of her insistence on entertaining the village postmistress, a woman on the verge of religious mania who has been spreading vicious rumours about the family. They go out to dinner, partly to avoid unpleasantness while Eunice Parchman is still in the house. 'Afterwards,' Ruth Rendell writes, 'the waiters and other diners were to wish they had taken more notice of this happy family, this doomed family.'

First edition London: Hutchinson, 1977
First US edition New York: Doubleday, 1978

88

WILLIAM McILVANNEY
Laidlaw

Here is a magnificent multi-layered crime novel. It was written by a poet, and indeed there are short passages in it that have almost the gem-hard concentration of poems. And 'hard' is the word. One is apt at the mention of a poet to think in terms of 'As I walked along the Strand with a lily in my hand,' but what makes most poets is their capacity for taking a hard look at what is, coupled with the gift of stating their findings memorably. Such a poet is William McIlvanney, and much of the pleasure of *Laidlaw* comes from the interaction of the sensitive seer of things and the raw brutality of the Glasgow at which he looks.

The first layer of the book, the man at its centre, Detective Inspector Laidlaw, incorporates all this contrast. He is as hard a man as a Glasgow policeman needs to be, ready to use his fists and, more, possessed of all that instant aggressiveness that marks out Glasgow Man, and Woman. Yet he is deep-seeing, a thinker; above all, a man with doubts, and one who makes use of those doubts.

'What I've got against men like Lawson,' he says once, 'isn't that they're wrong. It's just that they *assume* they're right. Bigotry's just unearned certainty, isn't it?' And in those two last words comes the saving doubt again.

From this picture of a highly unorthodox detective (yet one we can believe in as a real-life police officer), who is often successful where others fail or only half-succeed, comes another layer of the book. It can be read as a study of the philosophy of policing society. This comes out most clearly in the struggle that runs like a flailing chain through the pages between Laidlaw and his rival, Detective Inspector Milligan, who believes he has 'nothing in common with thieves, and con-men and pimps and murderers'; that they are 'another species' with whom he is simply at war. Laidlaw's view is, of course, the opposite. Society, he says, pretends crimes like the sexual killing of a girl (the nub of the book's story) are committed by monsters, not people. 'We can't afford to do that. We're the shitty urban machine humanised. That's policemen.'

Another layer to the book is the struggle between Milligan and Laidlaw for the allegiance—the soul, if you like—of a young detective constable, Harkness. But a layer that is much thicker, indeed almost the whole of the book, is McIlvanney's portrait of Glasgow and the sort of person who is a Glaswegian, whether it is the disappearing Glasgow where 'streets were places for living in, not just passing through', or the city whose inhabitants indulge in the aggressive pastime of insisting on giving strangers 'bulletins on your progress' with the parallel assumption that anybody doing anything unusual, like chasing a criminal, ought to be willing to stop and explain.

McIlvanney describes it all with a wit that has more than a little 'Glasgowness' itself. A character forks bacon into his mouth 'and it couldn't have tasted worse if he'd been a rabbi.' A doddery hotel porter opens its door 'with all the ease of the Venus de Milo cracking a safe.' Laidlaw visits a respectable house where 'the nearest thing to turmoil would be when the tea was stirred.' And McIlvanney, a fine craftsman, also has the gift of rendering Glasgow's thick argot in phonetics that make it miraculously possible to follow.

But there is one more layer still. It is McIlvanney's attempt to understand not simply the complex man, Laidlaw, who came into his head, not even the pulsating city he hymns, but life itself. He wrestles, in true Glasgow fashion, with the problem of what life is truly about. 'Take it far enough,' Laidlaw's pupil Harkness exclaims to his gropingly searching mentor, with a touch of exasperation, 'and it's all just an act of God.' And Laidlaw replies—in a way it sums up the book—'So maybe we should find out where He is and book him.'

First edition London: Hodder and Stoughton, 1977
First US edition New York: Pantheon, 1977

[1977]

89

DONALD E. WESTLAKE
Nobody's Perfect

I sometimes think that the hardest form of crime fiction to write—and it's all hard to write—is the combination of crime and the farcical. All the more pleasure, then, when in the hands of a writer of enormous adroitness the difficult mixture adds up to a satisfying whole. And Donald E. Westlake is that writer. One of crime's prolificoes (some half-dozen first-class tough novels of organised crime for a start, twenty books as Richard Stark with thief heroes, half a dozen books as Tucker Coe in the thoughtful Ross Macdonald private-eye vein, and more than twenty comedy crime novels), he has certainly learnt his craft.

It was something that needed to be learnt to bring off the difficult feat he has attempted time and again, and nowhere perhaps more successfully than in *Nobody's Perfect*. The title itself was a cheeky challenge to reviewers everywhere. You can imagine the easy put-down it invited: 'but Westlake, sad to say, is far from it.' In fact, when I reviewed the book I was happy to take that title the other way and say the writer was as near perfection as anyone was likely to get in his chosen field. Re-reading the book, I see no reason to go back on that verdict.

The challenge that faced Westlake when he wrote it was simply that crime is, of its nature, not funny. People get hurt when crimes take place. They get killed. At the least they lose things precious to them, or their illusions (which is worse). On the other hand, farce has to be funny or it is a deflated balloon.

To work his way out of this dilemma, Westlake brings a considerable battery of talents to bear. First, he knows exactly what is needed to write effective farce. If you want ridiculous and extraordinary events to be truly funny, you have first to create a firm base of the ordinary.

The beginning of this book, then, is a down-to-earth description, nowhere exaggerated, of a burglar awaiting swift trial in New York. Westlake gives us the setting straight, and tacky. The cubicle 'with its institutional green walls, its black linoleum floor, the great hanging globe of light, the frosted glass window in its door, its battered wooden table and two battered wooden chairs and one battered metal waste basket.' Only after a page or two of such plain description does he venture on the first flicker of upward flight with the attorney assigned to defend, an incompetent who cannot even get his briefcase open; 'he was young, possibly fourteen.' A tiny touch, but the first stirring of delightful, impossible (but somehow seeming just-possible) things to come.

Then Westlake brings to his difficult task a splendid skill with the basic words. He chooses time and again the best, the only, the unlikely but right. An empty bourbon glass with 'nothing but an amber echo round the bottom.' Or, 'he hadn't wanted to steal . . . but at the time it had seemed to him his need was greater than theirs; certainly his arithmetic was.' And, trickiest moment of all, making actual mayhem seem funny, as when the monstrous crook, Tiny, complains about the inept driver on his last robbery, 'Before we got outa the car, when the cops surrounded us, I broke his neck. We all said it was whiplash from the sudden stop.' You need the whole context to appreciate the joke properly, but somehow the words used and the order they are used in make even death a laugh.

Then there is the sheer skill of the plot. Farce crime needs a plot that provides incident after incident in swift, dazzling succession. Westlake's story of his unlucky burglar Dortmund (met in earlier books) and how he is persuaded to steal a painting in order to give it back to its owner is just such a story, taking one whirlingly through New York, to London and to Scotland at its romantic zaniest.

Pace, of course, is what does it. You are never left thinking 'I wonder if that is really likely.' Before you do, an event just one stage more unlikely, and funnier, has swept you up. Enormous inventiveness is what is needed to do this, and that Westlake triumphantly supplies.

First edition London: Hodder and Stoughton, 1978
First US edition New York: Evans, 1977

90

REGINALD HILL

A Pinch of Snuff

A Pinch of Snuff might well be the title of any of the detective stories of the so-called Golden Age, the time when sex was more or less confined to *He took her hand. 'Darling,' he said, 'it's all over'*. Much talk about variations in the manufacture of boxes holding different sorts of snuff is indicated, with perhaps a joke or two about sneezing and of course a murder, altogether bloodless. Reginald Hill's book, perhaps the best example of his output, is very far from all that.

The snuff of his title is snuff as in 'snuff movie', those pornographic films in which, it is reported, a real live victim is actually done to death in a horribly violent manner. Hill writes not detective stories but crime novels, books in which he examines in depth some aspect of human activity, generally contemporary. So in *A Pinch of Snuff* he muses, through the medium of an always-ongoing story, about precisely that combination of sex with violence which many people see as a particularly modern phenomenon.

He is not afraid, either, to do this at what might be called uncomfortably close quarters. Where a less probing writer might be content to present the theme of sex-cum-violence in general terms, by confining it for instance to the porno cinema and not-too-detailed descriptions of the films it shows, Hill not only describes the reactions of his young detective to one of these films (mixed voyeuristic pleasure and puritan disapproval), but he also describes later the detective's wife's reactions. And he goes further. Into his plot he weaves the fact that the murder victim had shortly before his death been the willing recipient of a caning.

But Hill does all this strictly within the confines of a crime story, even a story of detection. And he sets his tale in the large provincial town in Northern England used in a good many of his previous books (it is, adroitly, never named). He uses, too, the sleuths he invented for his first book, *A Clubbable Woman*:

Detective Superintendent Dalziel (you pronounce it, if you remember to, Dee-ell) and Detective Sergeant (in *A Pinch of Snuff*, Detective Inspector) Peter Pascoe.

The pair are a subtle variation, befitting a writer of considerable subtlety, on the traditional Holmes–Watson partnership, so useful to the writer wanting to conceal the meaning of clues while laying them fairly in front of the reader. Neither of the two is Holmes; neither is Watson. Instead, the two men learn from each other in a continuing clash of temperaments.

Dalziel is a 'copper' in the old style; down-to-earth, often unashamedly gross (Hill makes a good deal of his habit of scratching his groin), but an exemplar of all that traditional commonsense police work can achieve. Pascoe is a graduate—in sociology, no less—a typical sensitive liberal of the 1970s. He is aware, compassionate, and liable not to see the unpleasant facts in front of his face.

Thus in *A Pinch of Snuff* he remains unaware of who one of the principal villains must be until, intervening at a late stage, Dalziel produces the rabbit from the hat. But, on the other hand, Pascoe's sensitivity enables him to pierce the veils put up by other figures in the story. He is, one suspects, in many ways Hill himself, a writer endowed with sharp perceptions and a delightfully whimsical wit. Here he is writing about an elephant's-foot umbrella-stand that sets the tone for a house visited in the course of the investigation. 'The huge foot, which had been raised for the last time on some Indian plain and set down (no doubt to the ghostly beast's great amazement) here in darkest Yorkshire . . .'

The combining of light wit and an unflinching look at the darker sides of human existence is what marks Hill out as a writer of some stature, even among the ranks of non-crime novelists. But to this mix of the amusing and the alarming, with neither allowed to swamp the other, he brings, too, one of the chief gifts of the detection writer, the weaving together of an ingenious and credible plot. There are many strands in *A Pinch of Snuff* but at the final climax they come satisfyingly together to produce a pleasure not always to be found in the novel proper.

First edition London: Collins, 1978
First US edition New York: Harper and Row, 1978

91
JOSEPH HANSEN
Skinflick

The world of homosexuals has not been absent from crime fiction in the last half of the twentieth century, but almost always it has been there in the form of the exaggerated, show-off, camp world. With the Dave Brandstetter novels of Joseph Hansen we entered a new, saner era. Dave, Californian insurance investigator, is a homosexual who convinces without the author using any of the easy-label traits earlier writers grabbed at (and many later writers still grab) when they want to portray a gay. Brandstetter is a homosexual without hysteria.

As such he would be welcome in the *genre*. But he is more than this. He is the classical private-eye brought up to date, hence the fact that he is not strictly a private-eye but works in the death-claims division of insurance companies. But the way he works is the way in which the great private-eyes of an earlier day—Philip Marlowe, Sam Spade—worked: by putting themselves into the thick of things. If Dave Brandstetter does not often use his fists and does not carry a gun, it does not mean that he cannot act tough.

Here he is in action in *Skinflick*. 'Fullbright charged ... He lunged across the bar grabbing for Dave. Dave stepped out from behind the bar ... pushed his glasses into his pocket. "Take it easy," he said.' Fullbright, of course, charges again. Dave side-steps, puts out a foot. And before we know it he is mopping up Fullbright's broken nose.

Something else, too, of the classical private-eye story is to be seen here: the laconic, one-sentence-at-a-time prose. It is right for this sort of story, and Hansen uses it in the way it ought to be used. He says only what needs to be said. He avoids the temptation, wide open to every follower of Chandler and Hammett, to embroider, to put in favourite bits of their own world. Which is not to say that *Skinflick* is devoid of humour; far from it. Hansen's description of the actual making of a cheap porno movie is laugh-a-line stuff, but the laughs are not there just for laughs' sake. They are there to make us see that the people who make porno films are human beings too.

But another of Hansen's virtues in his portrayal of Dave Brandstetter needs to be pointed out. He does not make him sympathetic though he is, into any cardboard propaganda figure pleading for tolerance towards the homosexual community. He is simply a man. A man of determination, who, armed with only the slender evidence that the overly religious murder victim has not been killed by a supposedly vengeful porno bookshop owner, refuses to let go, even when the tttheory he has painfully arrived at proves not to be the true answer. He is a man, too, who happens to have a caring streak, which induced him to try to re-establish the drunk whose job he has succeeded to.

For some of the characters Brandstetter encounters in his search for the truth, Hansen does ask for our tolerance. There is, for instance, the transvestite actor in skinflick movies ('That's what skinflick means—what you see ain't what you think, but it makes you think it is.'). Randy is shown as happily cheerful for the most part: 'Ho hum,' he says when someone comments about him warily 'I don't think that's a girl.' But he is sometimes shown to be sad, as we all are at times. 'Randy looked at [the youth] bleakly. "God, to have a body like that!".' Dave tells him his body looks fine. But, says Randy, 'It came from the wrong outfitter.' Hansen, in short, knows how to bring to life characters who bear a real relationship to the human beings who breathe the air of our world.

He knows, too, how to make that world spring to life in his pages. He has an eye for the detail that says everything. In consequence, in just a few words, he can make vivid scene after scene in sun-soaked Southern California. Here is Dave getting back into his car after being peppered with shotgun pellets: 'The blood on the leather bucket seat had dried in the hot wind. It crackled when he sat on it.' It takes a real writer, not any mere propagandist for the homosexual way, nor any ordinary churner-out of private-eye stories, to see something as forcefully as that 'it crackled,' and to find the few short words needed to send the image winging into our imaginations, miles and miles away years and years later.

First edition New York: Holt, Rinehart and Winston, 1979
First UK edition London: Faber and Faber, 1980

[1979]

92

P.M. HUBBARD
Kill Claudio

P.M. Hubbard is a unique figure in crime literature. That, I realise, is something of a claim when there are writers as individual as Hammett and Simenon—to name but two—to be taken into account. Yet I have no hesitation in staking out a special area for Hubbard, one that he has made his own and one which no other writer could lay claim to. It lies in the view he had of the world and the sort of person who best inhabits it.

To anyone who has read any of his books what I have said will make immediate sense. The flavour comes over, unmistakable as that of a fine burgundy amid a myriad bottles of good red wine. I will, however, bring one witness to underpin my contention. He is Anthony Quinton, Lord Quinton, the distinguished philosopher of the British school. It must be rare for such a figure to review a crime novel, let alone in the learned pages of the *Times Literary Supplement*, but Quinton on one occasion reviewed a new Hubbard at some length there.

'The fact is,' he wrote, 'that Hubbard is a wholly original writer with an idiosyncratic vision of people and the way in which they interact ... Hubbard expresses his vision with wit, delightful verbal economy and the special unforgettable intensity of genuine commitment.' It is this last intense commitment, I believe, that puts the Hubbard novels into the topmost flight.

A word first, though, about that verbal economy. As with the style of any writer worth his salt, the style is the man, and the particular contained economy of Hubbard's writing expresses, I hazard, the author himself and certainly the sort of man he holds up for our admiration. The sentences are almost always short, but they do not seem to be making a virtue of shortness, as with some of the lesser writers of the American pulp school. Hubbard's sentences are short not to achieve the effect of the jab or a punch, but because he means to say only just what he wants to put over, and no more.

And these sentences may be said to paint for us equally the

Hubbard hero. He is a man who always works within himself, who never goes further than necessary. But that necessity may go, as it does in *Kill Claudio*, to what in other people would be considered extraordinary lengths.

The whole story of this book is based on the premise that Ben Selby, once an agent in some undisclosed organisation, finding a former colleague killed in mistake for himself, is perfectly willing to set out to discover and eliminate the killer. And he does so at the mere behest of the dead man's wife, a behest as terse and as unexpected as that of Shakespeare's Beatrice in *Much Ado About Nothing* when she says to Benedict simply, 'Kill Claudio.'

The Hubbard hero, then, is a man who would set about this task coolly, calmly and with no trace of heroics. 'I walked at my own pace,' he says after he has discovered his erstwhile friend's body. No feelings that he has a duty to the forces of the law will make him hurry to report the death.

In this he is very British, and in fact the Hubbard hero is a particular type of Briton held up for our admiration, one of the sort who with hardly more than a handful of similar colleagues administered the vast sub-continent of India for some two hundred years of quiet unassuming work.

He is also portrayed—for all that he is the essence of reticence—in depth. Not for nothing does Hubbard take his title, and the book's very mainspring, from Shakespeare. The Shakespearian understanding of man and his roots is there, as is a tremendous sense of Time. We get that in the very opening paragraph when Ben Selby says that had he not by chance come across his friend's body on the moor, 'the bones would have gone neatly down into the peat along with all the other riff-raff of the centuries.' And Time emerges at the book's climax when the mysterious, never-accounted-for treasure for which Selby's friend was killed is found at last—buried beneath an unshiftable rock fall, the effect of the slow erosion of a timeless landscape.

So, against such vast eternities Hubbard tells a story tingling with suspense, and portrays a hero he patently believes is one worth holding up to posterity as a true man.

First edition London: Macmillan, 1979
First US edition New York: Doubleday, 1979

93

JOHN D. MacDONALD
The Green Ripper

John D. MacDonald was an enormously prolific writer of tough crime stories, which over the years became thinking crime stories. He was best known for the series about Travis McGee, the six-foot-four ex-football player, living on a boat in Southern Florida called The Busted Flush, which he won in a poker game. McGee in his early days was something of a crookedish knight-errant, righting wrongs in what he called 'salvage operations'. Later, as here, he espoused causes.

The twenty-odd McGee books—each has a colour in the title—are, in fact, perhaps our best example of the crime story as a novel of feelings. In this it is not unfair to compare MacDonald to Charles Dickens, although Dickens had of course an infinitely wider range. But it is Dickens the novelist of feelings, of sentiment, and of sentimentality, that MacDonald brings to mind.

In *The Green Ripper* we get no hint in the opening of any crime puzzle or crime situation. Instead there is a rapid, and skilful, evocation of a warm and cosy world. It is the Dickens of *A Christmas Carol*, only in place of Tiny Tim exclaiming 'God bless us every one' we have the girl McGee has been living with exuding remembered sensuous pleasures; and in place of Scrooge, ready to be turned to treacle, we have McGee's old friend Meyer, the world-class economist, crying universal woe—but not yet.

Soon, of course, the action does begin. McGee's girl is killed. But there is no sudden extermination by a single shot or quick knife thrust before the action zooms off. Instead we get a death scene drawn out to the farthest point. McGee's Gretel, Grets for short, is killed with a slow-acting poison and we live her last hours very much as in the *The Old Curiosity Shop* we live the last hours of the girl always called Little Nell.

Again, after Grets' death we get Dickensian sentiment in the memorial service mourners: 'together we form a village. And share the trouble as much as we can. Take as much of it upon ourselves as is possible, and we know it is not very much. Okay?' It is not the language of Dickens: it is his way of feeling.

This also extends to the other side of the coin, as one might say. Dickens could portray a bad woman; in deference to his readers he seldom did, but he portrayed such a person in Edith Granger, who married Mr Dombey of *Dombey and Son* for his money, in what might be called sentimental terms reversed. It is in just such a way that MacDonald describes the almost-widow Anna Farmer, ready to give herself to McGee for sex.

Like Dickens, too, MacDonald can produce social comment with feeling. Where Dickens took his readers tremendously to task after the death of Jo the crossing-sweeper in *Bleak House*, with 'Dead, right reverend . . .', MacDonald castigates us more briefly but with almost as much feeling with 'They were promoting Christmas carols at the big shopping centre, pumping them out into the night wind. Jangle bells. And the silent stars go by.' MacDonald has, as well, something of the Dickensian skill with the feelings-charged pun, as in the title of this book. The Green Ripper, McGee tells us, is a child's irony-laden mispronunciation of the Grim Reaper. And before the book is done, that Grim Reaper has at McGee's hands added not a few to his harvest.

Nor is the Dickens catalogue yet over. We get the tart with a heart in *The Green Ripper*, a brainwashed religious nut willing to solace McGee when he has infiltrated himself into the organisation behind Grets death, just as Nancy in *Oliver Twist* comforts (though in a very different way) Oliver in Fagin's den. And finally, in a letter McGee writes before he sets off to penetrate the evil organisation, we have 'I have this very strong feeling that I am never coming back here, that this part of my life is ending . . . There is surely an echo there of Sidney Carton's 'This is a far, far better thing that I do . . .'.

Sometimes Dickens is accused of sentimentality, and the same charge could be levelled, at a different power, at MacDonald. But Dickens could, like none other, sound the note of true sentiment of strong and warm feeling. At his own level John D. MacDonald with Travis McGee does just this.

First edition London: Hale, 1980
First US edition Philadelphia: Lippincott, 1979

94

JOHN WAINWRIGHT
All On A Summer's Day

Of the sixty-four books John Wainwright wrote between 1965, when he began, and 1985 (he is still writing away), which should be chosen as typical? First, perhaps it should be said that I have no doubt that one at least ought to figure among my hundred best. The mere fact that a writer is more than usually prolific does not necessarily mean that the goods produced are shoddy. Look at Balzac. But there is a further complication in selecting one Wainwright: in the course of producing those sixty-four books he has worked with success in a good many of the sub-genres of the crime story. As a former police officer, however, he is primarily a chronicler of police life, and in the end I chose this police procedural as my example, although it is in some way untypical since it is one of the few—if not the only—multi-police procedural he has written.

But by selecting it—and it is certainly a fine, strongly-written book in itself—I have been able to point to more aspects of Wainwright's love affair with the police than I might otherwise have done. It gives us all aspects of policing, from the home life of a constable on the beat, a night-time 'door-knob-tryer,' through accurate accounts of the necessary bureaucratic routines of a typical British force (the Keyholders' Register, the correct form of an Arrest Report, the Telephone and Teleprinter Message Book) on to the politics of high office.

All On A Summer's Day is set in an imaginary Yorkshire town, Sopworth, and in the course of its 300 pages we meet a whole variety of policemen. There is the door-knob-tryer, happy on his perch at what is considered the bottom rung, content if when he retires they will say 'He was a cracker of a copper.' There is, at the top of the ladder, the Assistant Chief Constable (Crime) for the region in which grimy but wealth-producing Sopworth is situated.

But Wainwright's range is not only up and down the ladder of police ranks. It is also up and down the moral character scale.

197

And it is his ability to view his fellow human beings of all types with both judgement and compassion that marks Wainwright out from the common ruck of crime writers. It is this that underpins a style of writing that many have found crude and hectoring, though most have acknowledged that it is also compelling.

Thus in *All On A Summer's Day* we get pen-portraits, in depth, of policemen like Chief Superintendent Blakey, the clawer-up the rungs of the ladder who 'knew when to smile a sycophantic smile and agree...or *not* agree, as the case may be'—an example, by the way, of the Wainwright no-holds-barred way with the language. Blakey is shown, without compunction, as unpleasantly contemptuous of all beneath him in the ranks of the force, and as being convinced through and through of his own importance. Yet in the end, when he gets his comeuppance, Wainwright has for him more than a shade of understanding and compassion.

At the other extreme there are Wainwright's hero policemen, whether it is the contented constable happily doing his duty 'bobbying' as Wainwright frequently calls it, or Detective Chief Superintendent Robert Blayde, tough, determined, yet by no means without humanity, and fired by a wish to equal the great names of the police before him, while still modestly aware of his powers and limitations.

And as the varied events of a single period of exactly twenty-four hours unroll in Sopworth, ranging from murder (which is not a common occurrence in this solid Yorkshire town) to incidents of pure farce (which are more common) and on to the drudgery, loved by some, hated by others, of the every-day and all-night bobbying, we get both a picture and a philosophy of police life as it is and has to be, with variations, wherever men act against the necessary constraints of society.

First edition London: Macmillan, 1981
First US edition New York: St Martin's, 1981

AMANDA CROSS
Death in A Tenured Position

Death in A Tenured Position (known in Britain, where tenure of an academic post is not such a fraught matter as in the States, as *A Death in the Faculty*) shows that in the 1980s the classic detective story still has life in it, though it is a life that needs more than mere nostalgic imitation to keep air flowing in and out of the lungs. It shows too—it is a notably well-written book—that the genre is, in these 1980s, attractive to the probingly intelligent, sensitive writer. 'Amanda Cross' is the pseudonym of Carolyn Heilbron, Professor of English at Columbia University, New York.

In the pages of this, her sixth detection work, she brings together several strands of the *genre* into a well-woven and highly entertaining whole. Most obvious is the donnish school, with the Cross detective, Professor Kate Fansler, a worthy successor to Edmund Crispin's Professor Fen—if that is possible in a sleuth who in crossing the Atlantic has undergone a sex-change and lost much of that fey British eccentricity (perhaps not such a bad thing).

Kate Fansler acts as a detective chiefly by applying the methods of literary criticism to puzzles of human behaviour as particularly revealed by the advent of sudden death, in this case death by cyanide poisoning. Here she is explaining at last to a lawyer why the chief suspect is not guilty: 'He didn't have the opportunity, or the means, to take your *sine qua non*, and he didn't even have mine: the motive.' The motives of human beings are the stuff of the great novels that this Professor of English spends her working life pondering, and they are equally the key to the murders she takes time off to solve. (She has that final necessary qualification for the amateur detective: private means).

Then, too, *Death in A Tenured Position* is an 1980s instance of the 'backgrounder', popularised and established by Dorothy L. Sayers. Here the particular background is Harvard University with, behind it, academic life in general (described with knowledge and acuteness) and—an added important layer—what one might call the female status, anxious as one is to avoid that equivocal word 'feminism'.

There is also, of course, the familiar contest between reader and writer which, however attenuated in form, cannot be omitted from any book in the detection mould. Here Amanda Cross sets a pretty puzzle indeed: who administered that cyanide to the newly-appointed woman professor at stuffy Harvard, and why was her body found in the men's room, let alone why had she been found dead drunk in a bath in a woman's room together with an out-and-out libber some time earlier? Without giving much away, I can say that the answer is the very least likely person.

Finally, our old friend the Great Detective here makes a ghostly appearance. Ghostly, I say, because Amanda Cross treats this mythic figure with a decidedly wry reverence. Three times in the course of the book is Kate Fansler given the attribute, but on each occasion it is implied that she both is and is not such a figure. She is, because that is the rôle she may be seen as inheriting; she is not, because in these 1980s no one, perhaps, can be. The age of the hero, even the female hero, has departed. Now we knowing readers think, possibly wrongly, that we have learnt too much to be able to believe in simple heroes.

The author's yet more knowing, yet cooler eye looks more positively, however, at everything her book encompasses, which is what makes it more than a mere imitation. The Harvard background is not offered simply as interesting in itself, but critically—very critically most of the time—as a still-active bastion of male prejudices.

The same cool, appraising, deliciously sharp eye is brought to the central subject, that female rôle in the world. A true academic is above partisanship so, finally, we hear Kate answering another out-and-out libber named Joan Theresa: 'Is Fansler your husband's name?' 'No. It's my father's name. Theresa, I take it, is your mother's.' Long live the assessing, balanced novelist in detection's pages.

First edition New York: Dutton, 1981
First UK edition London: Gollancz, 1981
as *A Death in the Faculty*

96

JOSEPH WAMBAUGH
The Glitter Dome

In Britain the police procedural novels written by former officers have given us accounts of police work and police life that ring true and, while not glossing over the bad, present us on the whole with pictures of policemen as heroes. In America a former detective sergeant in the Los Angeles Police Department, Joseph Wambaugh, has written police procedurals, every bit as authentic-seeming, which to a large extent turn the British approach upside-down. They show police work as often making of insufficient heroes debased men. They are police procedurals as comedy, black and cutting-edged.

Not that Wambaugh has a jaundiced view of the police. He left the L.A.P.D. only when he found that his celebrity as a writer—his books were tremendous bestsellers—was interfering with the work he loved. One evening, called to the scene of an armed robbery, he asked the barman victim, who had blood streaming from his pistol-whipped face, which hand the gunman had used. Instead of answering, the man asked Wambaugh in his turn what George C. Scott (who starred in the films of his early books) was really like. Next day Wambaugh resigned.

The Glitter Dome is perhaps Wambaugh's finest work, especially if one regards *The Onion Field*, which Wambaugh calls a non-fiction novel, as falling outside the scope of this book. In *The Glitter Dome*, Wambaugh depicts in a realistic way (though on occasion, one suspects, succumbing a little to the temptation to overegg the pudding) the life of pairs of police officers; two detectives, two narcotics men, two patrolmen. He shows us their humour, which is frequently extremely crude, their difficulties and degradations, and—in vividly splashed-on detail—the sex lives that are inextricably bound up with the police way of life in California, if nowhere else.

He tells us of their many woes and occasional semi-triumphs, wandering round the murder of a Hollywood film mogul, in a strongly satirical manner and in short, chopped, juxtaposed fragments which have evoked comparisons with Joseph Heller.

This episodic way of telling a story not only makes the reader wonder time and again what is happening (and keep turning the pages in the hope of finding out) but, more importantly, it mirrors the chancy series of events which Wambaugh sees as constituting the usual way a murder gets investigated. The two detective sergeants in the book, Al Mackey and Marty Welborn, by sticking to procedure in a mad, whirling world, get no more than near to the solution of the mystery.

Wambaugh shows us, with (I imagine) a good deal of justice, that the police approach to a major murder can be primarily concerned not with discovering the actual murderer but with providing the public at large with an acceptable account of the matter. Thus his two principal heroes, after much work and many difficulties, contrive an explanation for the finding of the body of Nigel St Claire, the studio president, in the parking lot of a downtown bowling alley, and only afterwards do the true facts come to light, by chance.

The work and the difficulties are presented to us in a fine flow of easy writing, with dialogue that smacks everywhere of the way actual policemen talk. Make no doubt of it, Wambaugh is another of the ex-police officers who are also natural writers of fiction. Look at his description of the life of the then-in-fashion roller-skaters, a truly lyrical evocation. So the in-talk—the hints that are dropped and the digressions we get, or seem to get—swish by and we find ourselves at the end more or less clear about what has happened (and that's like much of life, after all), and certainly with a vivid idea of the way police action bites into the souls of the men who are foolish enough, or braggart enough, to take it up.

We are also left, perhaps above all, with the memory of the Glitter Dome; at once a garish, lights-swirling watering-hole where tired and randy police officers of both sexes meet and mingle, and a symbol for the false world of Hollywood. And that is a symbol, too, of the falsities and hollow glamour of Southern California life ('Nothing was for free in the Glitter Dome'), and perhaps of much of life in the wider world.

First edition New York: Morrow, 1981
First UK edition London: Weidenfeld and Nicolson

JUNE THOMSON
To Make A Killing

In America, for some reason, this book was re-titled *Portrait of Lilith* (and, for reasons almost as obscure, June Thomson's detective, Inspector Finch in Britain, becomes Inspector Rudd in the States). A title with 'portrait' in it is, however, not at all bad as describing the sort of books June Thomson writes, for though *To Make a Killing* is not a portrait of anyone called Lilith (it is a painting of 'Lilith' that figures in the story), it does contain splendid, life-threaded portraits of the characters who act out its murder mystery; a mystery to which the British title, a twisting of the old proverb 'It takes two to make a quarrel,' gives a faint, echoing clue.

The murder, the mystery and Inspector Finch (or Rudd) enter the book only after more than eighty pages have gone by. June Thomson uses those pages to give us three fine character-studies of people who come to seem as real as anyone we have known in the flesh.

There is Max Gifford, the now-crippled, once-flamboyant painter, first seen 'lying, a great, grey bull-seal of a man beached amongst the crumpled bedding, the neck of his nightshirt unbuttoned to reveal a broad chest, Jove the Ravisher's once magnificent torso grown flabby with age, and with one eye slyly open.' Mrs Thomson succeeds in depicting this stereotype figure in terms that make him by no means a stereotype but a living, awkward real human being. She does this, as much as anything, through his relationship with his mistress, Nina, the girl who while still of school age had run away with him nearly thirty years earlier. It is in the interplay of personalities, observed with tremendous subtlety and attention to the minute details of everyday life, that Mrs Thomson excels.

Take this early exchange between Max and Nina after she has given him a letter from an unknown gallery-owner offering, after many years of neglect, to hold a one-man show for him. He has pretended not to have thought about the offer, but now as she leaves he abruptly tells her to telephone an answer. This she must do from the house of a friend named Lionel, who, Max has said will offer to marry her as soon as he himself is dead. 'Straightening up, she said "You old sod." He grinned at her, unrepentant. "Give my love to Lionel." She slammed the door anyway, determined to have the last word.'

This is the to-and-fro of real life. You feel, from the very opening pages of the book that you are in safe hands. The dense, different, otherwise world of true fiction will never be ripped apart by crude statement in place of the quiet, natural emergence of such facts as you need to know.

And, note, that for all that this is the method of the pure novelist, some of the facts Mrs Thomson needs you to know are no less than the dear old clues to a murder mystery. She may go very much deeper into her people than, say, Agatha Christie, but she does not neglect to provide a who-done-it? tug and a surprise solution. Indeed, her puzzle—why it is that Eustace Quinn, the gallery-owner, is murdered on only the second time he comes to the house—is as intriguing as any from the great Golden Age.

I have said that the book begins with three fine character studies. The third is of Nina's brother, the waster, Danny, whom Nina sees as looking 'famished . . . and a little weird with those high, triangular cheekbones and prominent Adam's apple sticking out above the collar of his shirt which moved convulsively up and down as he answered her.' Again, it is through the relationship of brother and sister, rarely portrayed in this age of sex, that we get the deep-plunging picture of Danny.

Not that Mrs Thomson shirks sexuality, nor describing with precision its effects: 'that sudden jolt of desire, as much a real physical sensation as an electric shock.' Sex, indeed, is at the root of her story, that gradual series of discoveries ending with, at the same point, the revelation of what lies behind the tense, complex relation of Max to Nina, Nina to Max and the revelation of who did kill Eustace Quinn. This is what the detective novel, as distinct from the detective story, ought to be able to do. At its best, as here, it does it with a final coming-together that makes one think of a master symphony's final chords.

First edition London: Constable, 1982
First US edition New York: Doubleday, 1983

98

PETER LOVESEY

The False Inspector Dew

There is a passage in the prizewinning *The False Inspector Dew*—it gained the Gold Dagger of the Crime Writers' Association for 1982—that goes: 'He dealt two hands of five on to a glass-topped table. "Look at yours." She had the eight, nine, ten, jack and queen of clubs. "I just dealt you a straight flush," he said. "What would you bet on that stake, Poppy? Your new dress? Better not. Mine's a royal." He turned over the ace, king, queen, jack and ten of diamonds.'

It is merely an incident in the complex story Peter Lovesey tells in this book, intriguingly set for the most part aboard the liner *Mauretania* swirling its way from Southampton to New York in the year 1921. But it also describes what Lovesey does in the book. He produces a whole series of infinitely cunning surprises, one after another. No sooner has he lulled us into accepting one version of what is going on than he ups and neatly reverses the whole. So it would be quite unfair to give any account of the book's plot, and in less than fifty pages it would be impossible.

Lovesey made his reputation with a series of books set in Victorian days and featuring a lowly detective hero, Sergeant Cribb, with a yet lowlier Watson, Constable Thackeray. They put before us for our delectation various little-known aspects of Victorian life, researched with extraordinary thoroughness, and *The False Inspector Dew* owes its success in part to that same thoroughness, here devoted to another period.

Its major success, I am sure, is to be attributed to that legerdemain in plotting combined with steadily forward-driving narration. However much it was necessary for Lovesey to hop us readers from one set of characters to another, from one scene to another, in the interests of his plot—and for the better part of the first half of the book, hop we do—he contrives always to keep you reading. He employs no fireworks of style to achieve this. Instead he puts a never-ending series of little questions into one's mind. What will so-and-so do next?, one constantly asks. And constantly keeps reading to find out.

But the historical background is there from the very beginning; a solid, four-page, factual account (with one or two tiny fictional interpositions) of the sinking of another liner, the *Lusitania*, which succumbed to a torpedo attack in 1915 with the loss of 1,210 lives, including those of the millionaire Alfred Vanderbilt and the impresario Carl Frohman. This—it contains a key to the eventual solution—is recounted in a tone of sober, almost newspaper-reporting factuality. And, cleverly, Lovesey keeps this tone as his story unfolds, so one is left believing.

There is much to believe in, on board the peacetime *Mauretania* plunging to her destination. There are dances featuring the tango and the foxtrot. There is much Bridge playing. There are deck games. There is an amateur variety concert. There is the statutory fancy-dress party, with passengers ingeniously teasing lengths of rope into false beards and fashioning togas out of Company bedspreads. And there is the working area of the huge ship, the main hold 'big as a warehouse and stacked high with boxes and crates and near it the hold containing a line of motor-cars ... roped to the deck and secured with wooden blocks under the wheels.' Those wooden blocks are typical of the detail Lovesey has at his command, as is the perfume, Essence of Stephanotis, typical of the 1920s, which one of the characters wears.

Out of it all, and aided by his steady prose, Lovesey creates a reality. This is his aim. Historical mystery, he has said, 'provides an escape from modern life. But we are not at the mercy of a science-fiction writer's fantasising. The world we enter is real.' In this book, Lovesey has added to that escape into a real world of the past his dazzling plot: no wonder the book was a prizewinner.

First edition London: Macmillan, 1982
First US edition New York: Pantheon, 1982

JAMES McCLURE
The Artful Egg

The Artful Egg is the culminating volume in the series of crime
novels James McClure has written featuring the white South
African police detective Lieutenant Tromp Kramer and his Zulu
side-kick, Bantu Detective Sergeant Mickey Zondi. The subtlety
and truth with which Kramer is shown as both inherently
colour-prejudiced and as a complex, caring human being is
remarkable. Writing of one of the series in the London *Sunday
Times*, the critic John West has said: 'The seedbed of future good
fiction probably lies in the best of current crime writing; the best
novels about South Africa today are McClure's stories of the
Trekkersburg police.'

In *The Artful Egg*, McClure succeeds in making a credible
progression for Kramer from the cheerful beater-up of black
suspects in the earliest books to a 1980s 'kaffir-lover', friend as
well as comrade-in-arms to Mickey Zondi, but in doing so he has
yielded not an inch to an easy sentimentality. The book, too, is
McClure's most ambitious attempt to use the crime story in
order to put into the minds of his readers a theme with all its
implications, a considerable advance from his early aim of simply
acquiring readers through detective stories who would be made
to think about the South African situation.

The Artful Egg is decidedly complex, with two cases taking
place simultaneously, but it succeeds splendidly in putting
forward its deeper theme. Each part of its double denouement is
equally surprising and satisfactory as both detection pay-off and
final coming-to-light of that theme, a hymning of the irrepressible force of life.

The book's odd title is, in fact, an almost poetic statement of
this (McClure wrote poetry in his early manhood days); he puts
it in the book's very opening words, 'A hen is an egg's way of
making another egg.' In other words, the urge of life will force its
way upwards through any and every necessary tortuosity, in the
way that a plant will twist and bend in stone-thick earth to come

to the light.

That almost comical expression about the artful egg is put into the mind of one of the most sympathetic characters to have come from McClure's pen, Asiatic Postman 2nd Class Ramjut Pillay, and it is Ramjut Pillay's delivery of the morning mail in a middle-class suburb of McClure's imaginary Trekkersburg that precipitates the book's complex plot. His subsequent writhings and twistings after discovering a body in a house where he has been too conscientious in delivering a letter—delightfully humorous in the telling—are a vital thread in the story and a fine, active illustration of the theme.

The Artful Egg, then, is a fine summing-up of all that McClure does best. It draws for us South African society, a society at which all the world looks. It gives us heart-based humour. It presents us with a gallery of credible and deeply-seen human beings. And—a particular gift of McClure's—it contrasts, time and again, life's delights and life's horrors. Take this passage: 'it was as near to a perfect day as anyone could wish. A butcher bird came to sit on a branch above him. It had a fledgling in its beak, still struggling feebly.' It is in such insights, in the recognition that the bad exists as well as the good, or the good as well as the bad, that differentiates McClure from a hundred lesser practitioners of crime fiction.

Yet he has always been content to remain a crime writer. Crime, he has said, he finds fascinating. It is through crime, as he sees it, that a society is judged; through its attitudes towards crime, through the way it controls crime, and—this has special reference to the South Africa where he was born and spent his early years—through what is considered by any particular society to *be* a crime. And let me add that McClure has shown, and nowhere better than in *The Artful Egg*, that in writing about crime it is possible, too, to write about life.

First edition London: Macmillan, 1984

First US edition New York: Pantheon, 1985

100

P.D. JAMES
A Taste for Death

With a book written as recently as 1986 I am clearly deprived of the assistance of my colleague, O.F. Time, in making my judgement that this is something worthy of my hundred-strong Temple of the Criminous Muse. But I have no hesitation in including it.

First, it is by any standards a very good novel of detection with a mystery, clues, suspects—and suspects presented at a fascinatingly deep level—and a genuine surprise solution. Second, P.D. James has succeeded here, I believe, in widening the scope of the crime novel in a way that has hardly been done before. By entering the worlds and minds of all her main characters—suspects, investigators, bystanders—she has been able to say more about life than has hitherto been attempted in the crime form. But, third, and most important to my mind, she has succeeded in writing, in the form of the crime novel, a book that has let her express her most profound beliefs.

Never before has there been a crime novel about religious faith. Yes, we have had dozens set in monasteries and convents or with churches, vicars and rabbis in them, but what P.D. James has done here is to achieve what Conan Doyle abandoned Sherlock Holmes in order to do: to write a book expressing his deepest beliefs. With Doyle it was historical novels that were intended to set a pattern of behaviour for all Britain to follow, a mighty ambition to which he was unable to rise. I believe that P.D. James, aiming rather less high, has succeeded. She has convincingly, if at times a little obscurely, put into a book all her feelings, doubts, fears and hopes concerning faith in God. This is something that may not be obvious at a first reading when, as P.D. James intended, one is caught up in the outward story of who killed Sir Paul Berowne, just-resigned Minister of the Crown, and the dilapidated tramp, Harry Mack. But at a second reading, or a thoughtful look back, the theme can hardly help but emerge.

Consider first where Sir Paul and Harry Mack were murdered: in the vestry of a church. Consider why Sir Paul was there to be murdered: because, visiting the building out of a mere interest in architecture, he had been struck by a divine revelation. Consider where the clinching clue is found: in that same church—a tiny simple thing like a button in the box meant for candle money. Turn then to the book's last pages, where an author is completing what he or she has to say. Are they concerned with Commander Dalgliesh? With the murderer? With any of the major characters? No, P.D. James chooses to end with the character she began with, the church mouse spinster who discovered the bodies. And what do we find her doing? Praying. But not praying any easy prayers; she is praying that her fast-failing faith may return. And in doing so she makes us, the readers, ponder on precisely the mystery of faith.

Or look at what might seem quite an incidental passage in this long book (long because it has a great deal to say). Chapter eight begins with a sketch of the pathologist coming to examine the bodies. A piece of necessary filling-out, you might say. But no: P.D. James gives us Doc Kynaston as a man who has 'a taste for death,' one fascinated by 'each new piece of evidence which might, if rightly interpreted, bring him closer to the central mystery.' Because the central mystery of death is surely what comes after, the sustaining key to religious faith.

Or consider what Lady Ursula, Sir Paul's aged, sharp-tongued mother, says to Dalgliesh when he comes to see if he can extract from her evidence which he needs. She puts him off by telling him she has been visited by the priest of the murder church: 'He seemed to me a man who has long ago given up the expectation of influencing anyone. Perhaps he has lost his faith. Isn't that fashionable in the Church today? But why should that distress him? The world is full of people who have lost faith; politicians who have lost faith in politics . . . for all I know, policemen who have lost faith in policing and poets who have lost faith in poetry.' Home jabs these, for doubting Dalgliesh. But, even more, the expression of P.D. James's central preoccupation in a long, ideas-crowded, wonderfully powerful book.

First edition London: Faber and Faber, 1986
First US edition New York: Knopf, 1986

The One-Hundred-and-
First Choice

H.R.F. Keating is far too modest. No account of crime fiction would be complete without some mention of his own contribution, and any list of the '100 Best' in this genre must surely include at least one of Keating's own novels. Since his list is now complete let us add, on our own account, one of these as the 101st choice.

But which one? Should it be one of the strange trio of novels with which Keating introduced himself in the early 1960s—*A Rush on the Ultimate*, perhaps, with its almost surreal atmosphere and its curious plot? Many critics would opt for *The Perfect Murder*, the dazzling (and award-winning) début of Inspector Ghote, whose adventures have since filled more than a dozen volumes. Or perhaps it might be an affectionate period-piece such as *The Murder of the Maharaja*, another award-winner. In fact it is none of these.

Inspector Ghote has no crime to solve in *Under a Monsoon Cloud*, his most recent exploit, and there are no clues for the reader to pounce on, no suspects, no thrilling chase—none of the traditional 'hooks'. Yet the book grips from the first page to the last, it is unequivocally a crime novel, and it is completely original. It is about anger.

Posted as a relief officer to a remote village during the scorching lull before the monsoon breaks, Ghote has to submit to an inspection by his long-time hero, the formidable 'Tiger' Kelkar, who in a burst of annoyance flings a brass inkstand at a subordinate, which kills him. Ghote, reluctant to arrest Tiger and appalled that such a mishap could ruin a magnificent career, comes up with a plan to remove the body and conceal the accident, and in a grisly charade he and Tiger execute the scheme as the monsoon breaks. The deed is hastily covered-up and a year passes before Ghote, back in Bombay, learns that suspicions have at last been aroused and that an investigation is underway. He alerts the proud Tiger, whose response is to commit suicide, leaving a note accepting all the blame but exposing Ghote to some extremely awkward questioning.

All this is merely a prologue to the Inquiry, however, the prospect of which faces Ghote with a colossal moral dilemma; to tell the truth would obviously be the 'right' thing, but it would certainly mean dismissal and the end of everything he has worked for, when he was simply trying to protect a man he admired and to be a good policeman himself. After much internal anguish, Ghote confides in his wife Protima and at once they are at odds: 'Then there is one thing to do only,' she insists. 'You must give out a lie.' As the Inquiry begins the monsoon rages again, turning the pathetic fallacy splendidly on its head.

The Inquiry occupies the whole of the last two-thirds of the book, and the twists and turns of its progress would bemuse even a Perry Mason. Ghote's conscience is strikingly personified in the form of Mrs Ahmed, the civil-liberties-walli who acts as council for his defence between rushing off to assist the beggars whose dwellings have been swept away by the monsoon. To her Ghote also has to tell the lie. The problem for the reader is not who did it (we know that all too well), nor even will he get away with it, but how on earth can this ethical paradox be resolved? It speaks volumes for the author's ability that such an adult theme can be not merely incorporated into the fabric of a detective story but also made as exciting as any thriller.

Apparently, Keating had not visited Bombay when he wrote the first Inspector Ghote novel, although he has been several times since. In this book the background is wonderfully evoked in a host of vivid details—but authenticity is not the overriding concern, for this is also a Bombay of the mind, where the heat and the confusion mirror the world beneath the ordered, determinate one that we would like to think we inhabit, and where Ghote, a good though by no means a perfect man, barely copes, but does his best and just about muddles through somehow. As, much of the time, do we.

First edition London: Hutchinson, 1986
First US edition New York: Viking, 1986

Index

213